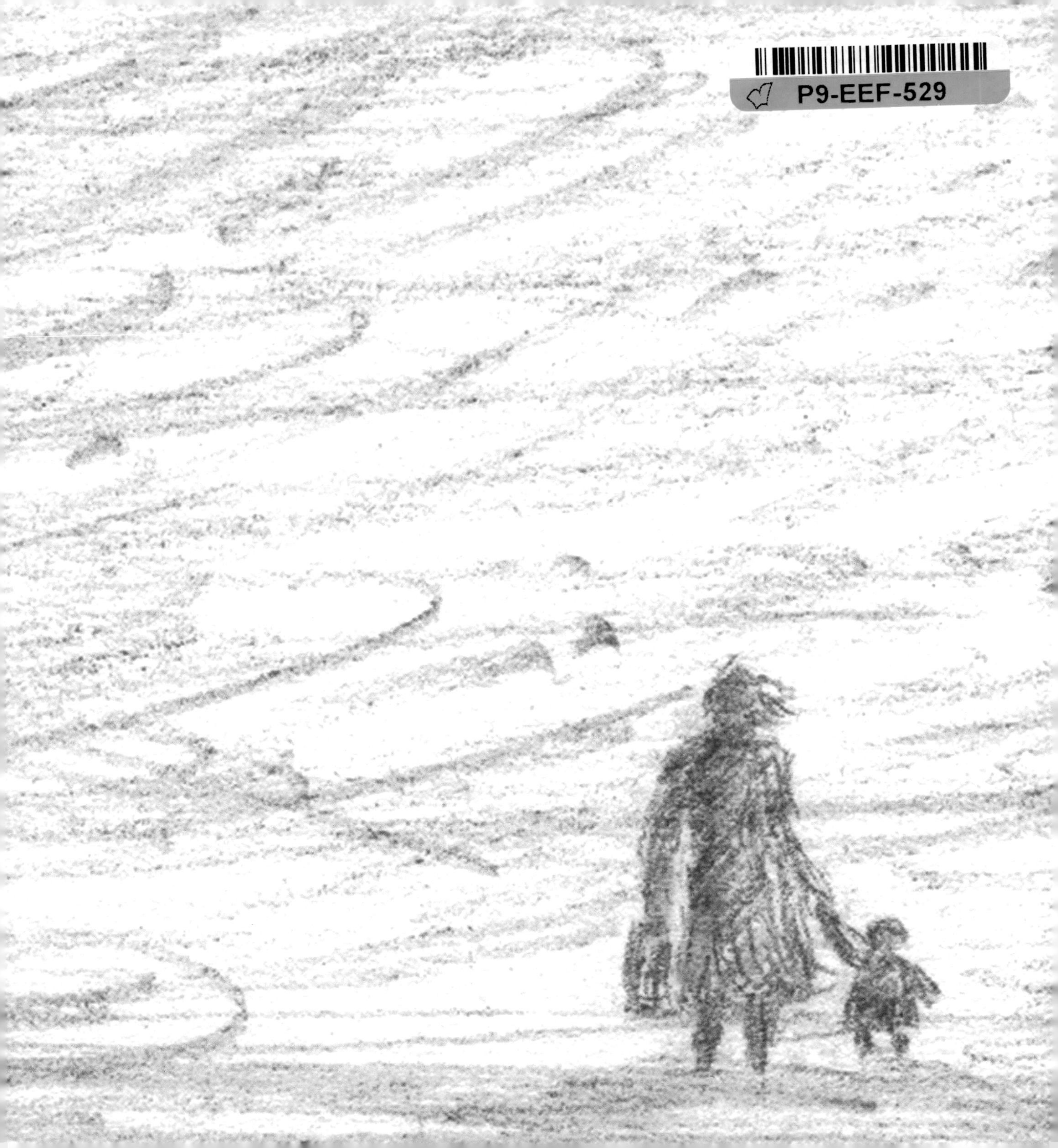

WE ARE ON OUR OWN

ACKNOWLEDGEMENTS:

I would like to thank Chris Oliveros and Peggy Burns for their constant help and encouragement throughout this journey and for believing in the book. Also thanks to Tom Devlin for his talent and caring to make it look right and a very special thanks to Geoff Katin, Aaron Katin and Ilan Katin.

PUBLISHER: Chris Oliveros.
PUBLICITY: Peggy Burns and Jamie Quail.
PRODUCTION: Jeremy Morris, Shawn Kuruneru, Chris Oliveros, and Tom Devlin.
COVER DESIGN: Tom Devlin.

FIRST HARDCOVER EDITION: May 2006.
Printed in Singapore.

Katin, Miriam
    We Are On Our Own / Miriam Katin.
ISBN 1-896597-20-3
                    I. Title.
PN6727.K29W43 2006   741.5'973   C2005-906360-2

Drawn & Quarterly
Post Office Box 48056
Montreal, Quebec
Canada H2V 4S8
www.drawnandquarterly.com

DISTRIBUTED IN THE USA AND ABROAD BY:
Farrar, Straus and Giroux
19 Union Square West
New York, NY 10003
Orders: 888.330.8477

DISTRIBUTED IN CANADA BY:
Raincoast Books
9050 Shaughnessy Street
Vancouver, BC V6P 6E5
Orders: 800.663.5714

WE ARE ON OUR OWN
A MEMOIR BY MIRIAM KATIN

DRAWN & QUARTERLY

MONTREAL

FOR MY MOTHER
WHO TAUGHT ME
TO LAUGH
AND TO FORGIVE.

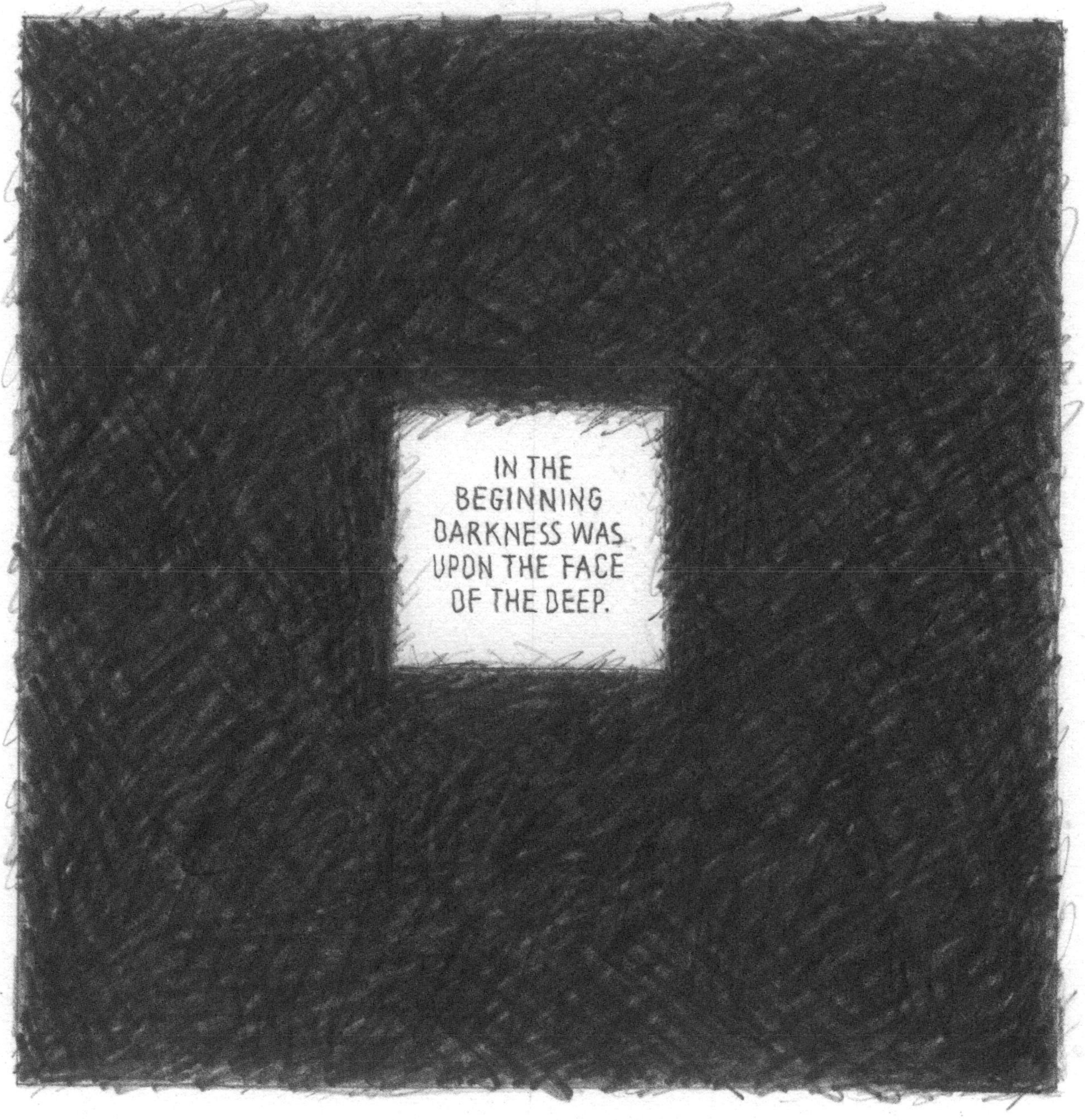
IN THE BEGINNING DARKNESS WAS UPON THE FACE OF THE DEEP.

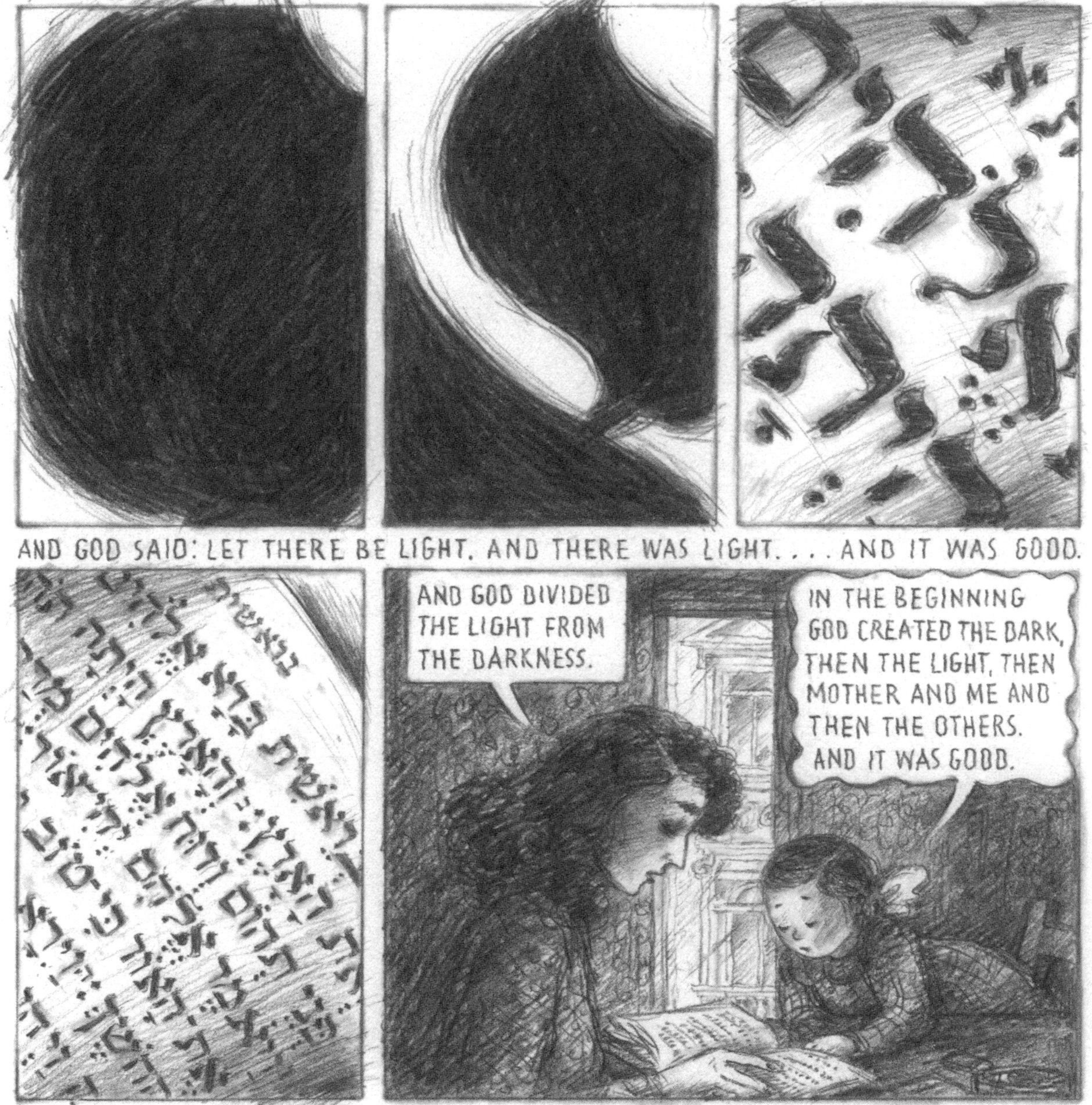
AND GOD SAID: LET THERE BE LIGHT. AND THERE WAS LIGHT. . . . AND IT WAS GOOD.
AND GOD DIVIDED THE LIGHT FROM THE DARKNESS.
IN THE BEGINNING GOD CREATED THE DARK, THEN THE LIGHT, THEN MOTHER AND ME AND THEN THE OTHERS. AND IT WAS GOOD.

אֱלֹהִים: GOD

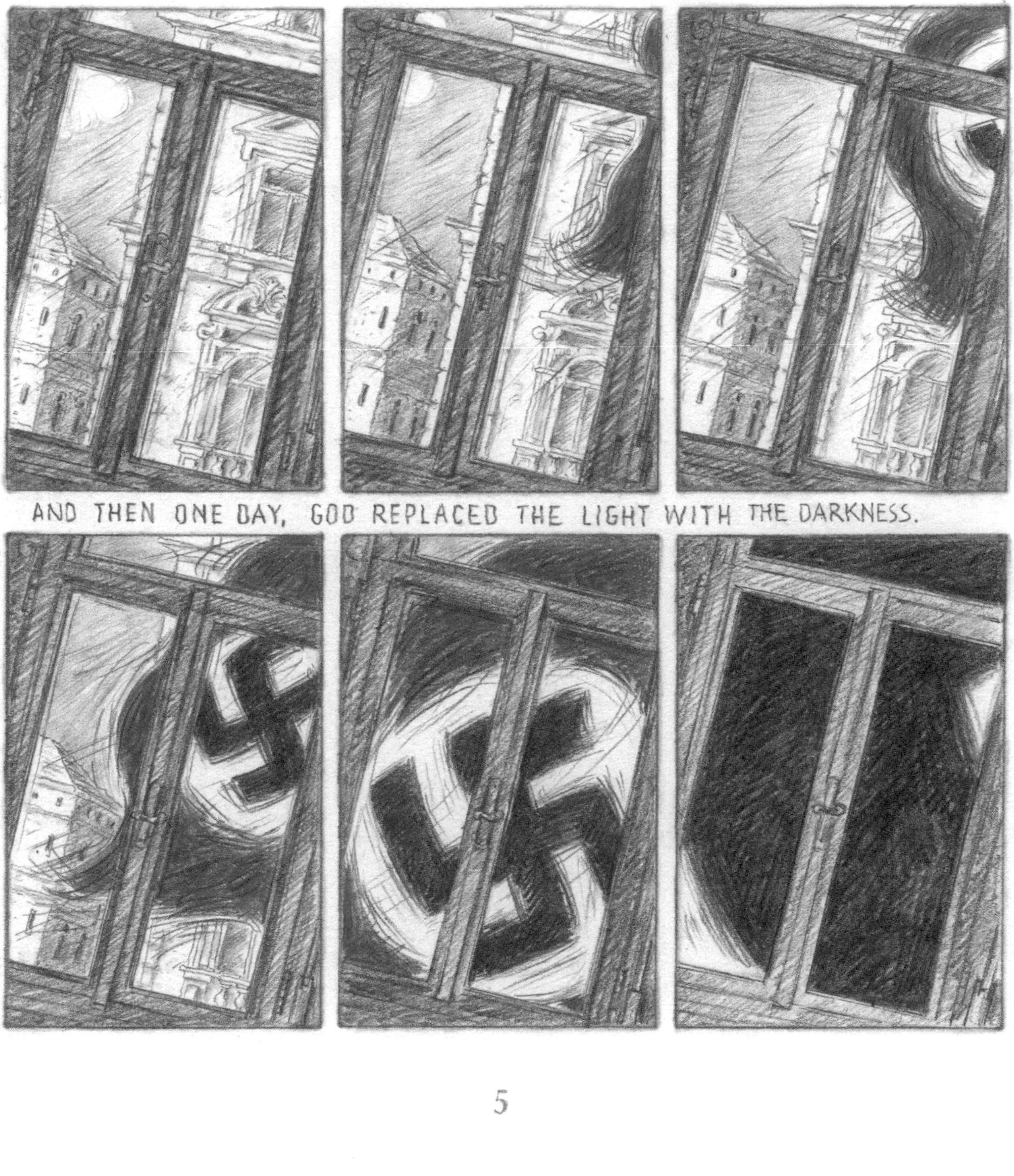
AND THEN ONE DAY, GOD REPLACED THE LIGHT WITH THE DARKNESS.

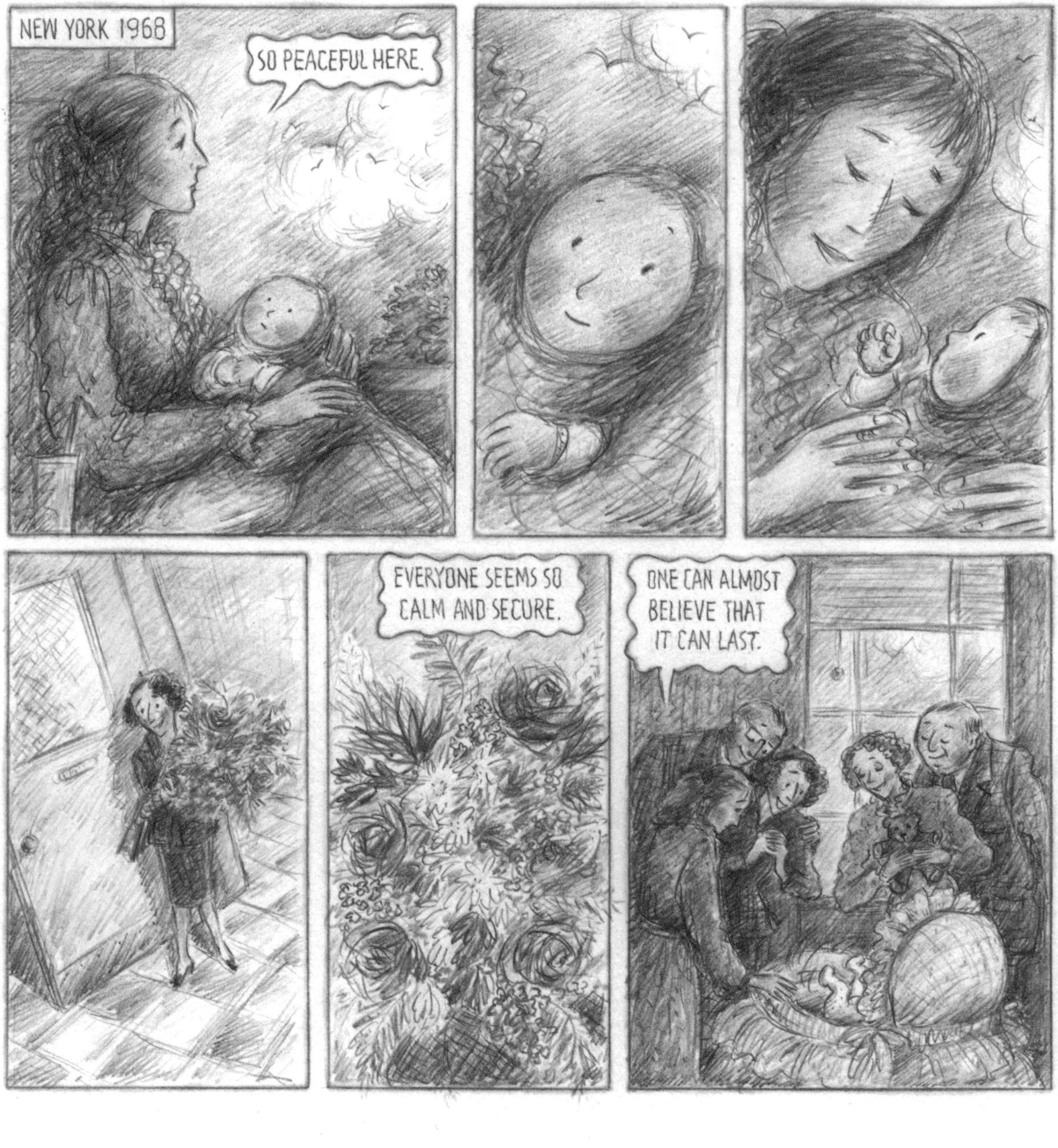
NEW YORK 1968
SO PEACEFUL HERE.
EVERYONE SEEMS SO CALM AND SECURE.
ONE CAN ALMOST BELIEVE THAT IT CAN LAST.

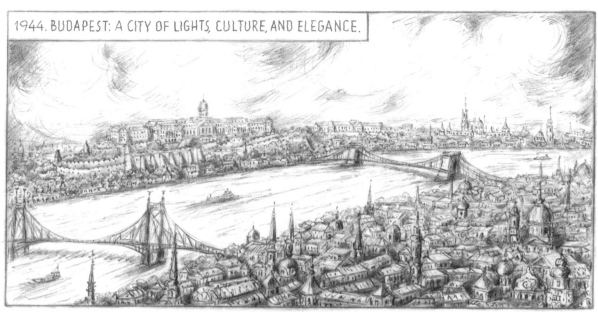

1944. BUDAPEST: A CITY OF LIGHTS, CULTURE, AND ELEGANCE.

I NEED SOME COFFEE. LET'S SIT DOWN.

OH ÉVA. I CAN'T SPEND MONEY NOW.

IT IS ON ME. PLEASE.

STOP REXY! STOP!

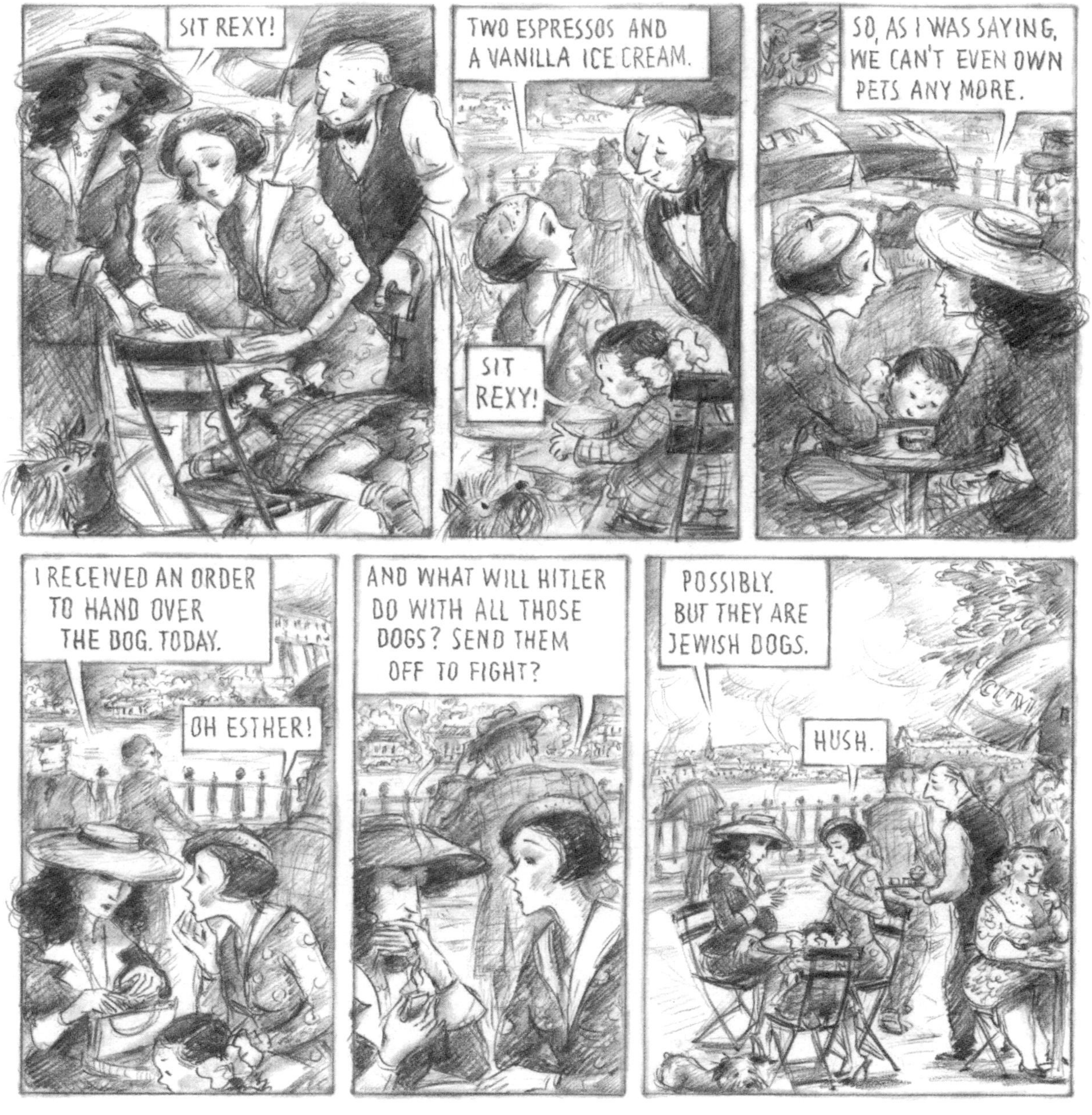
SIT REXY!
TWO ESPRESSOS AND A VANILLA ICE CREAM.
SIT REXY!
SO, AS I WAS SAYING, WE CAN'T EVEN OWN PETS ANY MORE.
I RECEIVED AN ORDER TO HAND OVER THE DOG. TODAY.
OH ESTHER!
AND WHAT WILL HITLER DO WITH ALL THOSE DOGS? SEND THEM OFF TO FIGHT?
POSSIBLY. BUT THEY ARE JEWISH DOGS.
HUSH.

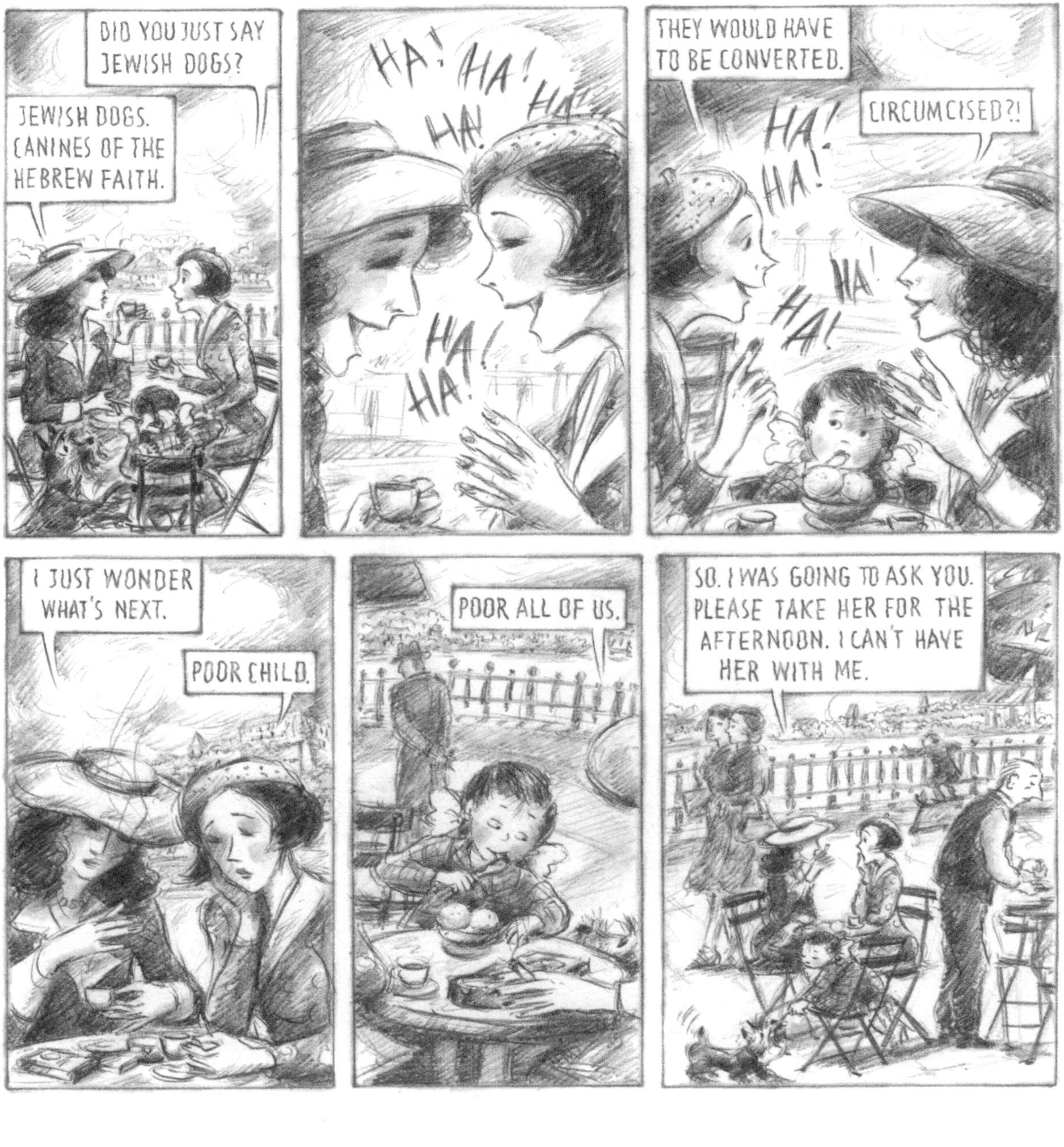
DID YOU JUST SAY JEWISH DOGS?
JEWISH DOGS. CANINES OF THE HEBREW FAITH.
HA! HA! HA! HA! HA! HA!
THEY WOULD HAVE TO BE CONVERTED.
CIRCUMCISED?!
HA! HA! HA! HA!
I JUST WONDER WHAT'S NEXT.
POOR CHILD.
POOR ALL OF US.
SO. I WAS GOING TO ASK YOU. PLEASE TAKE HER FOR THE AFTERNOON. I CAN'T HAVE HER WITH ME.

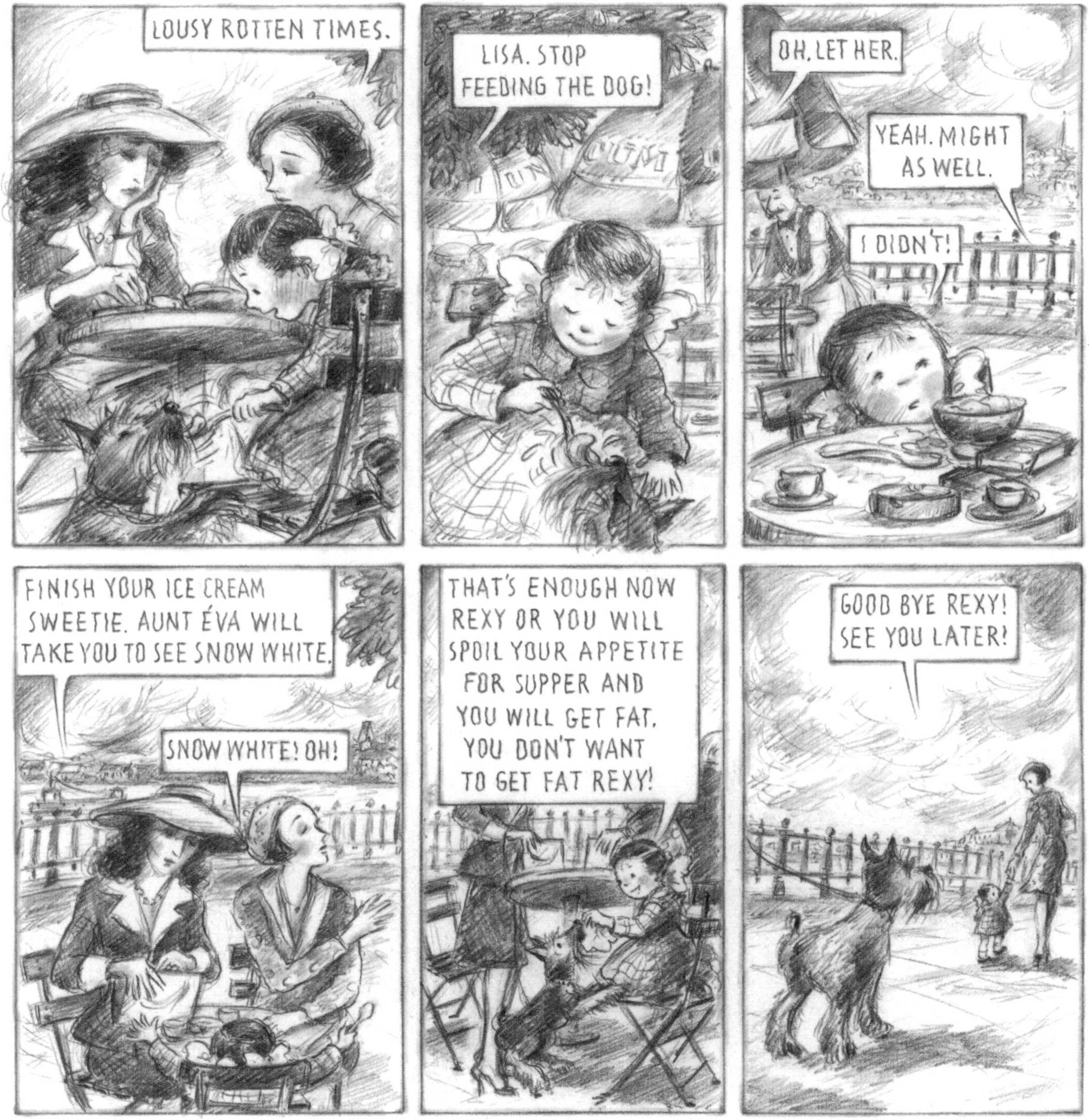
LOUSY ROTTEN TIMES.
LISA. STOP FEEDING THE DOG!
OH, LET HER.
YEAH. MIGHT AS WELL.
I DIDN'T!
FINISH YOUR ICE CREAM SWEETIE. AUNT ÉVA WILL TAKE YOU TO SEE SNOW WHITE.
SNOW WHITE! OH!
THAT'S ENOUGH NOW REXY OR YOU WILL SPOIL YOUR APPETITE FOR SUPPER AND YOU WILL GET FAT. YOU DON'T WANT TO GET FAT REXY!
GOOD BYE REXY! SEE YOU LATER!

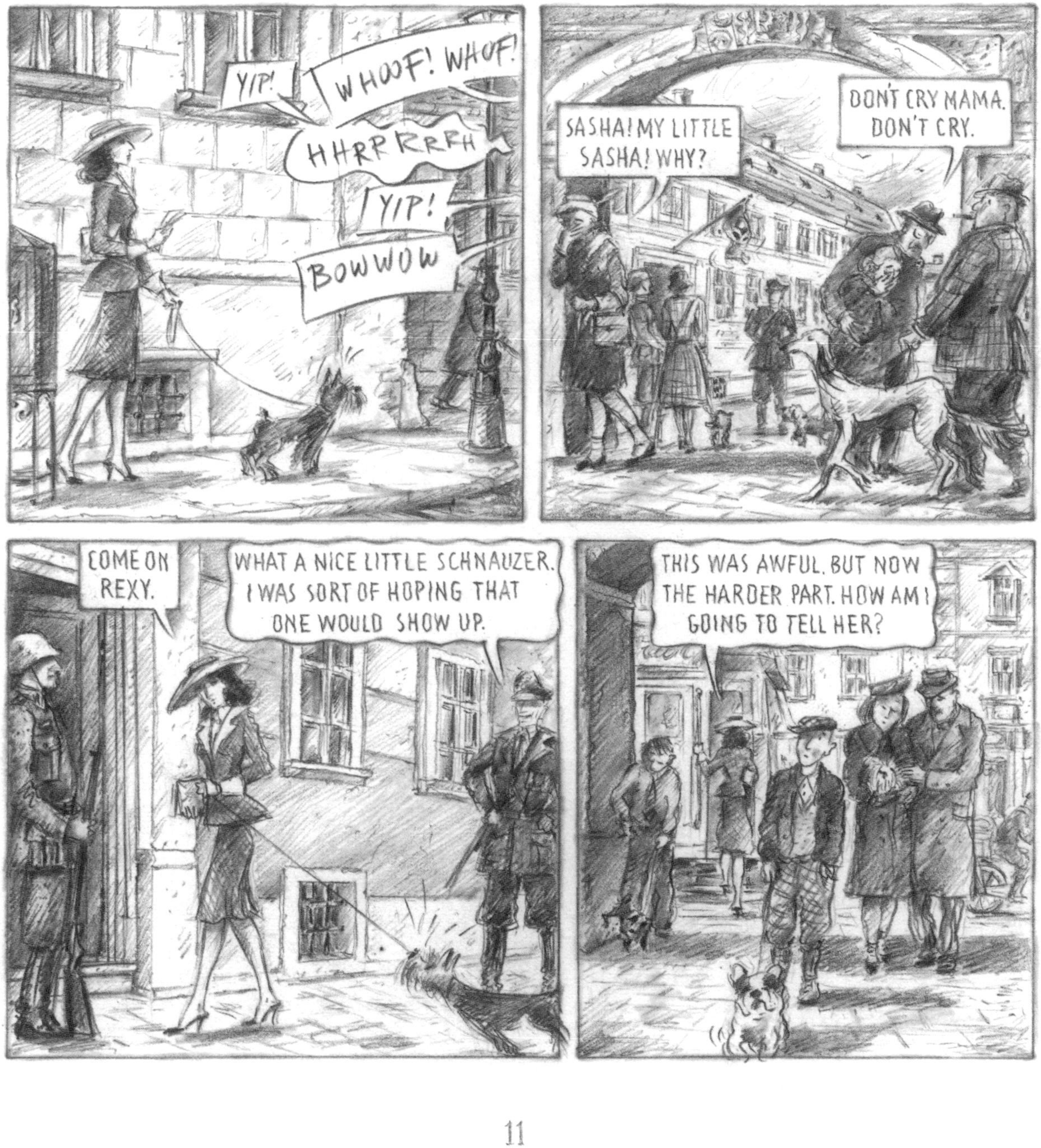
YIP!
WHOOF! WHOF!
HHRRRRRFH
YIP!
BOWWOW
SASHA! MY LITTLE SASHA! WHY?
DON'T CRY MAMA. DON'T CRY.
COME ON REXY.
WHAT A NICE LITTLE SCHNAUZER. I WAS SORT OF HOPING THAT ONE WOULD SHOW UP.
THIS WAS AWFUL. BUT NOW THE HARDER PART. HOW AM I GOING TO TELL HER?

My dearest Esther!
I received your card and the package. It is most welcome as there is not much food around here. I thank you.

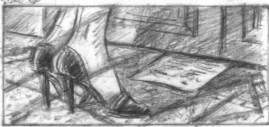

The weather is very bad but my coughing is gone thanks to the medicine you sent to me. Someone took a picture of me resting and here we are with the supper. Dearest, take good care of yourself and our little girl, this war will end soon.

12

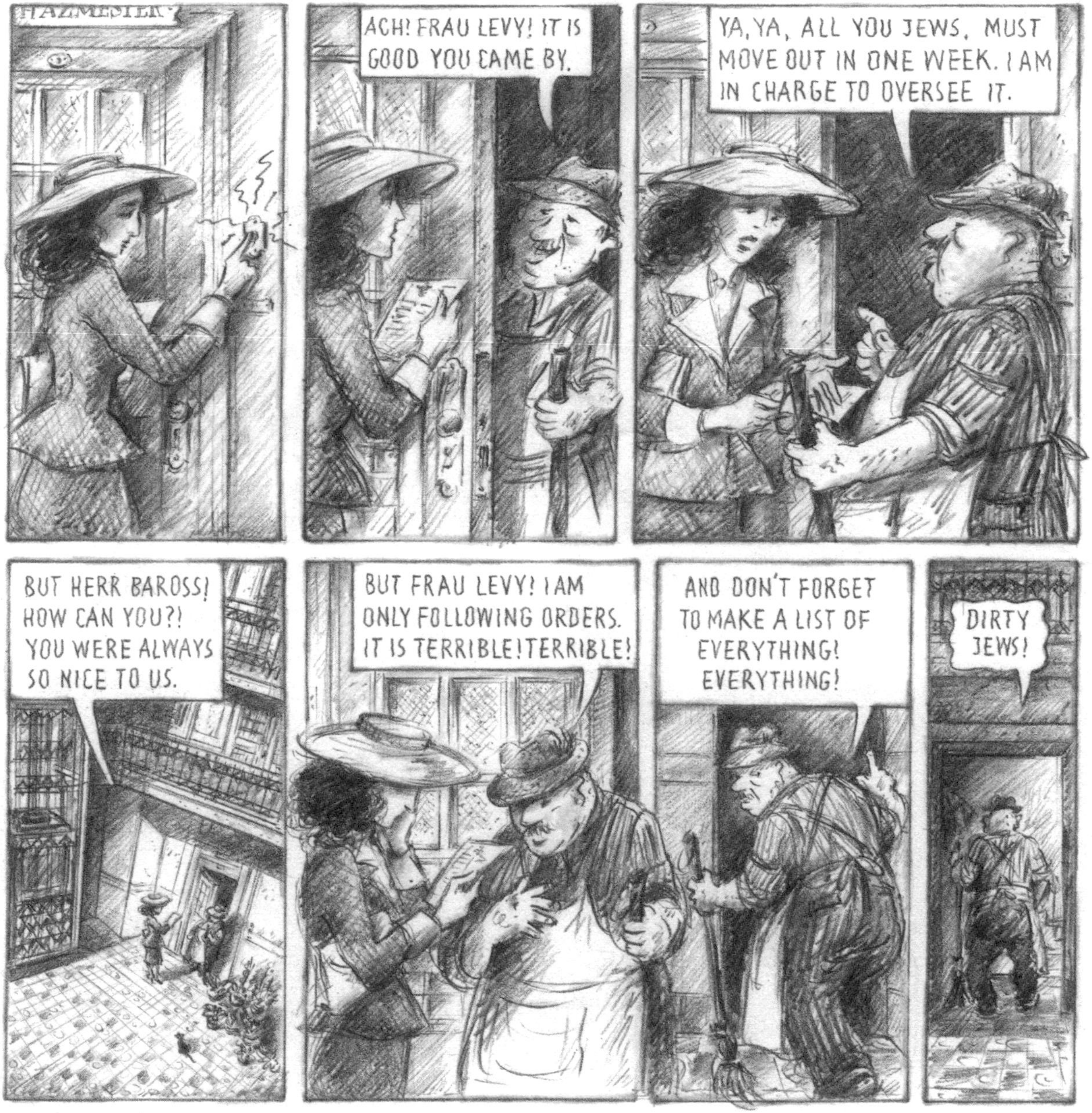
HAZMESTER
ACH! FRAU LEVY! IT IS GOOD YOU CAME BY.
YA, YA, ALL YOU JEWS, MUST MOVE OUT IN ONE WEEK. I AM IN CHARGE TO OVERSEE IT.
BUT HERR BAROSS! HOW CAN YOU?! YOU WERE ALWAYS SO NICE TO US.
BUT FRAU LEVY! I AM ONLY FOLLOWING ORDERS. IT IS TERRIBLE! TERRIBLE!
AND DON'T FORGET TO MAKE A LIST OF EVERYTHING! EVERYTHING!
DIRTY JEWS!

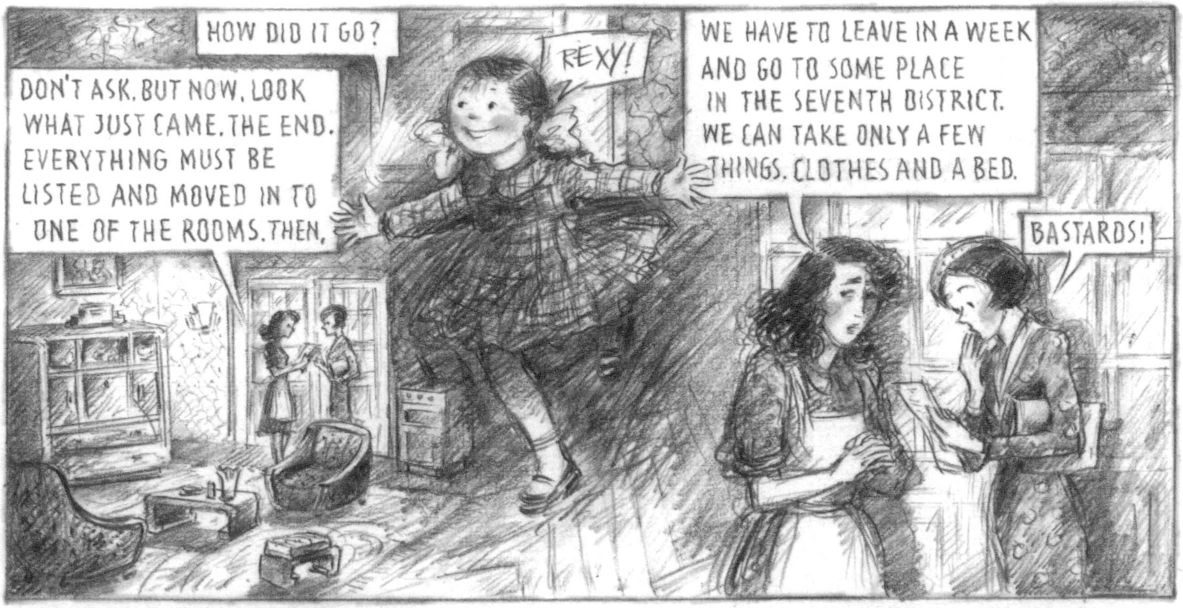
HOW DID IT GO?
DON'T ASK. BUT NOW, LOOK WHAT JUST CAME. THE END. EVERYTHING MUST BE LISTED AND MOVED IN TO ONE OF THE ROOMS. THEN,
REXY!
WE HAVE TO LEAVE IN A WEEK AND GO TO SOME PLACE IN THE SEVENTH DISTRICT. WE CAN TAKE ONLY A FEW THINGS. CLOTHES AND A BED.
BASTARDS!

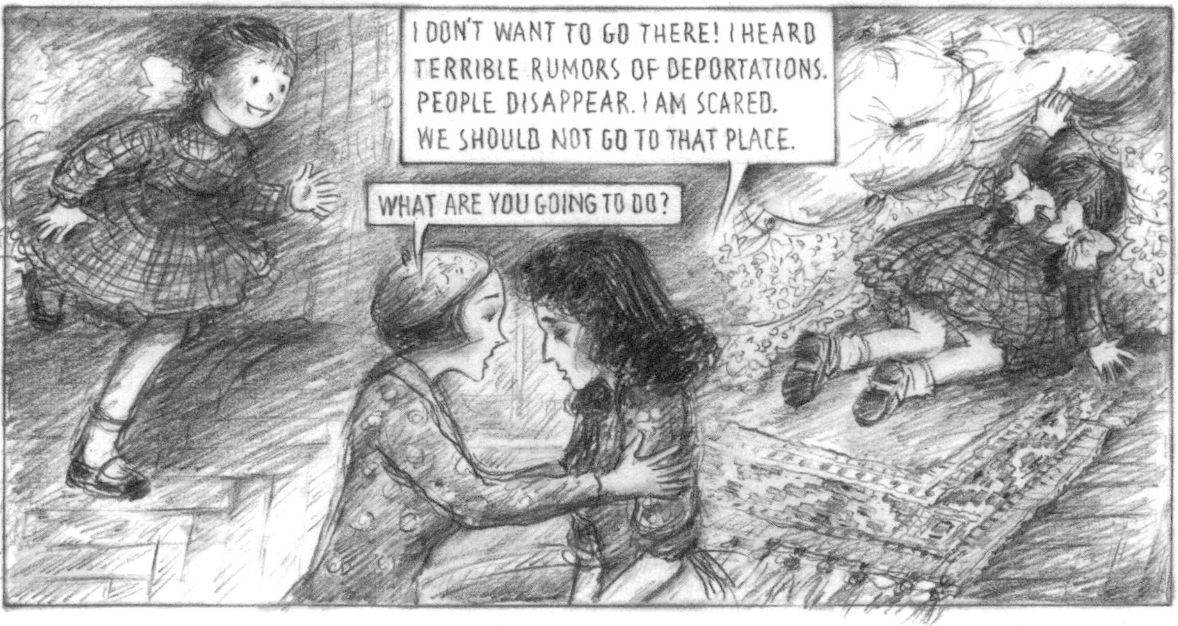
I DON'T WANT TO GO THERE! I HEARD TERRIBLE RUMORS OF DEPORTATIONS. PEOPLE DISAPPEAR. I AM SCARED. WE SHOULD NOT GO TO THAT PLACE.
WHAT ARE YOU GOING TO DO?

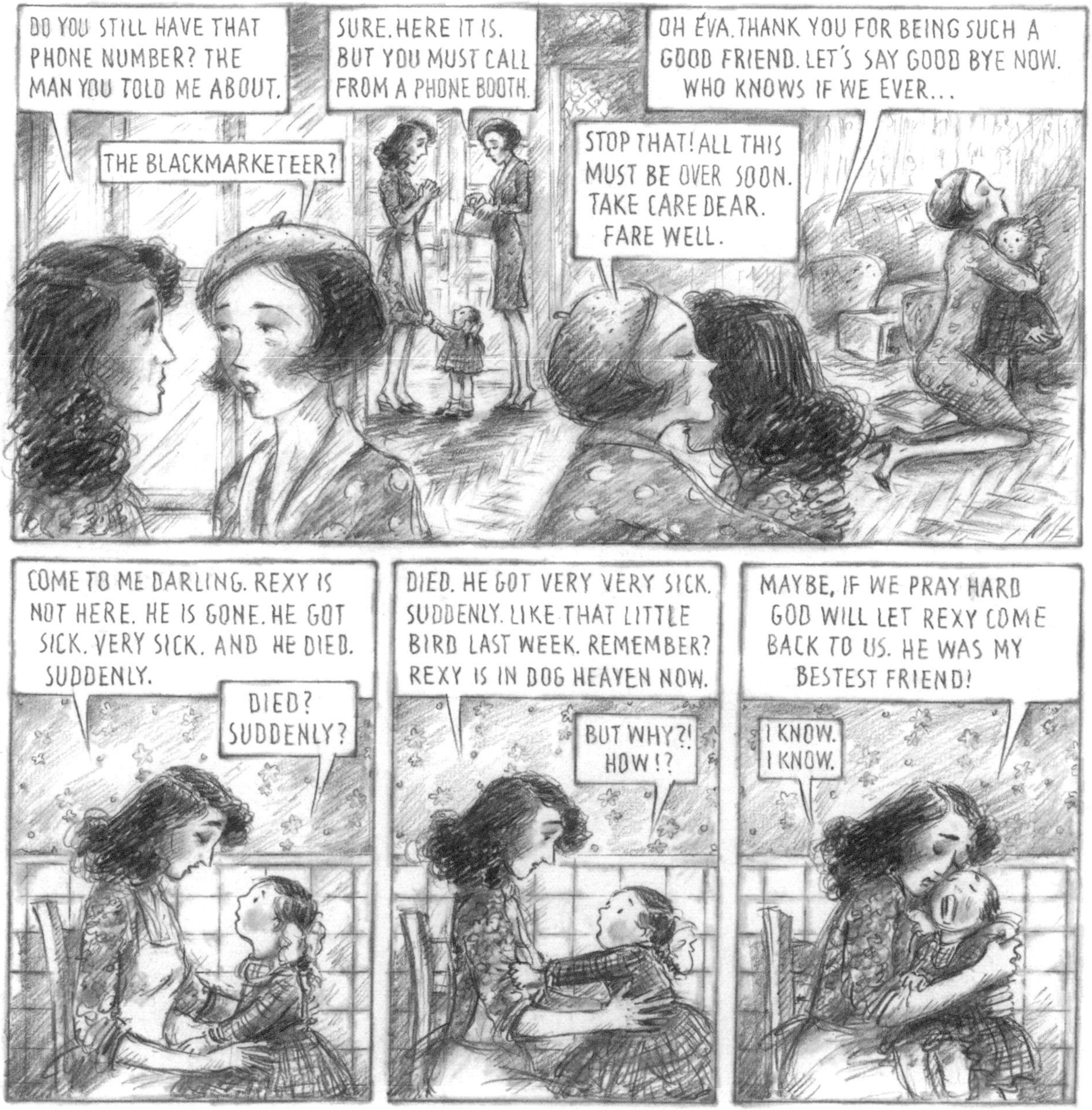
DO YOU STILL HAVE THAT PHONE NUMBER? THE MAN YOU TOLD ME ABOUT.
THE BLACKMARKETEER?
SURE. HERE IT IS. BUT YOU MUST CALL FROM A PHONE BOOTH.
OH ÉVA. THANK YOU FOR BEING SUCH A GOOD FRIEND. LET'S SAY GOOD BYE NOW. WHO KNOWS IF WE EVER...
STOP THAT! ALL THIS MUST BE OVER SOON. TAKE CARE DEAR. FARE WELL.
COME TO ME DARLING. REXY IS NOT HERE. HE IS GONE. HE GOT SICK. VERY SICK. AND HE DIED. SUDDENLY.
DIED? SUDDENLY?
DIED. HE GOT VERY VERY SICK. SUDDENLY. LIKE THAT LITTLE BIRD LAST WEEK. REMEMBER? REXY IS IN DOG HEAVEN NOW.
BUT WHY?! HOW!?
MAYBE, IF WE PRAY HARD GOD WILL LET REXY COME BACK TO US. HE WAS MY BESTEST FRIEND!
I KNOW. I KNOW.

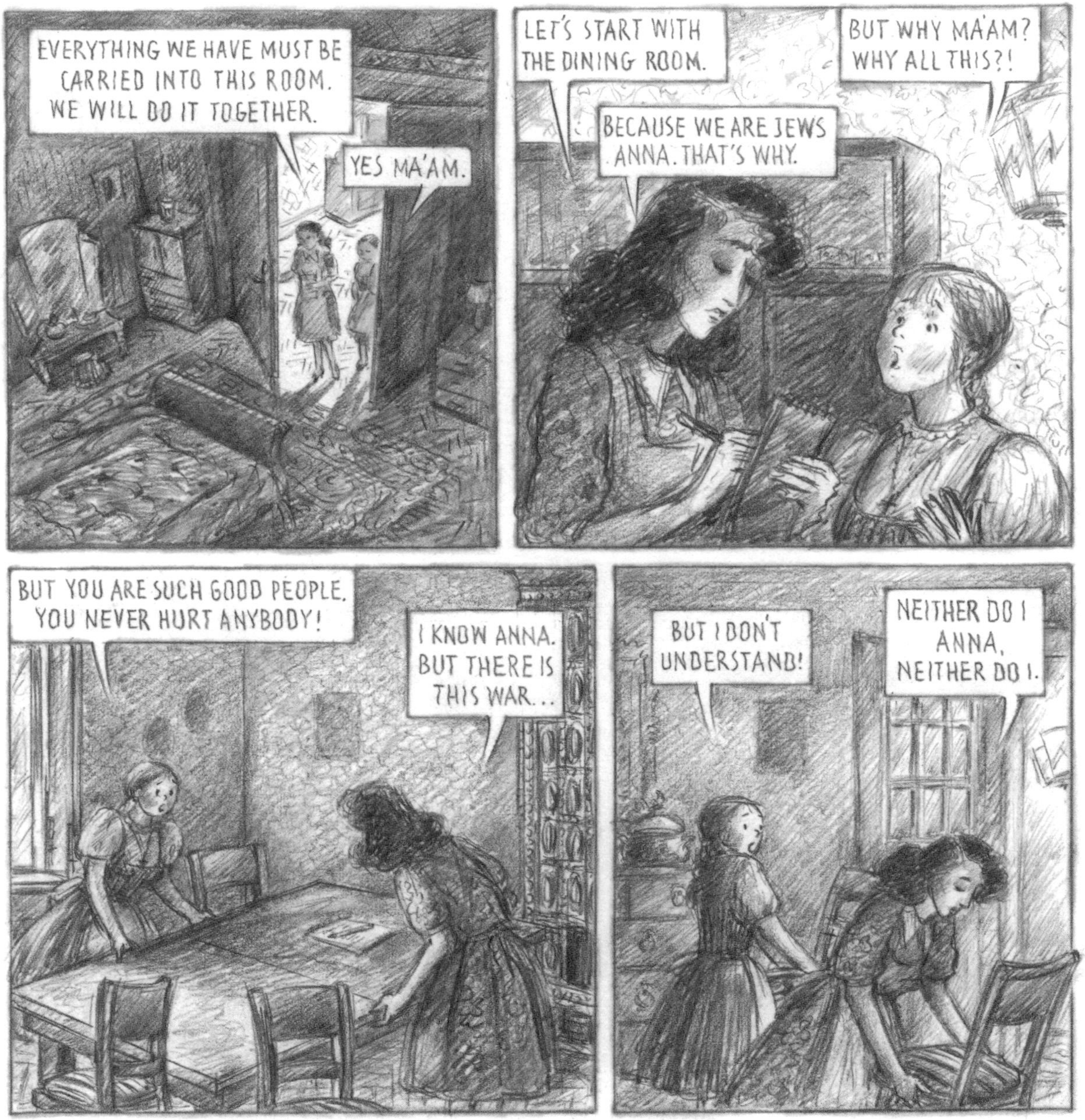
EVERYTHING WE HAVE MUST BE CARRIED INTO THIS ROOM. WE WILL DO IT TOGETHER.
YES MA'AM.
LET'S START WITH THE DINING ROOM.
BUT WHY MA'AM? WHY ALL THIS?!
BECAUSE WE ARE JEWS ANNA. THAT'S WHY.
BUT YOU ARE SUCH GOOD PEOPLE. YOU NEVER HURT ANYBODY!
I KNOW ANNA. BUT THERE IS THIS WAR...
BUT I DON'T UNDERSTAND!
NEITHER DO I ANNA, NEITHER DO I.

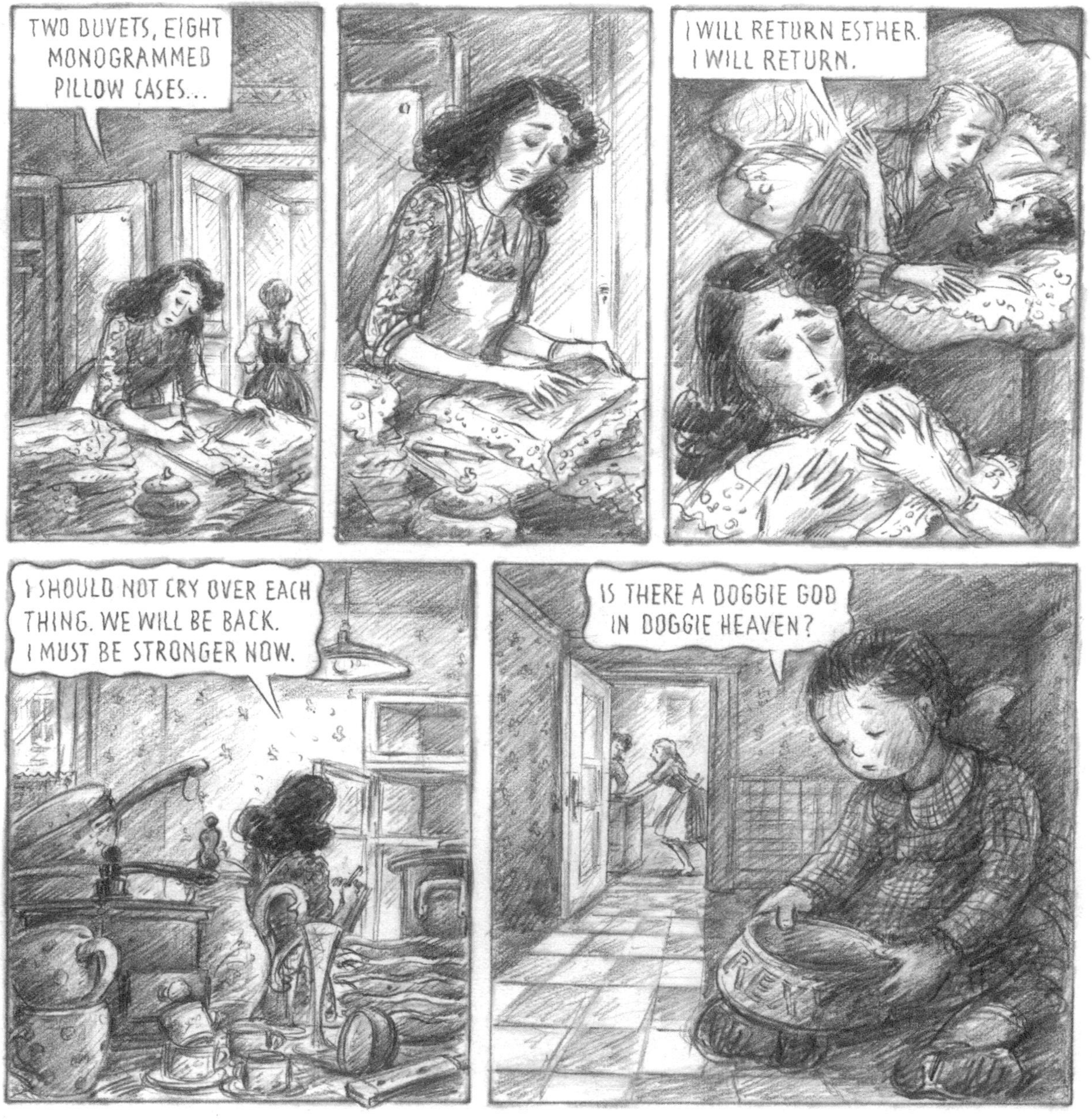
TWO DUVETS, EIGHT MONOGRAMMED PILLOW CASES...
I WILL RETURN ESTHER. I WILL RETURN.
I SHOULD NOT CRY OVER EACH THING. WE WILL BE BACK. I MUST BE STRONGER NOW.
IS THERE A DOGGIE GOD IN DOGGIE HEAVEN?
REX

YES. YES. I HAVE THE MONEY. I AM READY.
I WILL COME AFTER DARK. KEEP THE LIGHTS LOW.
BE SURE NOBODY ELSE IS THERE. DON'T TRUST ANYONE.
HERE ARE YOUR FAKE DOCUMENTS MADAME. THEY CERTIFY THAT YOU ARE A VILLAGE GIRL WITH AN ILLEGITIMATE CHILD. A SERVANT IN THE CITY.
THE CHILD'S NAME, MÁRIA VASZARI. FATHER UNKNOWN. A BASTARD. I HOPE IT WILL WORK. IT IS AN AWFUL LOT OF MONEY.
IT IS GOOD. YOU WILL BE SAFE. TAKE THE TRAIN. I HAVE A TICKET FOR YOU AND AN ADDRESS. MY UNCLE'S. GOOD PEOPLE.

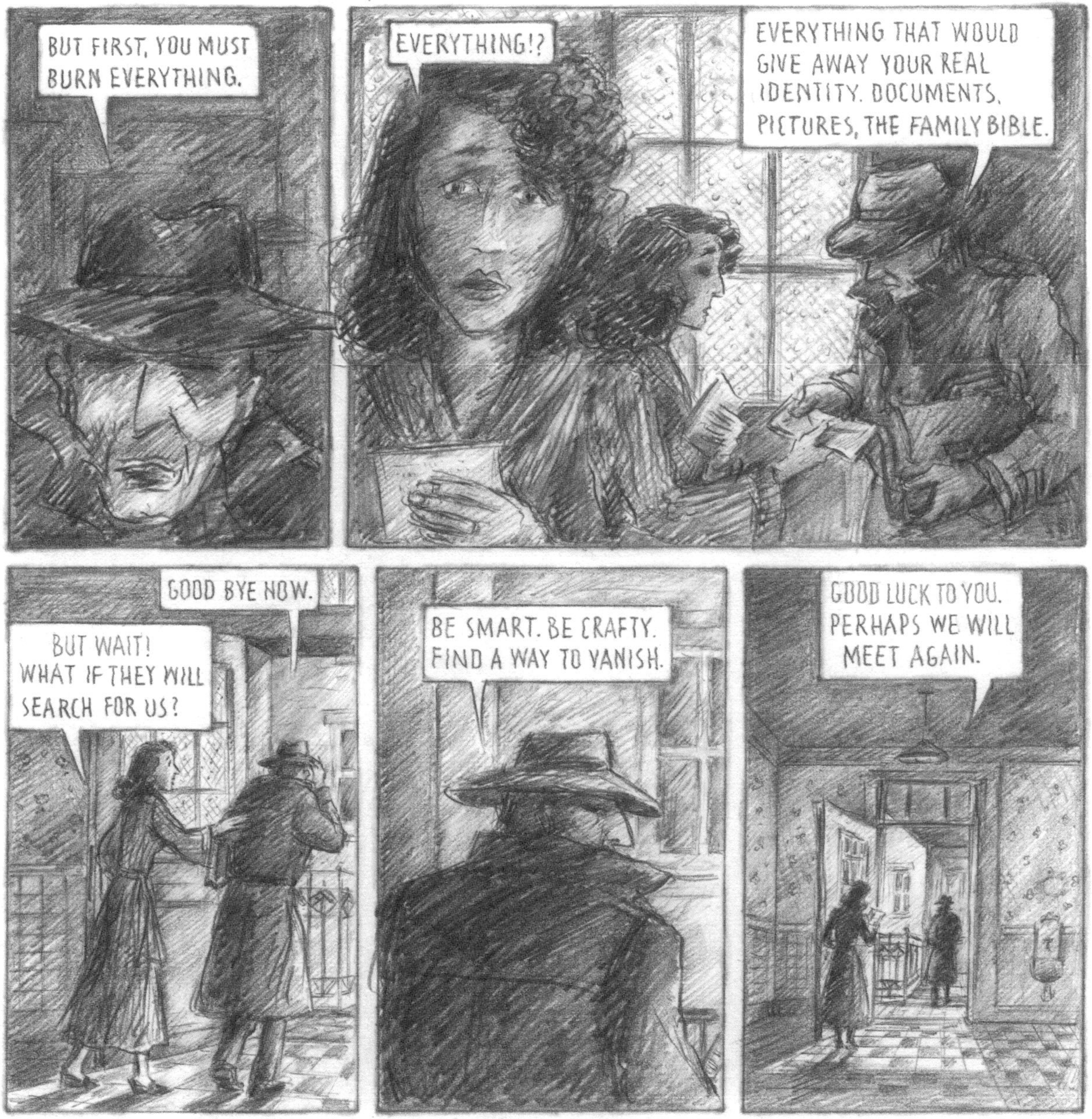
BUT FIRST, YOU MUST BURN EVERYTHING.
EVERYTHING!?
EVERYTHING THAT WOULD GIVE AWAY YOUR REAL IDENTITY. DOCUMENTS, PICTURES, THE FAMILY BIBLE.
GOOD BYE NOW.
BUT WAIT! WHAT IF THEY WILL SEARCH FOR US?
BE SMART. BE CRAFTY. FIND A WAY TO VANISH.
GOOD LUCK TO YOU. PERHAPS WE WILL MEET AGAIN.

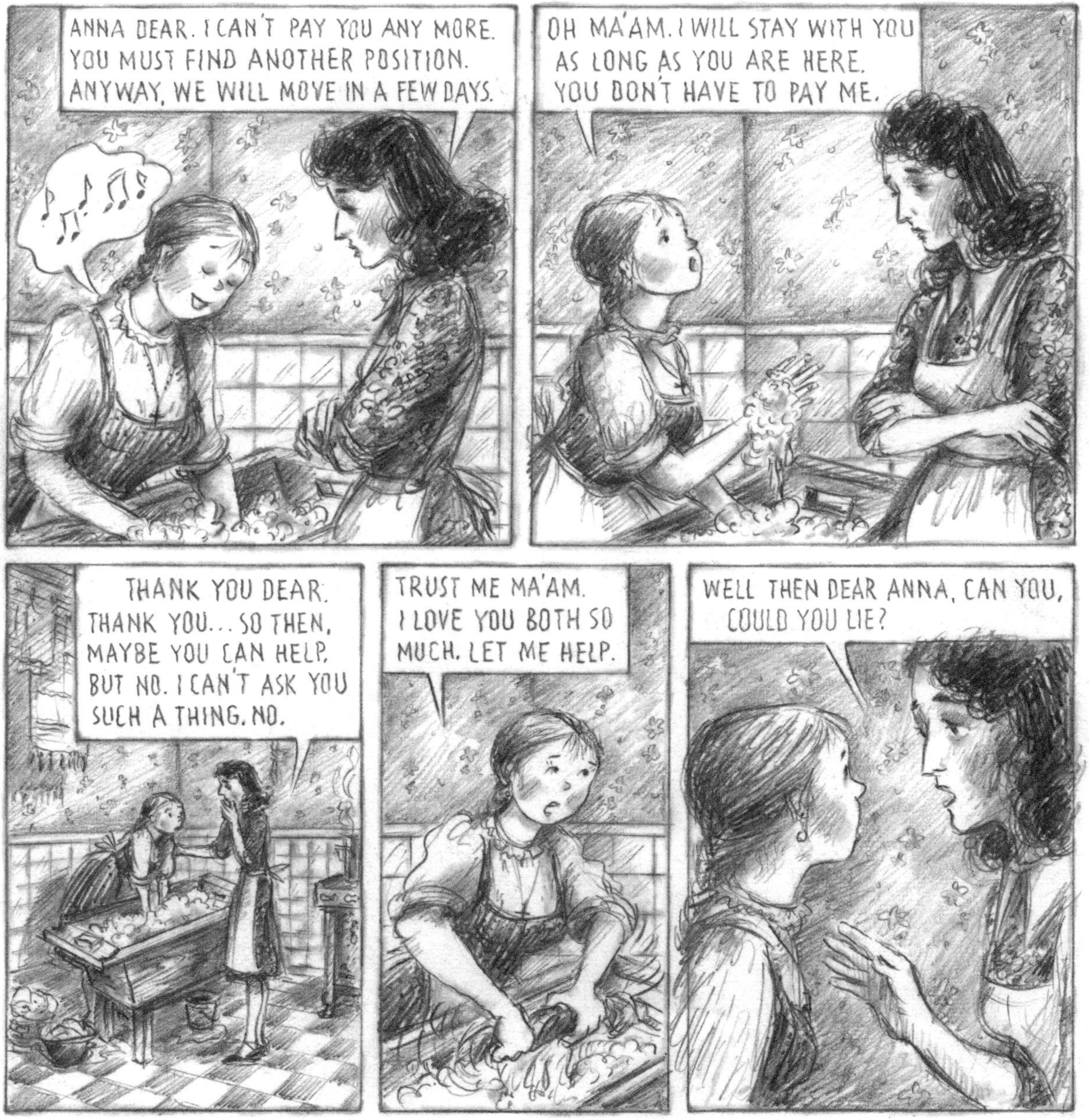
ANNA DEAR. I CAN'T PAY YOU ANY MORE. YOU MUST FIND ANOTHER POSITION. ANYWAY, WE WILL MOVE IN A FEW DAYS.
OH MA'AM. I WILL STAY WITH YOU AS LONG AS YOU ARE HERE. YOU DON'T HAVE TO PAY ME.
THANK YOU DEAR. THANK YOU... SO THEN, MAYBE YOU CAN HELP. BUT NO. I CAN'T ASK YOU SUCH A THING. NO.
TRUST ME MA'AM. I LOVE YOU BOTH SO MUCH. LET ME HELP.
WELL THEN DEAR ANNA, CAN YOU, COULD YOU LIE?

GO TO SLEEP NOW SWEETIE. I STILL HAVE SOME WORK TO DO.

EVERYTHING I HAVE TO BURN IS IN HERE.

MOTHER, SHE WAS ABOUT MY AGE HERE. HOW VERY BEAUTIFUL, WEARING HER SABBATH WHIG.

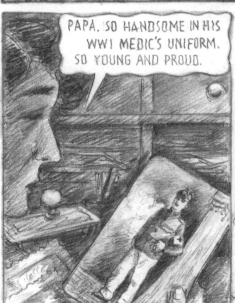

PAPA. SO HANDSOME IN HIS WWI MEDIC'S UNIFORM. SO YOUNG AND PROUD.

OUR WEDDING DAY. OH THE PLANS WE HAD. THE PLANS WE MADE.

LETTERS FROM THE FRONT. IF THEY KEEP COMING, WHO WILL READ THEM? WHO WILL ANSWER THEM?

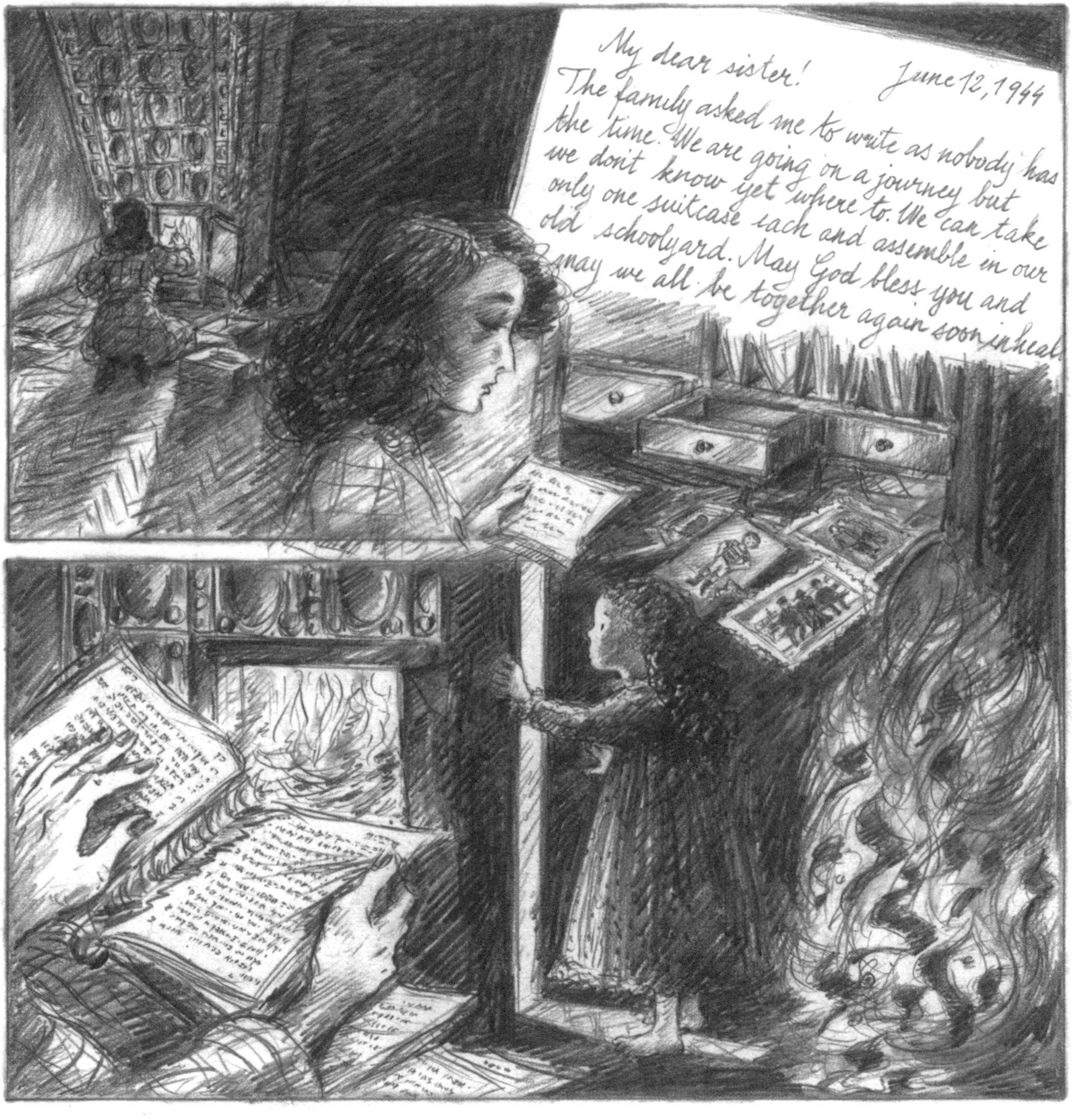
My dear sister! June 12, 1944
The family asked me to write as nobody has
the time. We are going on a journey but
we don't know yet where to. We can take
only one suitcase each and assemble in our
old schoolyard. May God bless you and
may we all be together again soon in heal

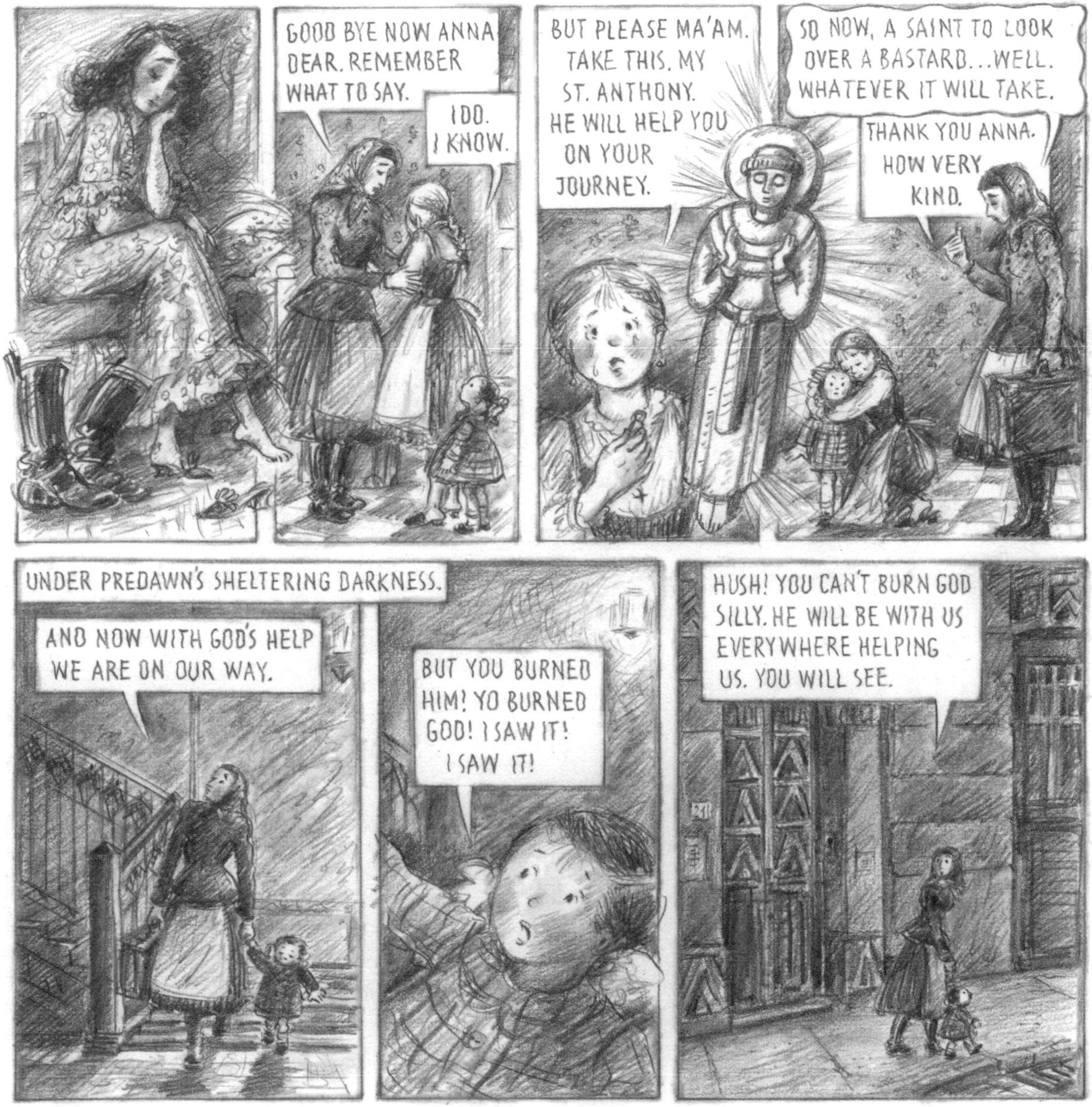
GOOD BYE NOW ANNA DEAR. REMEMBER WHAT TO SAY.
I DO. I KNOW.
BUT PLEASE MA'AM. TAKE THIS. MY ST. ANTHONY. HE WILL HELP YOU ON YOUR JOURNEY.
SO NOW, A SAINT TO LOOK OVER A BASTARD...WELL. WHATEVER IT WILL TAKE.
THANK YOU ANNA. HOW VERY KIND.
UNDER PREDAWN'S SHELTERING DARKNESS.
AND NOW WITH GOD'S HELP WE ARE ON OUR WAY.
BUT YOU BURNED HIM! YO BURNED GOD! I SAW IT! I SAW IT!
HUSH! YOU CAN'T BURN GOD SILLY. HE WILL BE WITH US EVERYWHERE HELPING US. YOU WILL SEE.

I AM ON MY OWN. GOOD BYE COSMOPOLITAN LADY. I MUST ACT THIS NEW ROLE. MUST NOT LOOK SCARED. LOOK DEFIANT.
WHY IN SUCH HURRY ANGEL?
HEY! CUTIE!
ACT VULGAR. TALK BACK.
PIECE OF ASS YAH?
MANY ATTEMPT TO FLEE THE CITY ILLEGALLY. WE TRY TO CATCH THOSE.
HALT!
UTASOK BALRA

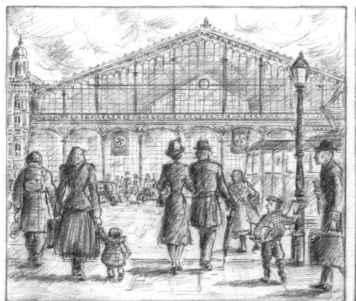

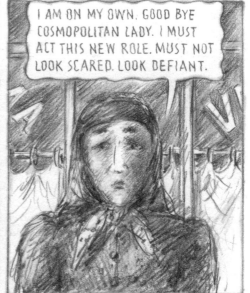

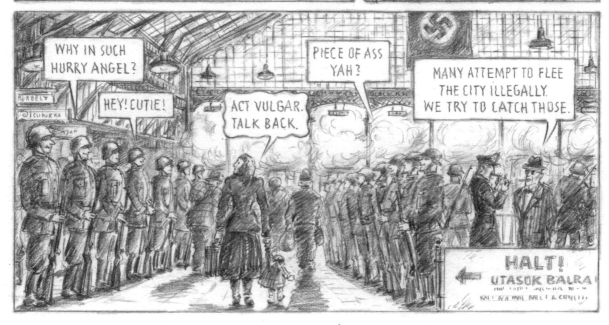

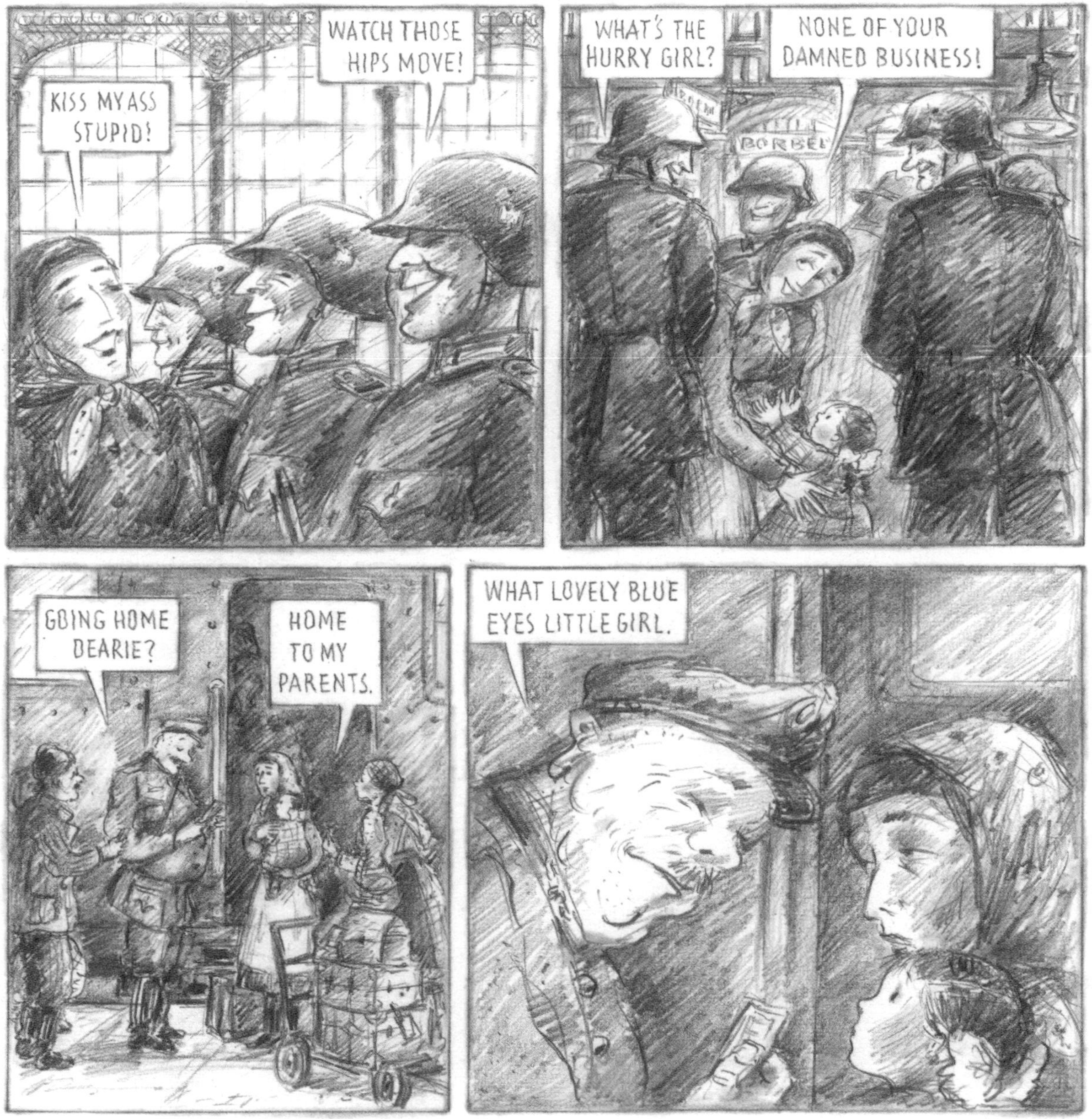

WATCH THOSE HIPS MOVE!
KISS MY ASS STUPID!
WHAT'S THE HURRY GIRL?
NONE OF YOUR DAMNED BUSINESS!
GOING HOME DEARIE?
HOME TO MY PARENTS.
WHAT LOVELY BLUE EYES LITTLE GIRL.

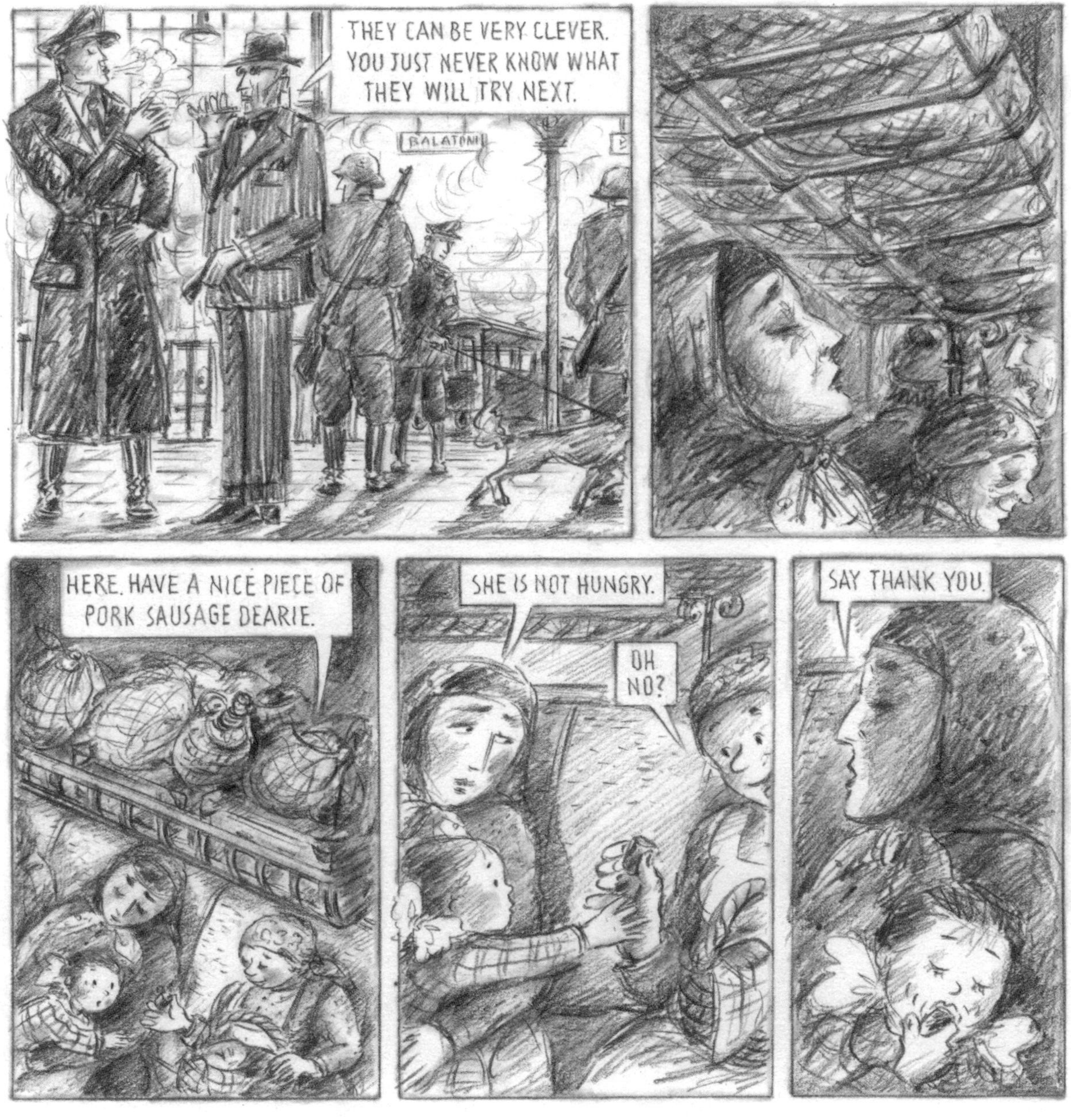
THEY CAN BE VERY CLEVER. YOU JUST NEVER KNOW WHAT THEY WILL TRY NEXT.
BALATONI
HERE. HAVE A NICE PIECE OF PORK SAUSAGE DEARIE.
SHE IS NOT HUNGRY.
OH NO?
SAY THANK YOU.

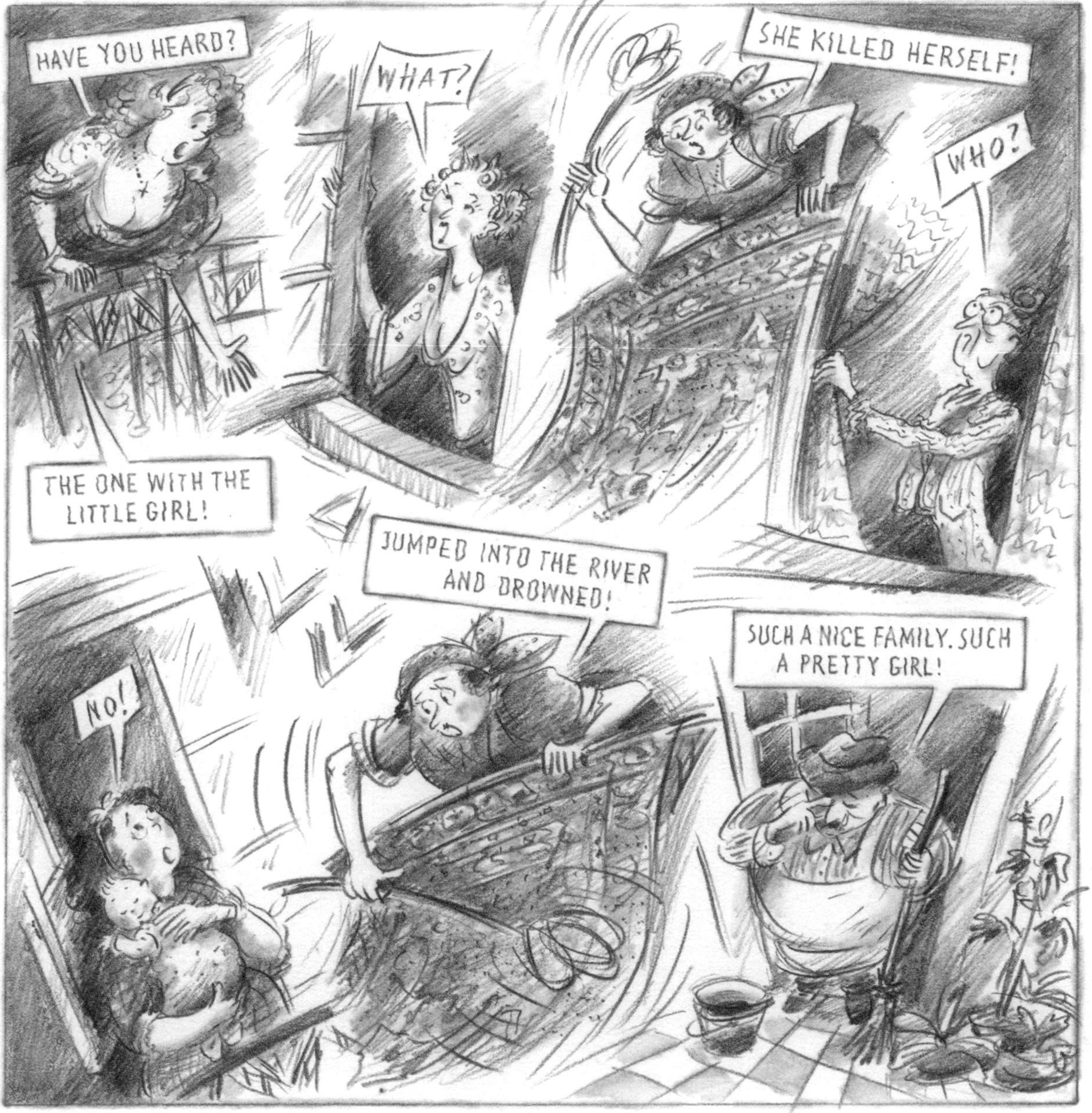
HAVE YOU HEARD?
WHAT?
SHE KILLED HERSELF!
WHO?
THE ONE WITH THE LITTLE GIRL!
NO!
JUMPED INTO THE RIVER AND DROWNED!
SUCH A NICE FAMILY. SUCH A PRETTY GIRL!

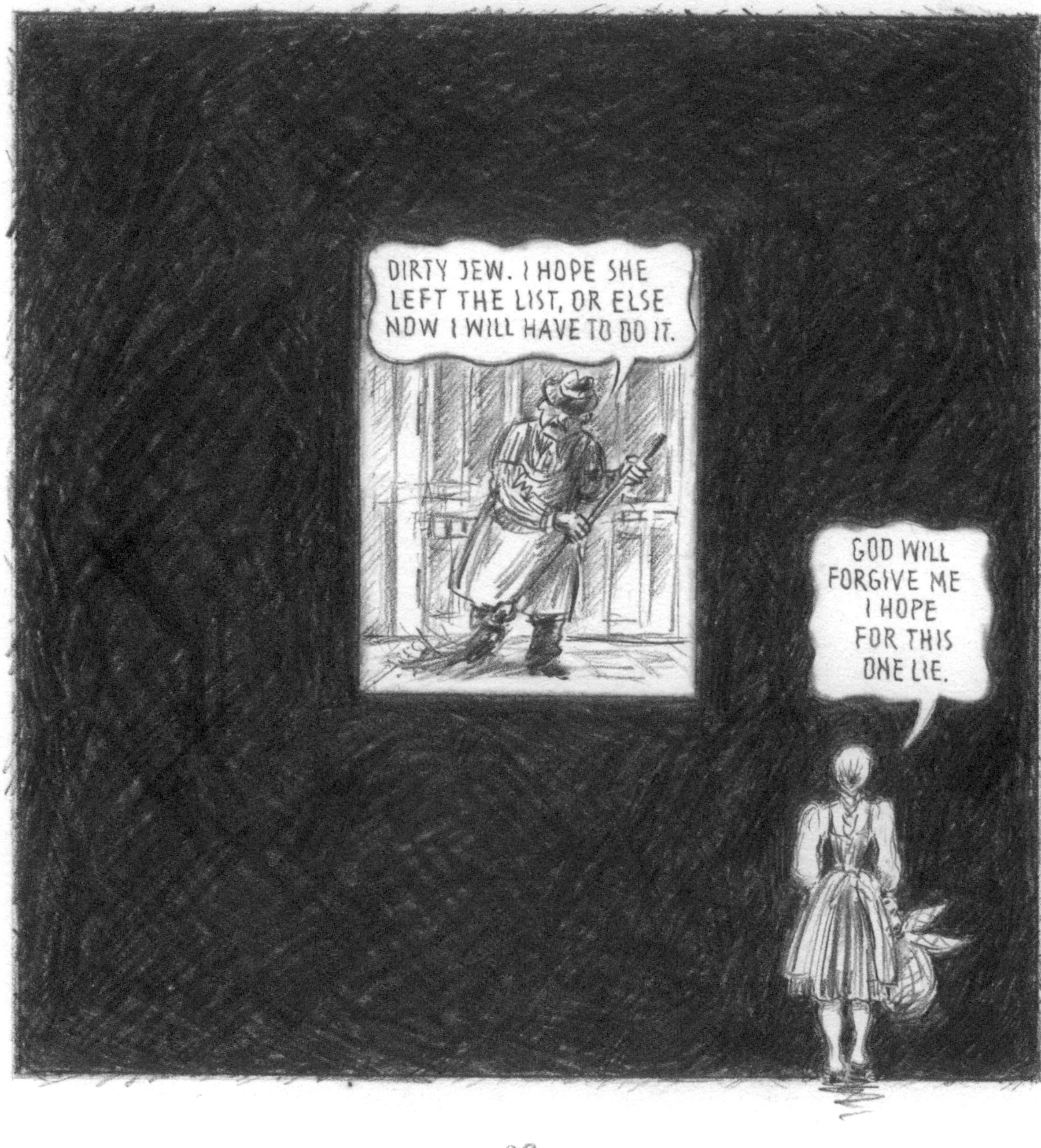
DIRTY JEW. I HOPE SHE LEFT THE LIST, OR ELSE NOW I WILL HAVE TO DO IT.
GOD WILL FORGIVE ME I HOPE FOR THIS ONE LIE.

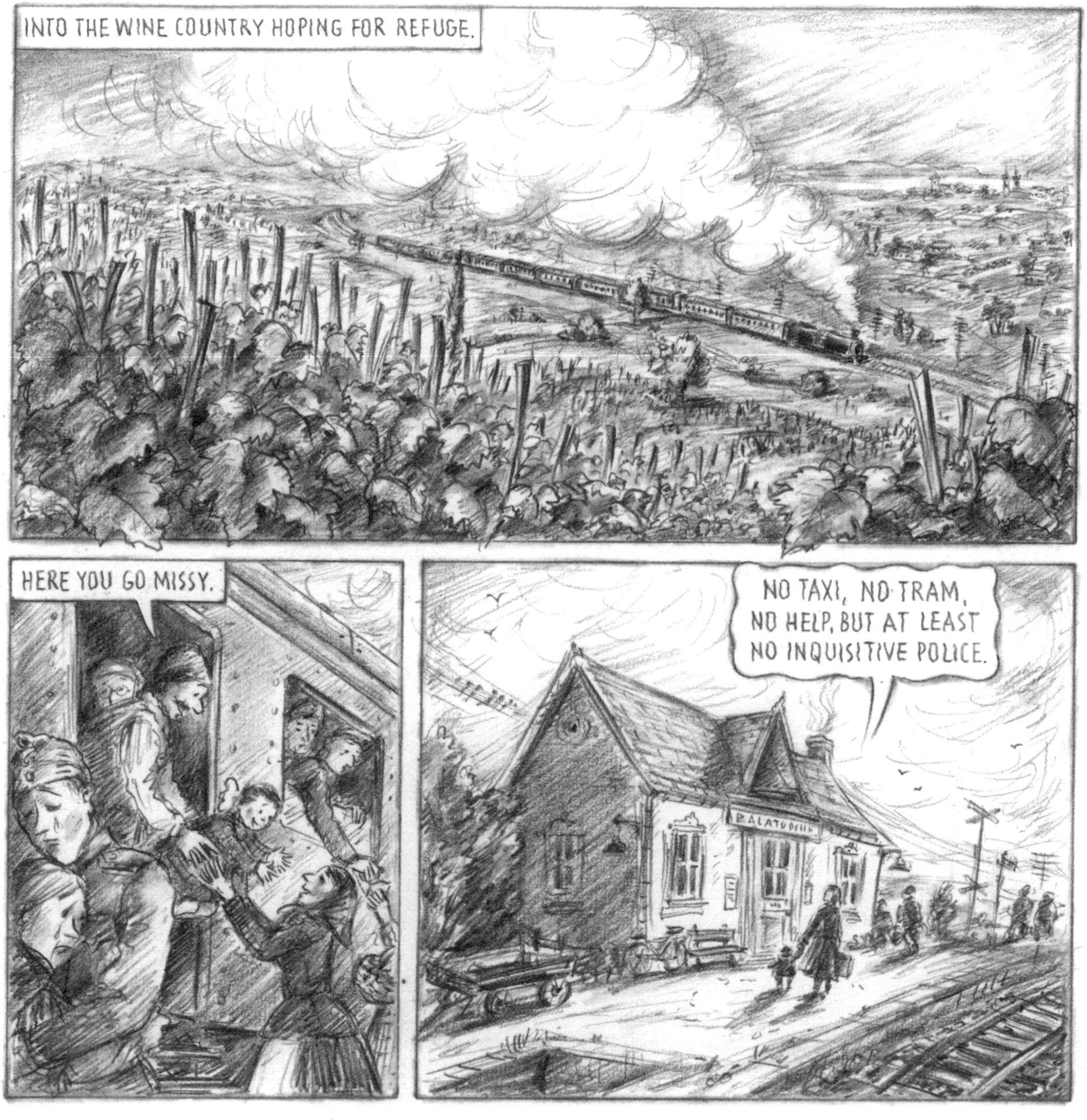
INTO THE WINE COUNTRY HOPING FOR REFUGE.
HERE YOU GO MISSY.
NO TAXI, NO TRAM, NO HELP, BUT AT LEAST NO INQUISITIVE POLICE.

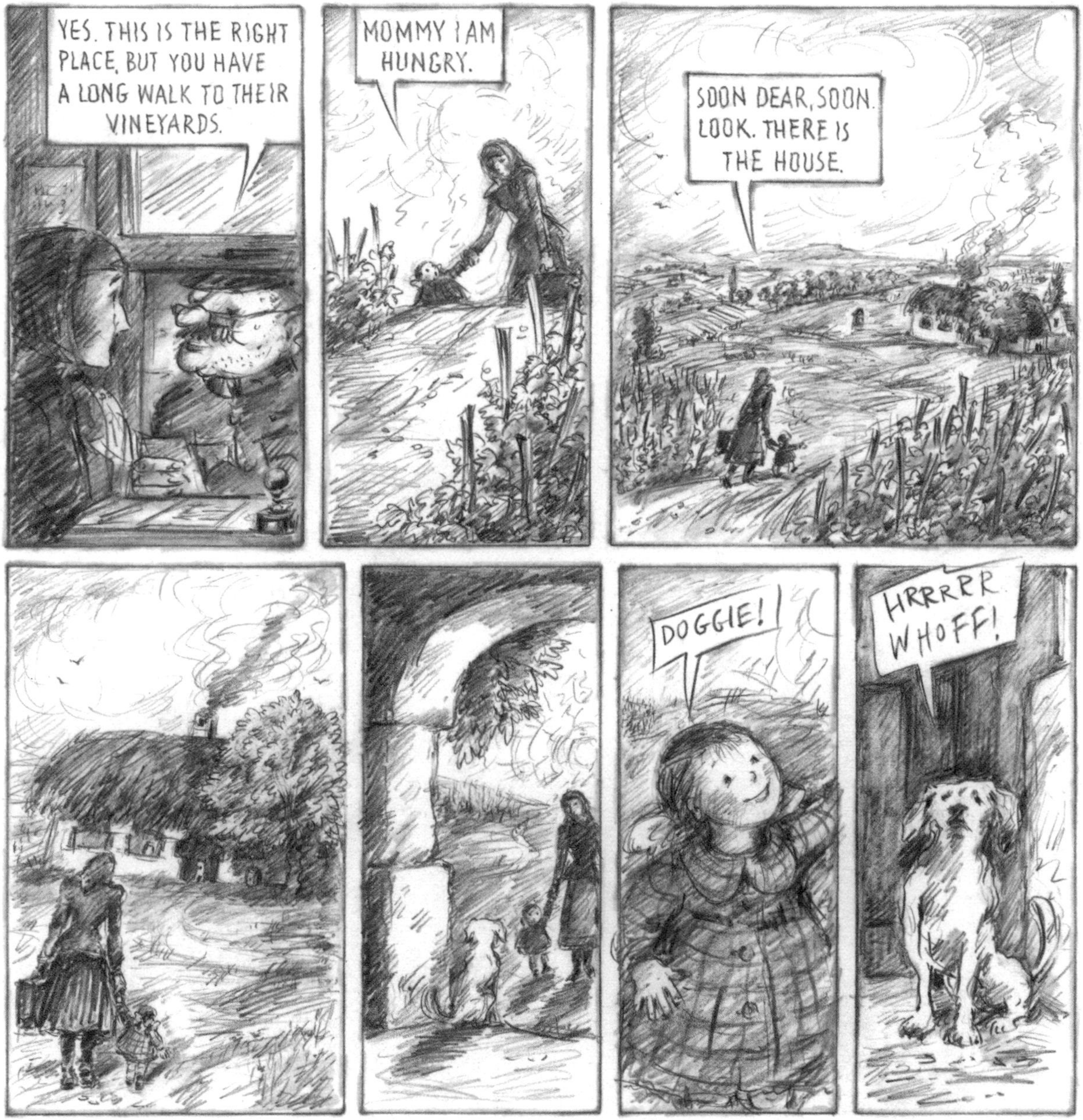
YES. THIS IS THE RIGHT PLACE, BUT YOU HAVE A LONG WALK TO THEIR VINEYARDS.
MOMMY I AM HUNGRY.
SOON DEAR, SOON. LOOK. THERE IS THE HOUSE.
DOGGIE!
HRRRRR WHOFF!

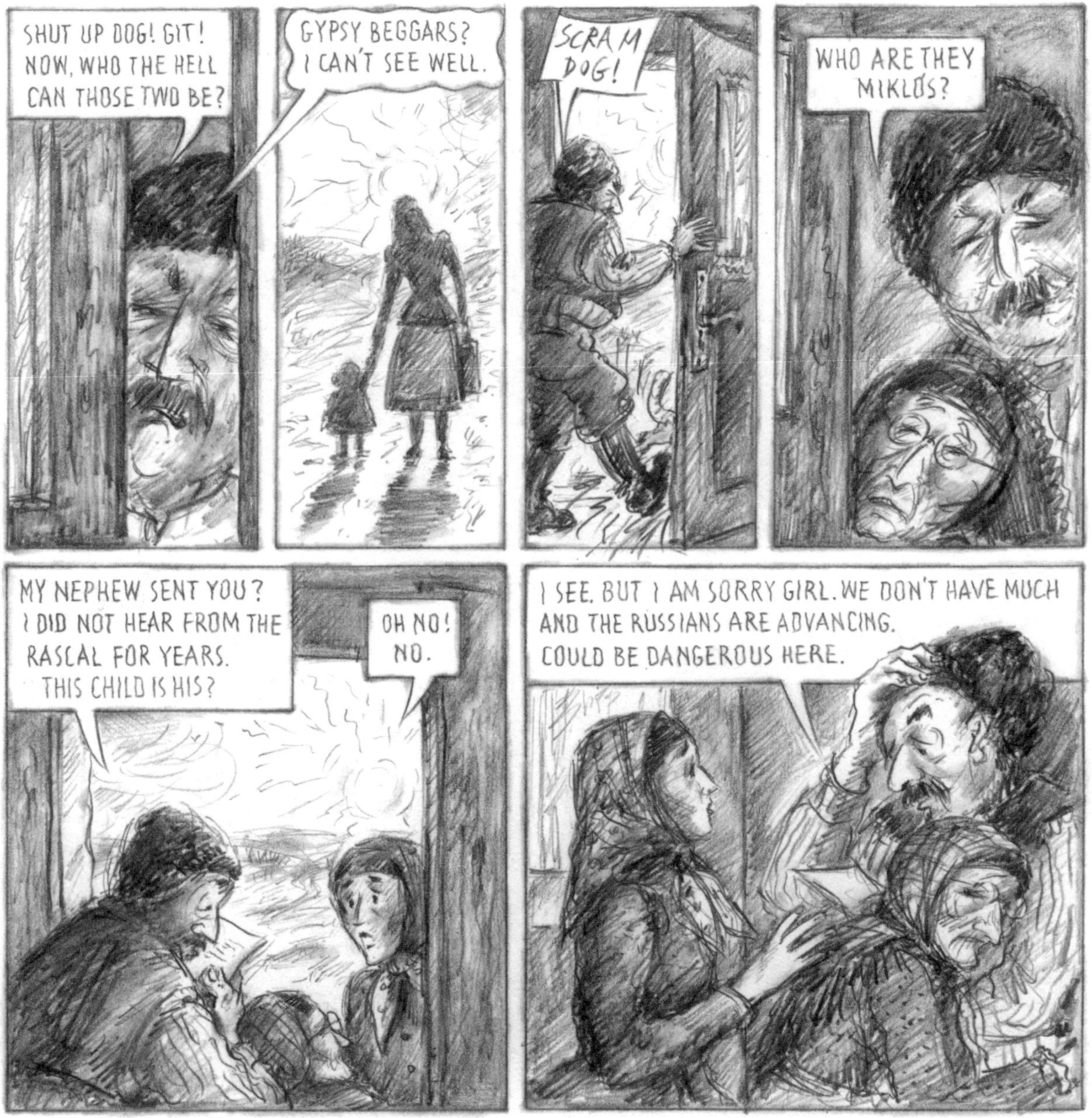

SHUT UP DOG! GIT! NOW, WHO THE HELL CAN THOSE TWO BE?
GYPSY BEGGARS? I CAN'T SEE WELL.
SCRAM DOG!
WHO ARE THEY MIKLOS?
MY NEPHEW SENT YOU? I DID NOT HEAR FROM THE RASCAL FOR YEARS. THIS CHILD IS HIS?
OH NO! NO.
I SEE. BUT I AM SORRY GIRL. WE DON'T HAVE MUCH AND THE RUSSIANS ARE ADVANCING. COULD BE DANGEROUS HERE.

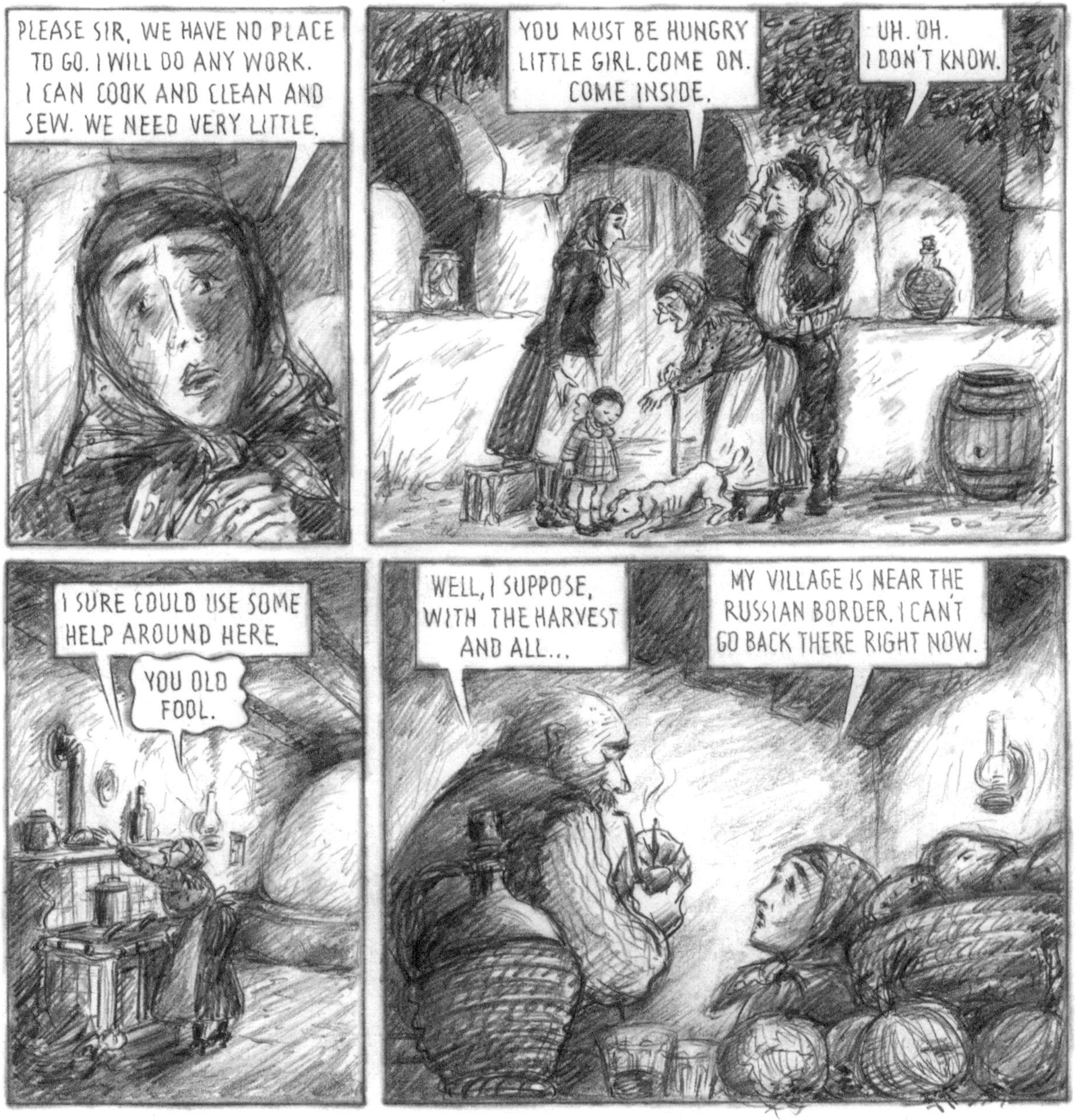
PLEASE SIR, WE HAVE NO PLACE TO GO. I WILL DO ANY WORK. I CAN COOK AND CLEAN AND SEW. WE NEED VERY LITTLE.
YOU MUST BE HUNGRY LITTLE GIRL. COME ON. COME INSIDE.
UH. OH. I DON'T KNOW.
I SURE COULD USE SOME HELP AROUND HERE.
YOU OLD FOOL.
WELL, I SUPPOSE, WITH THE HARVEST AND ALL...
MY VILLAGE IS NEAR THE RUSSIAN BORDER. I CAN'T GO BACK THERE RIGHT NOW.

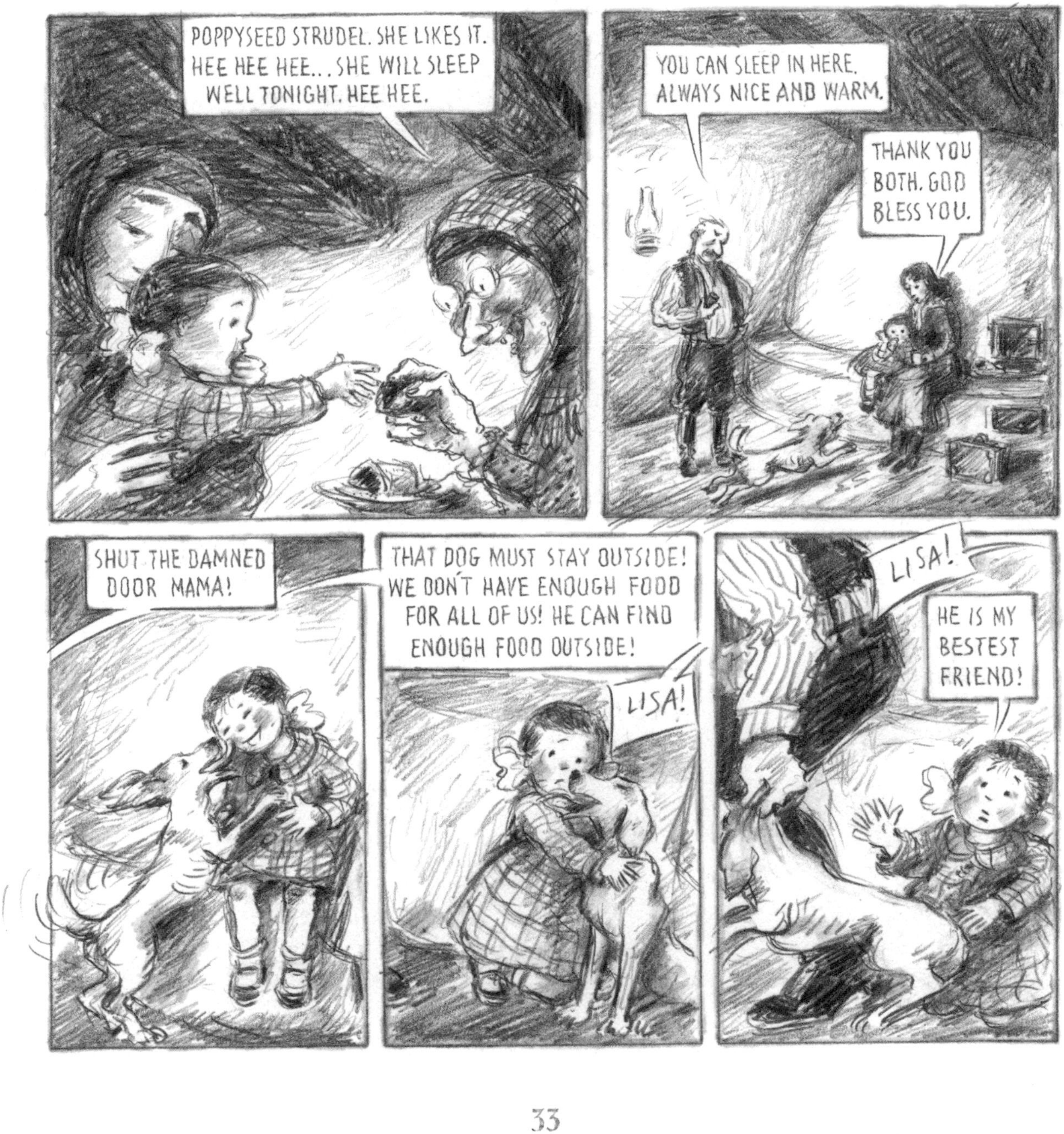
POPPYSEED STRUDEL. SHE LIKES IT. HEE HEE HEE... SHE WILL SLEEP WELL TONIGHT. HEE HEE.
YOU CAN SLEEP IN HERE. ALWAYS NICE AND WARM.
THANK YOU BOTH. GOD BLESS YOU.
SHUT THE DAMNED DOOR MAMA!
THAT DOG MUST STAY OUTSIDE! WE DON'T HAVE ENOUGH FOOD FOR ALL OF US! HE CAN FIND ENOUGH FOOD OUTSIDE!
LISA!
LISA!
HE IS MY BESTEST FRIEND!

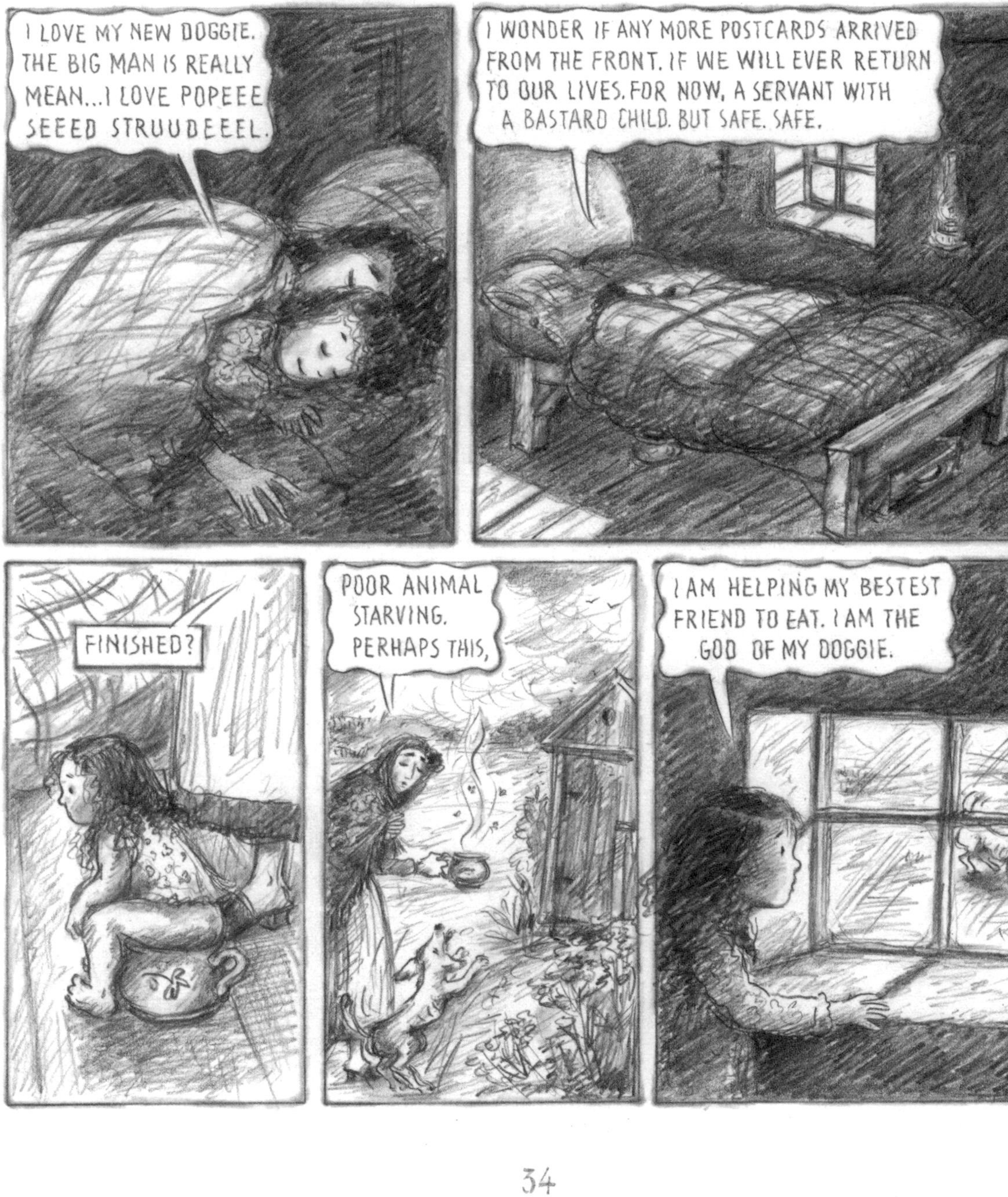
I LOVE MY NEW DOGGIE. THE BIG MAN IS REALLY MEAN...I LOVE POPEEE SEEED STRUUDEEEL.
I WONDER IF ANY MORE POSTCARDS ARRIVED FROM THE FRONT. IF WE WILL EVER RETURN TO OUR LIVES. FOR NOW, A SERVANT WITH A BASTARD CHILD. BUT SAFE. SAFE.
FINISHED?
POOR ANIMAL STARVING. PERHAPS THIS,
I AM HELPING MY BESTEST FRIEND TO EAT. I AM THE GOD OF MY DOGGIE.

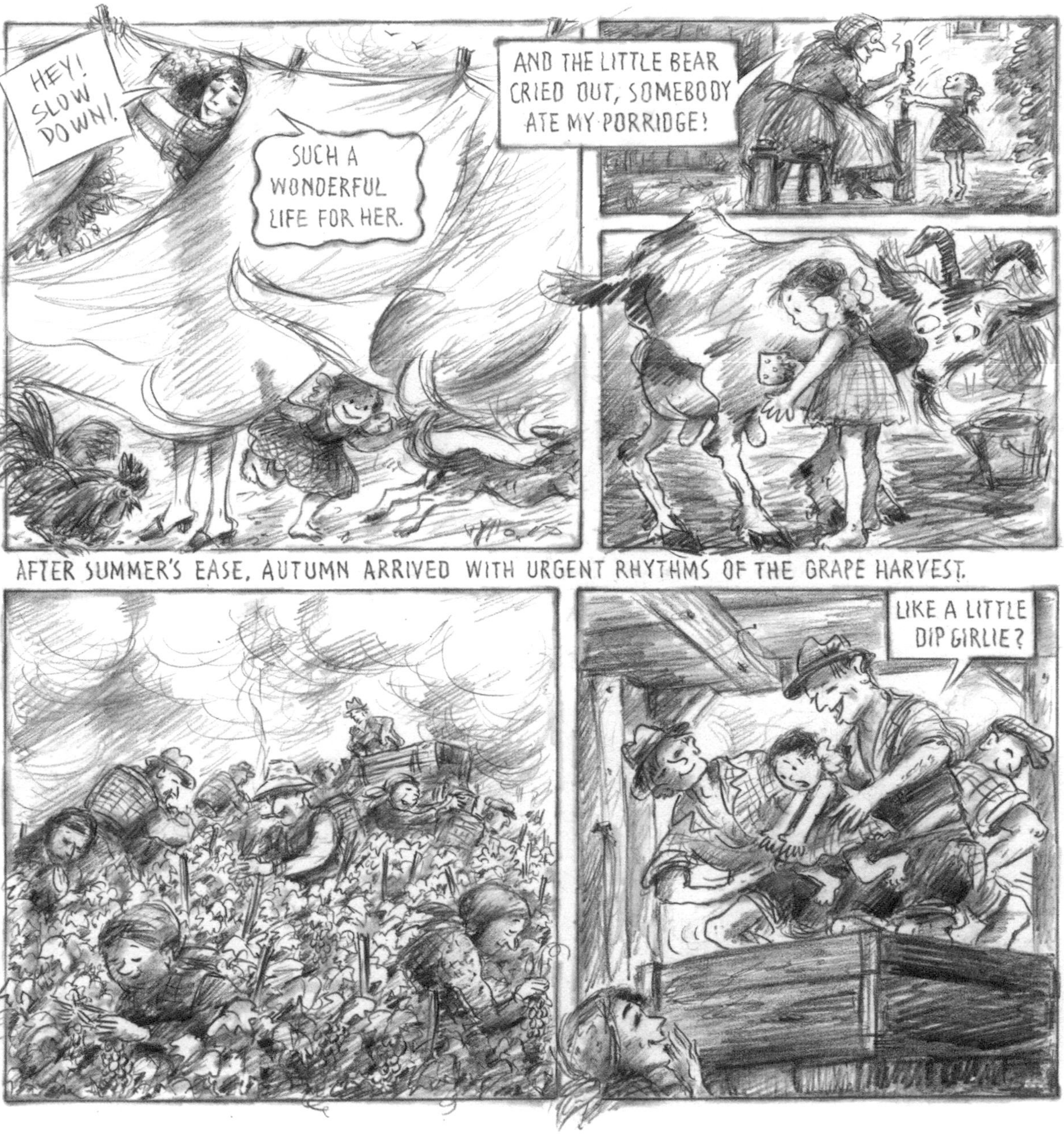
HEY! SLOW DOWN!
SUCH A WONDERFUL LIFE FOR HER.
AND THE LITTLE BEAR CRIED OUT, SOMEBODY ATE MY PORRIDGE!
AFTER SUMMER'S EASE, AUTUMN ARRIVED WITH URGENT RHYTHMS OF THE GRAPE HARVEST.
LIKE A LITTLE DIP GIRLIE?

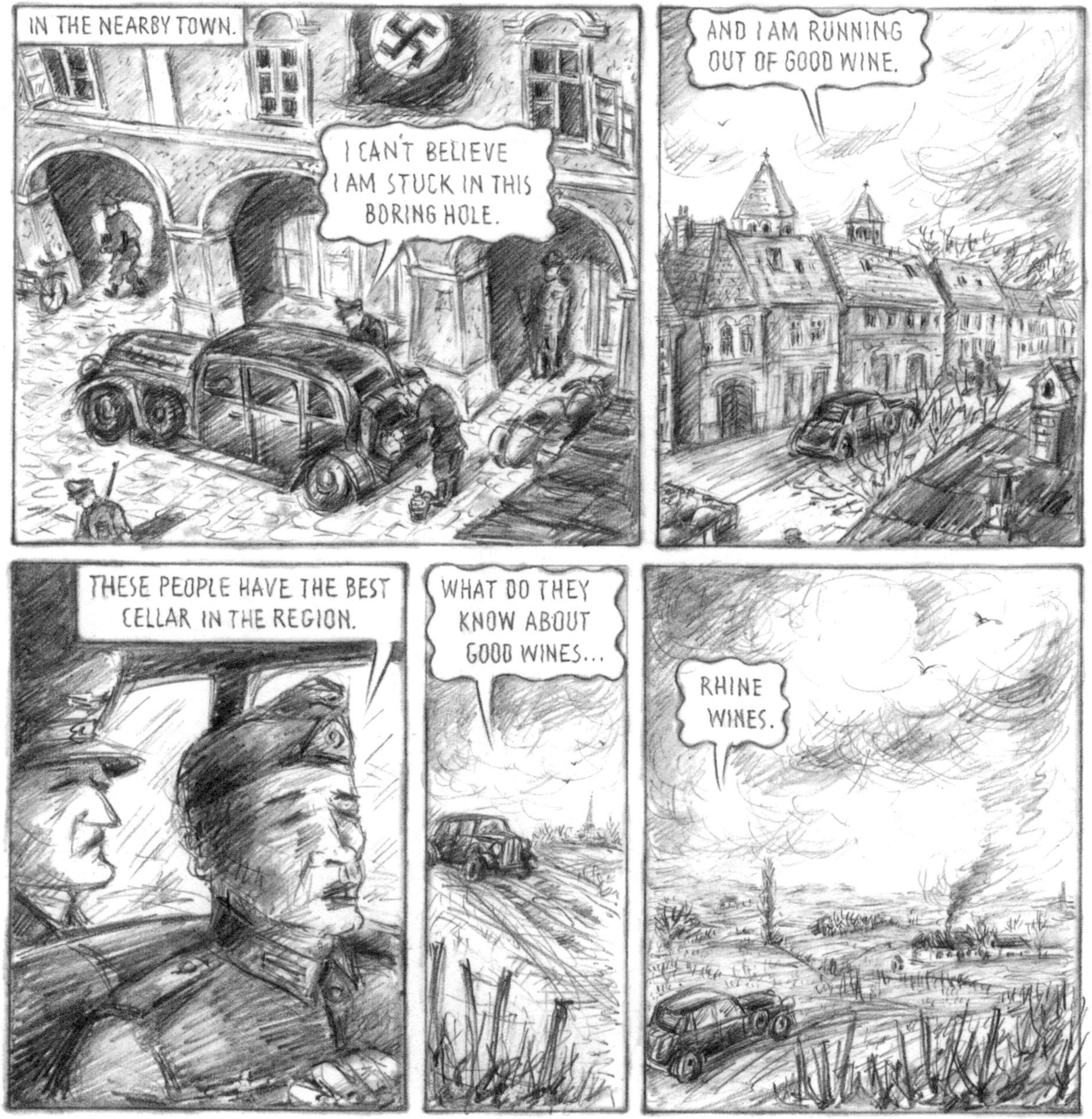
IN THE NEARBY TOWN.
I CAN'T BELIEVE I AM STUCK IN THIS BORING HOLE.
AND I AM RUNNING OUT OF GOOD WINE.
THESE PEOPLE HAVE THE BEST CELLAR IN THE REGION.
WHAT DO THEY KNOW ABOUT GOOD WINES...
RHINE WINES.

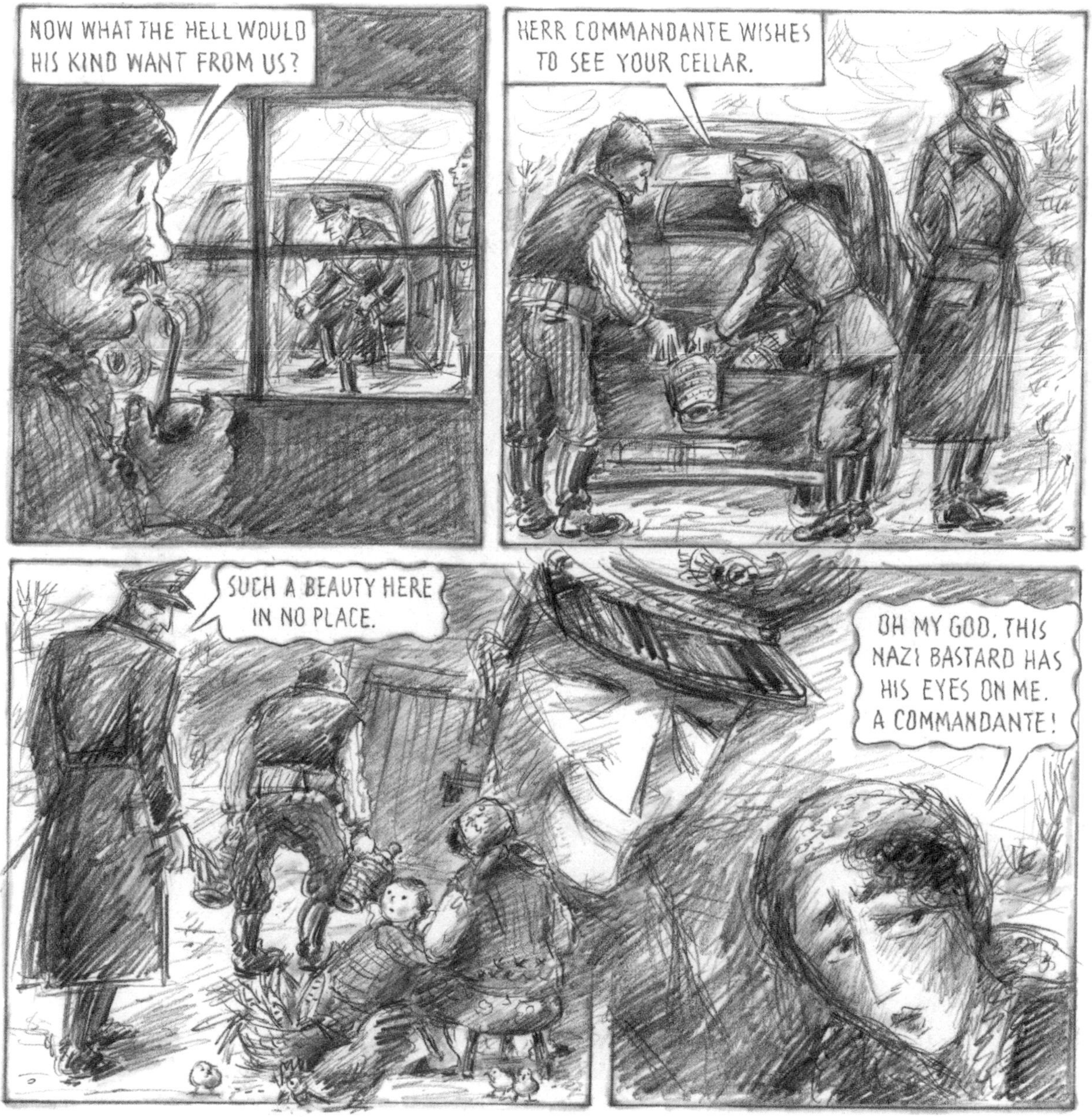
NOW WHAT THE HELL WOULD HIS KIND WANT FROM US?
HERR COMMANDANTE WISHES TO SEE YOUR CELLAR.
SUCH A BEAUTY HERE IN NO PLACE.
OH MY GOD. THIS NAZI BASTARD HAS HIS EYES ON ME. A COMMANDANTE!

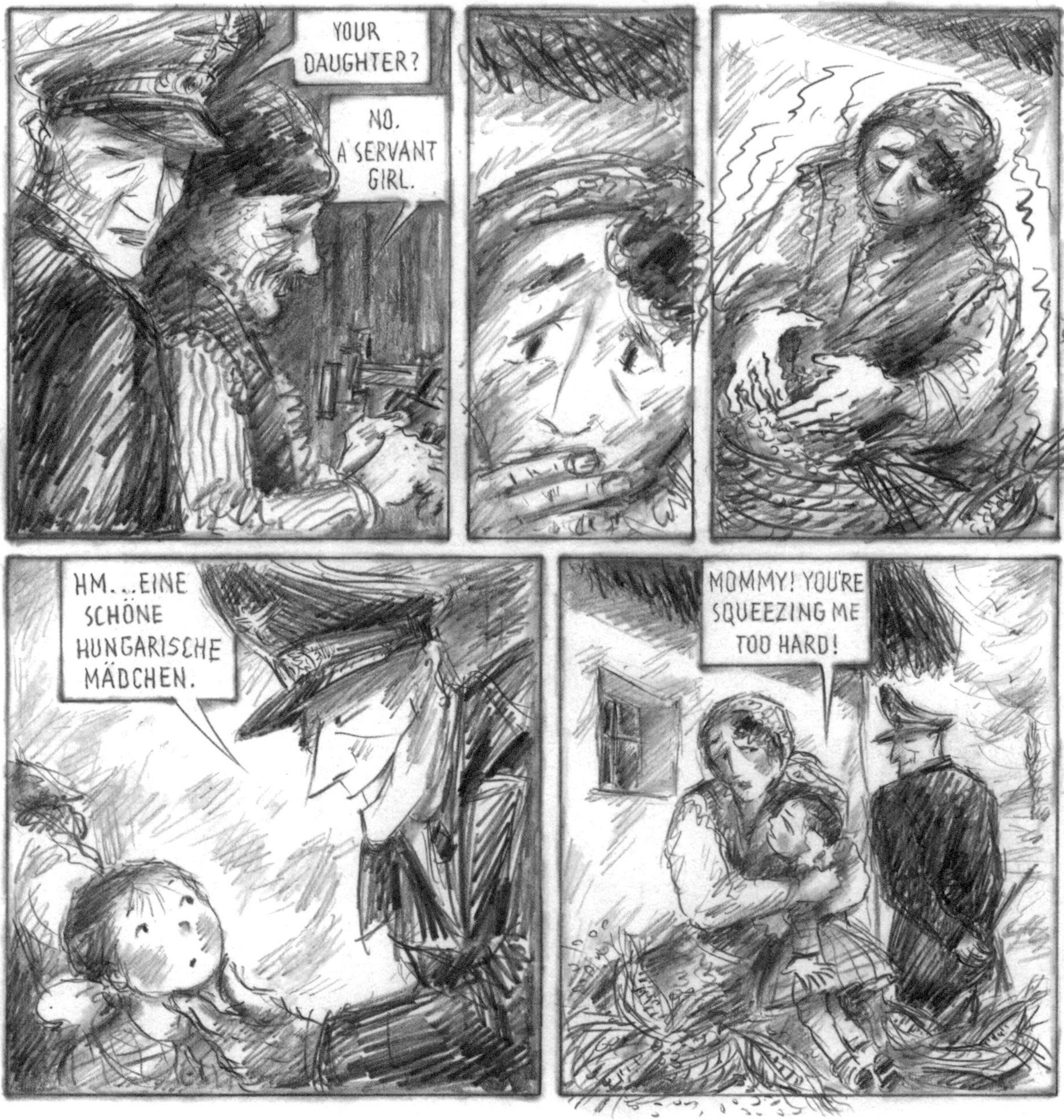
YOUR DAUGHTER?
NO. A SERVANT GIRL.
HM...EINE SCHÖNE HUNGARISCHE MÄDCHEN.
MOMMY! YOU'RE SQUEEZING ME TOO HARD!

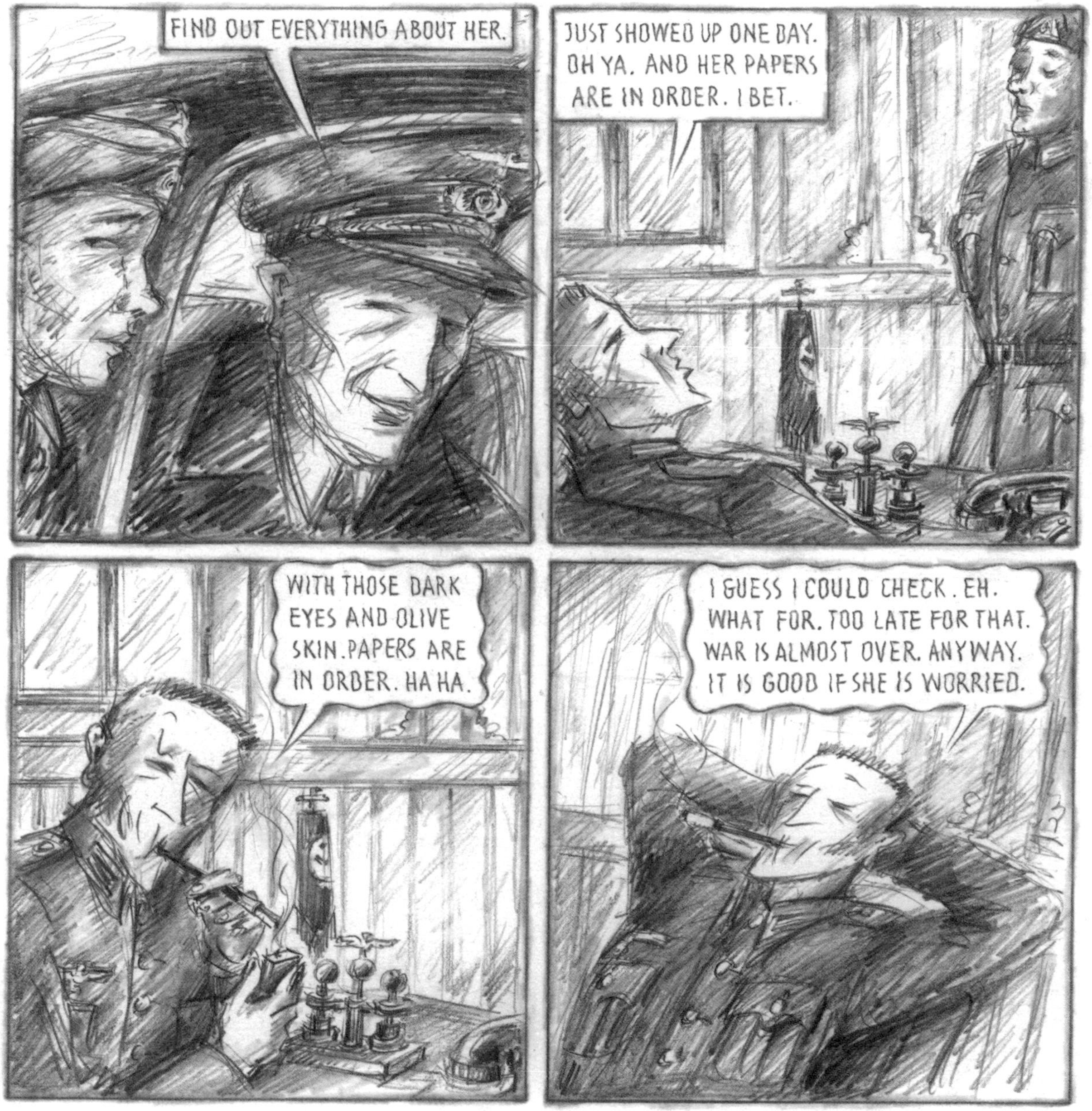
FIND OUT EVERYTHING ABOUT HER.
JUST SHOWED UP ONE DAY. OH YA. AND HER PAPERS ARE IN ORDER. I BET.
WITH THOSE DARK EYES AND OLIVE SKIN. PAPERS ARE IN ORDER. HA HA.
I GUESS I COULD CHECK. EH. WHAT FOR. TOO LATE FOR THAT. WAR IS ALMOST OVER. ANYWAY. IT IS GOOD IF SHE IS WORRIED.

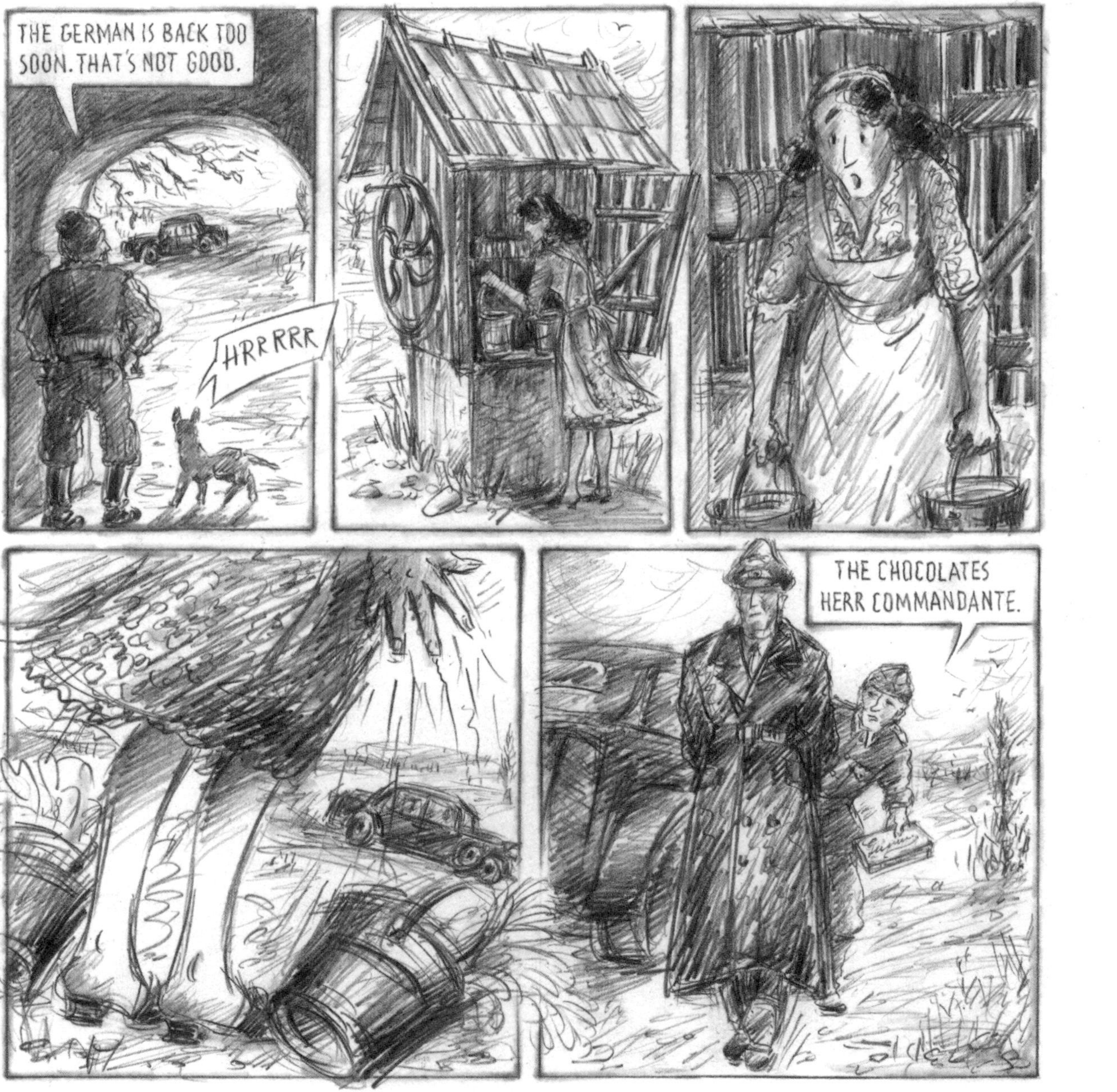
THE GERMAN IS BACK TOO SOON. THAT'S NOT GOOD.
HRRRRR
THE CHOCOLATES HERR COMMANDANTE.

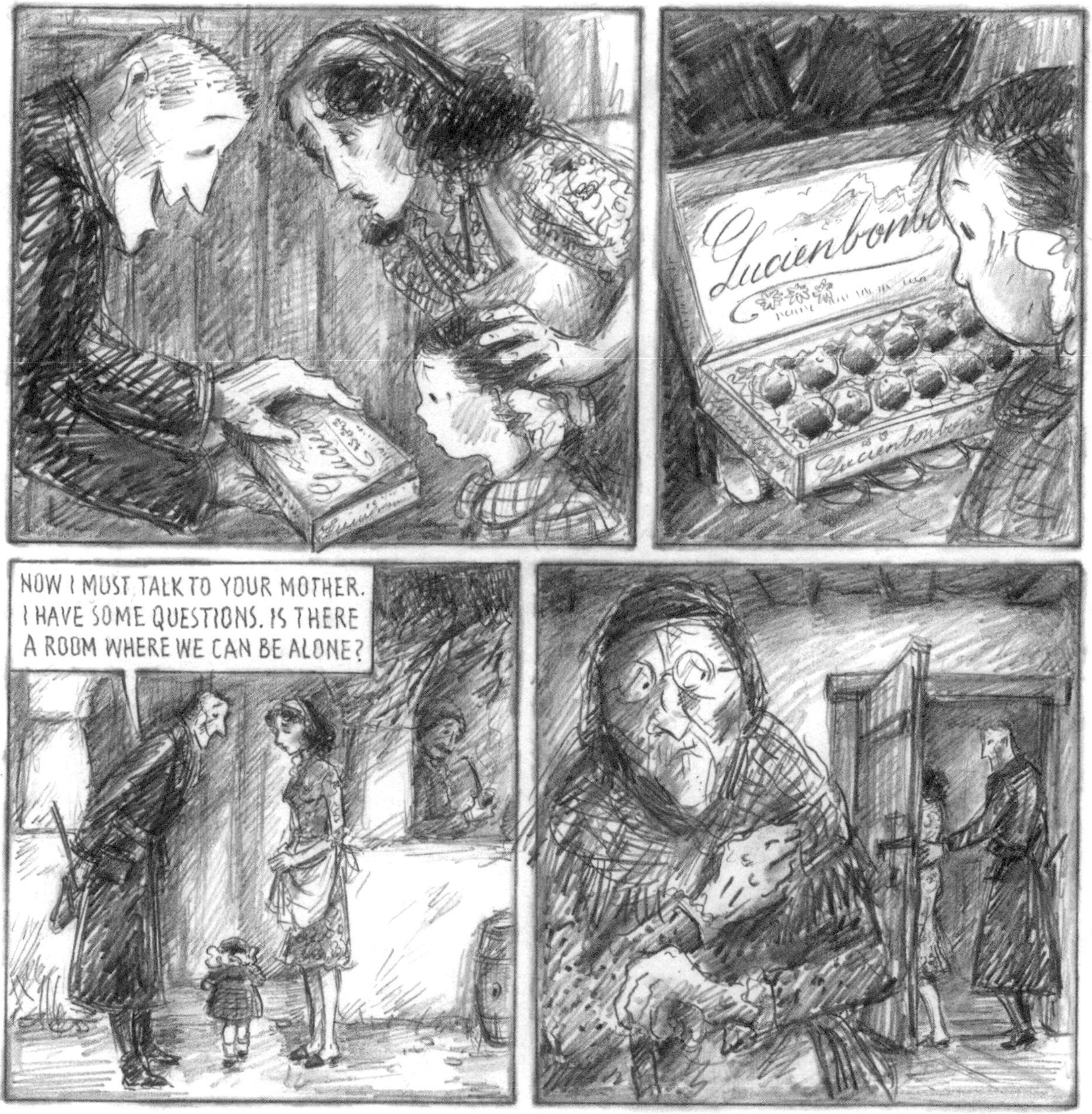
NOW I MUST TALK TO YOUR MOTHER. I HAVE SOME QUESTIONS. IS THERE A ROOM WHERE WE CAN BE ALONE?

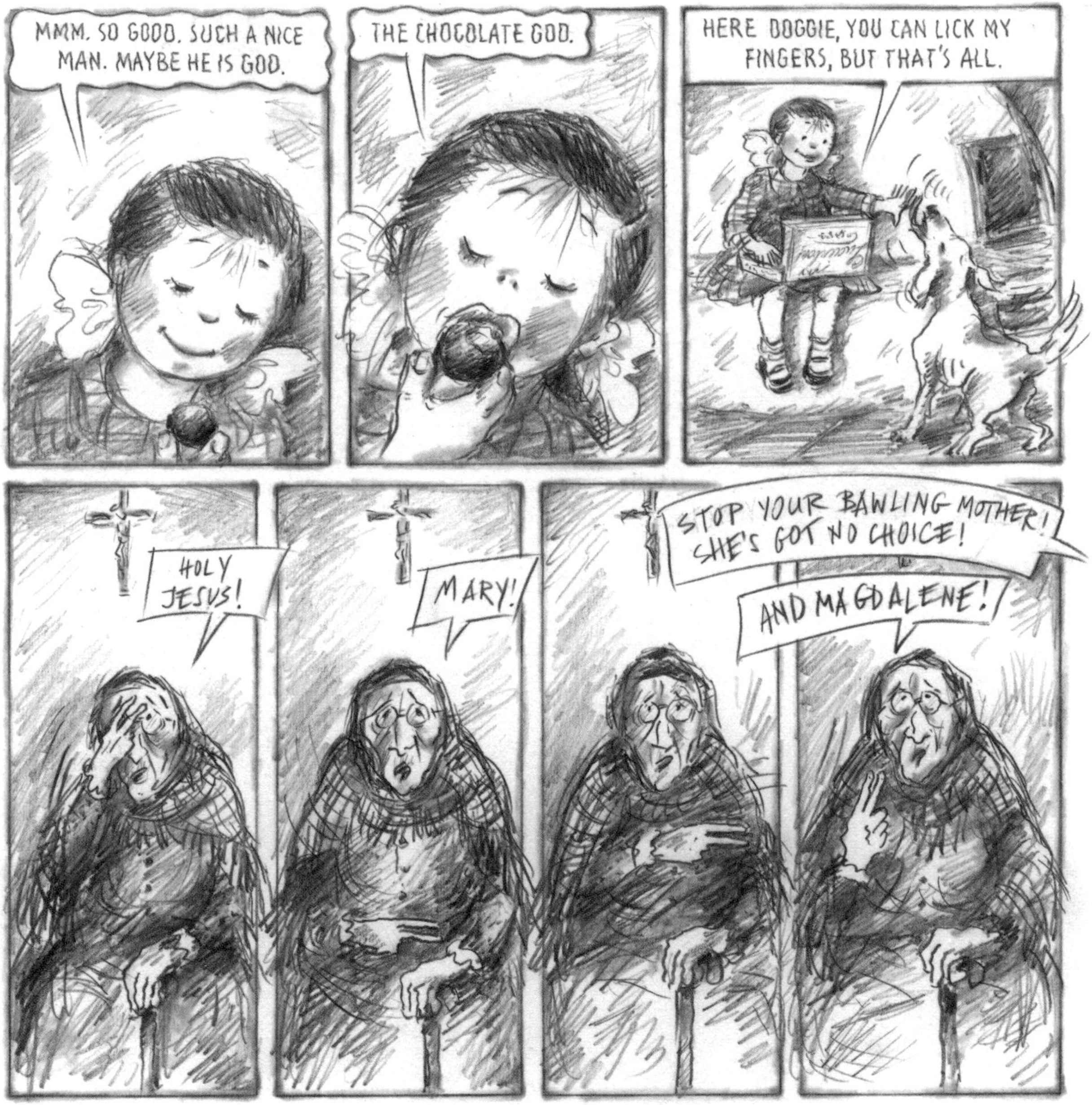
MMM. SO GOOD. SUCH A NICE MAN. MAYBE HE IS GOD.
THE CHOCOLATE GOD.
HERE DOGGIE, YOU CAN LICK MY FINGERS, BUT THAT'S ALL.
HOLY JESUS!
MARY!
STOP YOUR BAWLING MOTHER! SHE'S GOT NO CHOICE!
AND MAGDALENE!

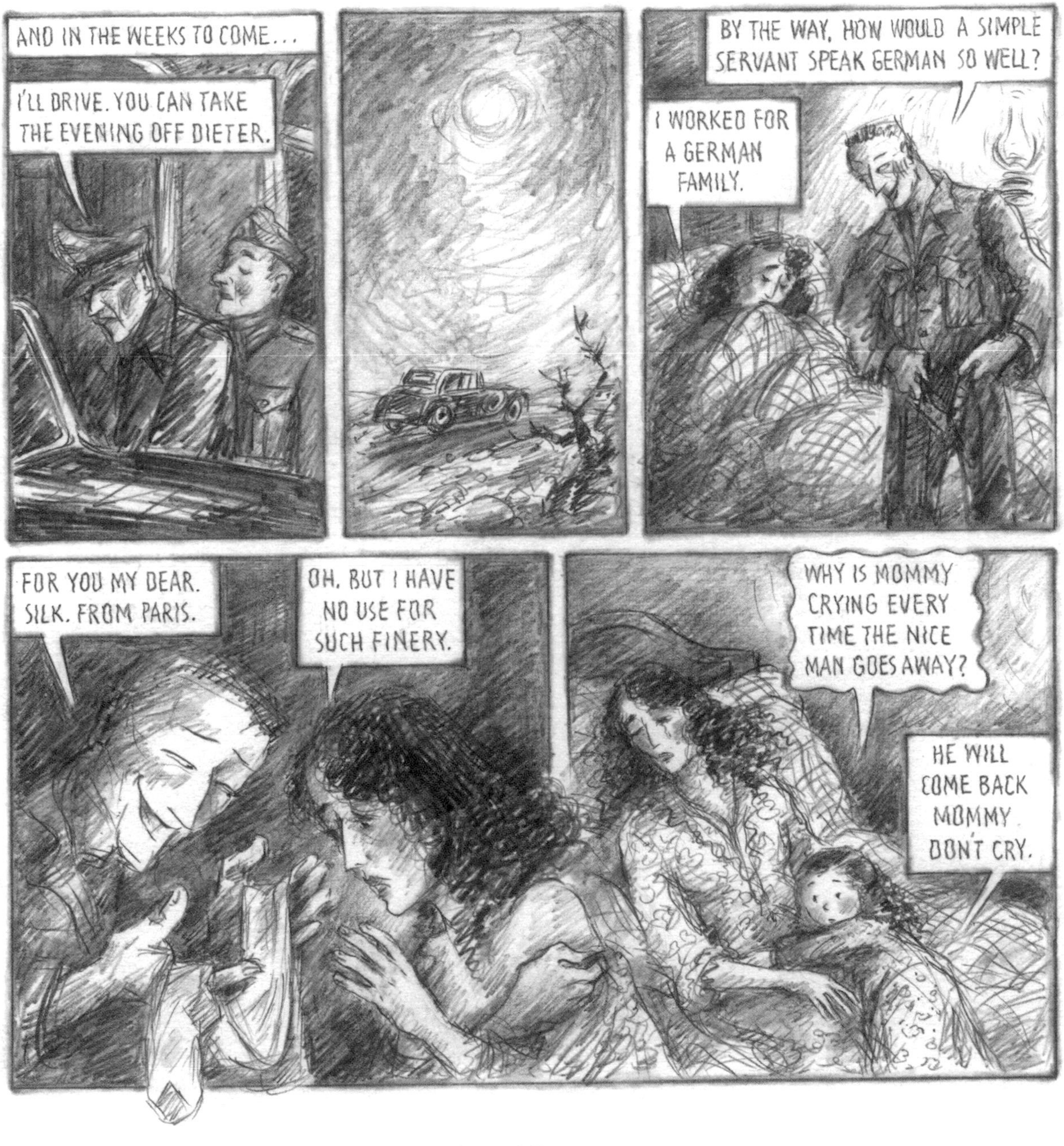
AND IN THE WEEKS TO COME...
I'LL DRIVE. YOU CAN TAKE THE EVENING OFF DIETER.
BY THE WAY, HOW WOULD A SIMPLE SERVANT SPEAK GERMAN SO WELL?
I WORKED FOR A GERMAN FAMILY.
FOR YOU MY DEAR. SILK. FROM PARIS.
OH, BUT I HAVE NO USE FOR SUCH FINERY.
WHY IS MOMMY CRYING EVERY TIME THE NICE MAN GOES AWAY?
HE WILL COME BACK MOMMY DON'T CRY.

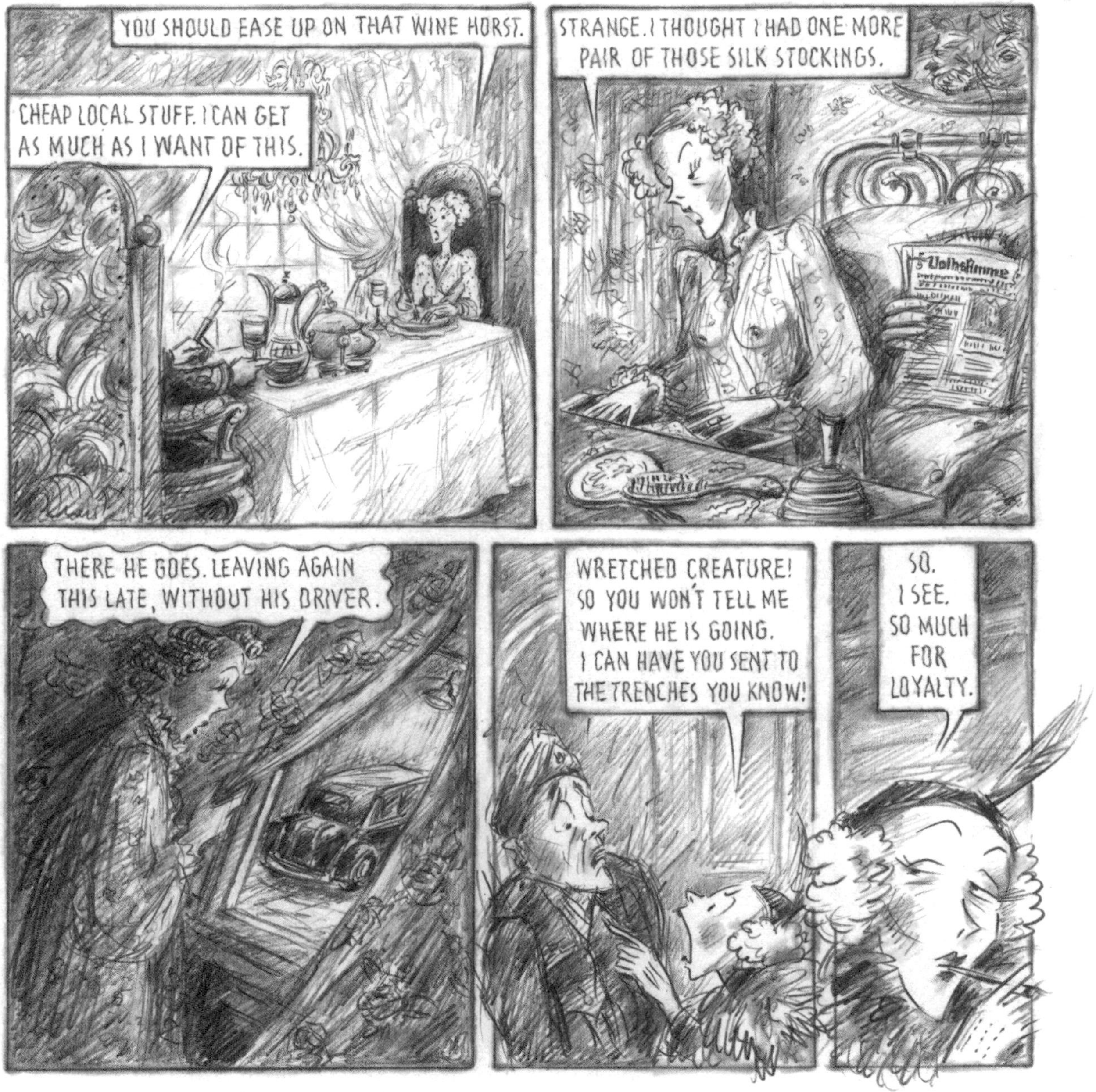
YOU SHOULD EASE UP ON THAT WINE HORST.
CHEAP LOCAL STUFF. I CAN GET AS MUCH AS I WANT OF THIS.
STRANGE. I THOUGHT I HAD ONE MORE PAIR OF THOSE SILK STOCKINGS.
THERE HE GOES. LEAVING AGAIN THIS LATE, WITHOUT HIS DRIVER.
WRETCHED CREATURE! SO YOU WON'T TELL ME WHERE HE IS GOING. I CAN HAVE YOU SENT TO THE TRENCHES YOU KNOW!
SO. I SEE. SO MUCH FOR LOYALTY.

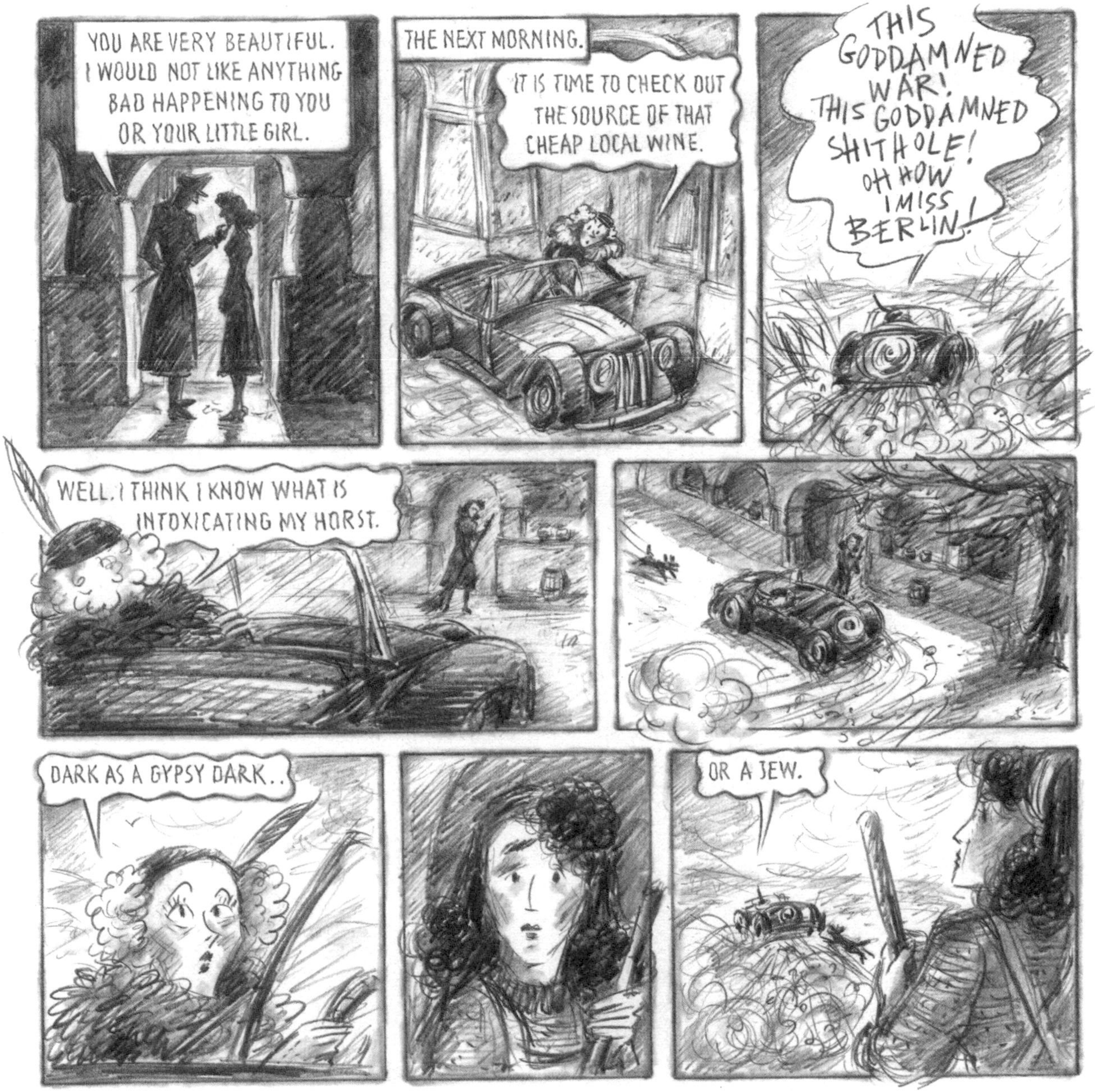
YOU ARE VERY BEAUTIFUL. I WOULD NOT LIKE ANYTHING BAD HAPPENING TO YOU OR YOUR LITTLE GIRL.
THE NEXT MORNING.
IT IS TIME TO CHECK OUT THE SOURCE OF THAT CHEAP LOCAL WINE.
THIS GODDAMNED WAR! THIS GODDAMNED SHITHOLE! OH HOW I MISS BERLIN!
WELL, I THINK I KNOW WHAT IS INTOXICATING MY HORST.
DARK AS A GYPSY DARK..
OR A JEW.

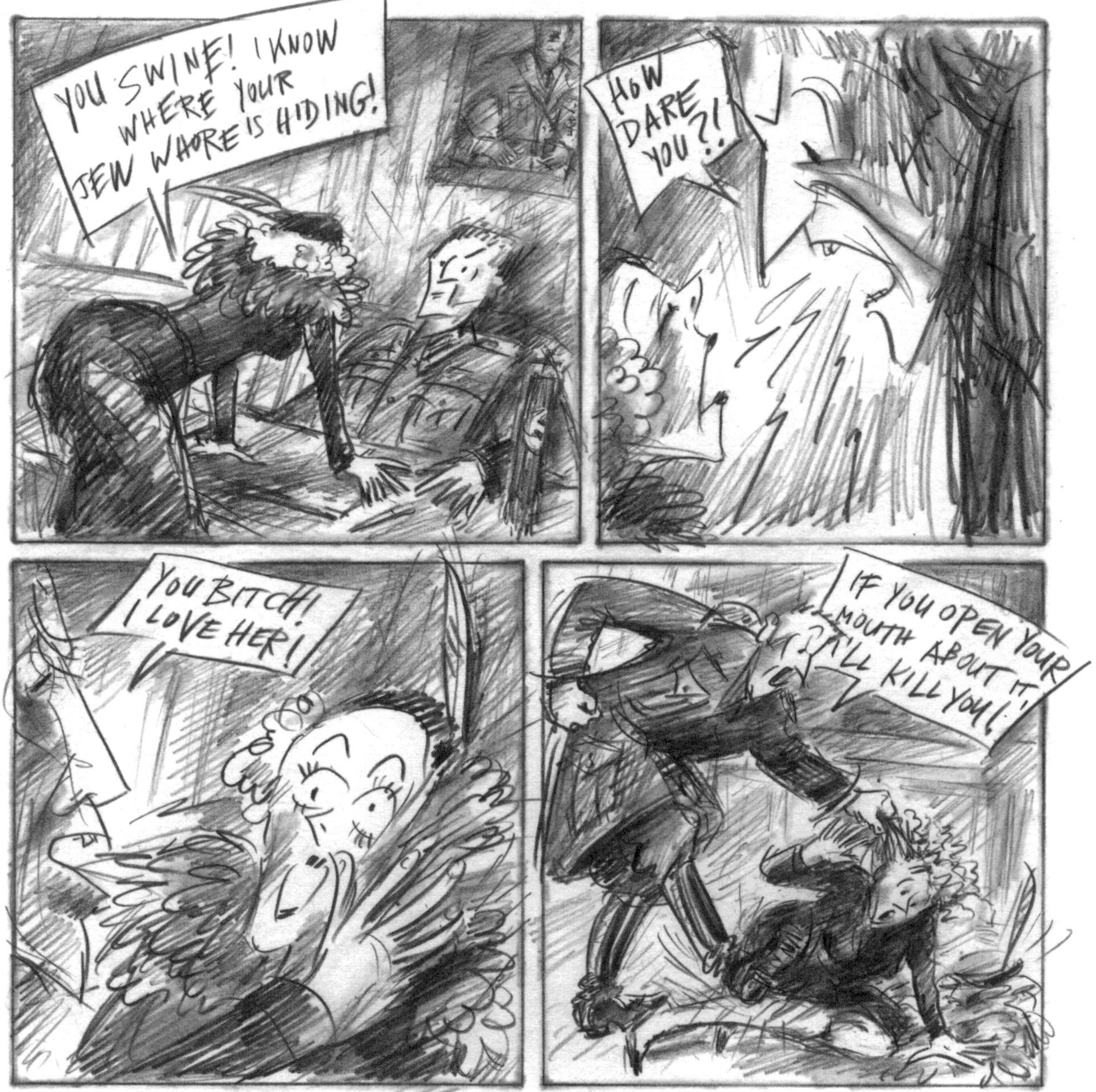
YOU SWINE! I KNOW WHERE YOUR JEW WHORE IS HIDING!
HOW DARE YOU?!
YOU BITCH! I LOVE HER!
IF YOU OPEN YOUR MOUTH ABOUT IT, I'LL KILL YOU!

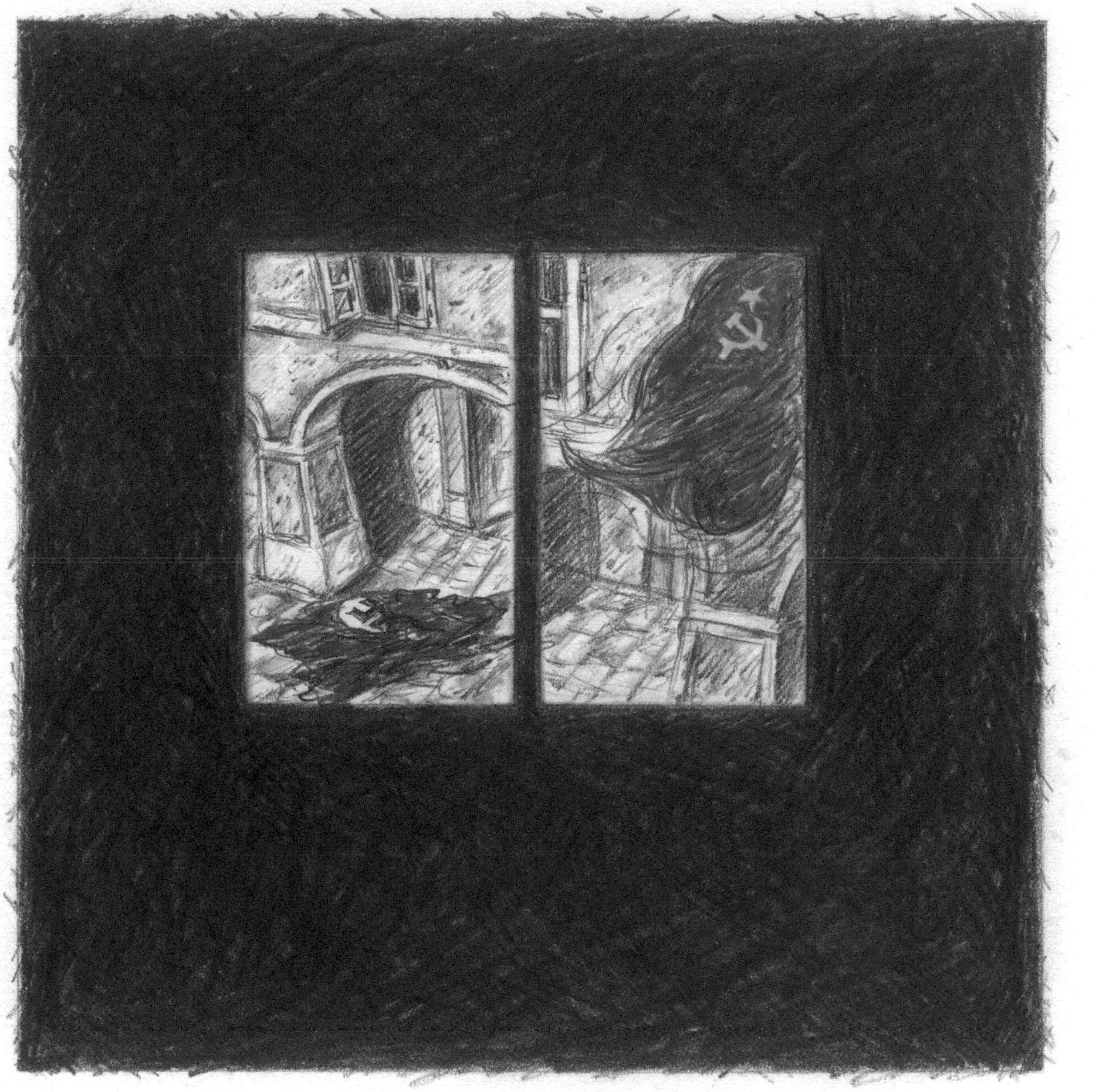

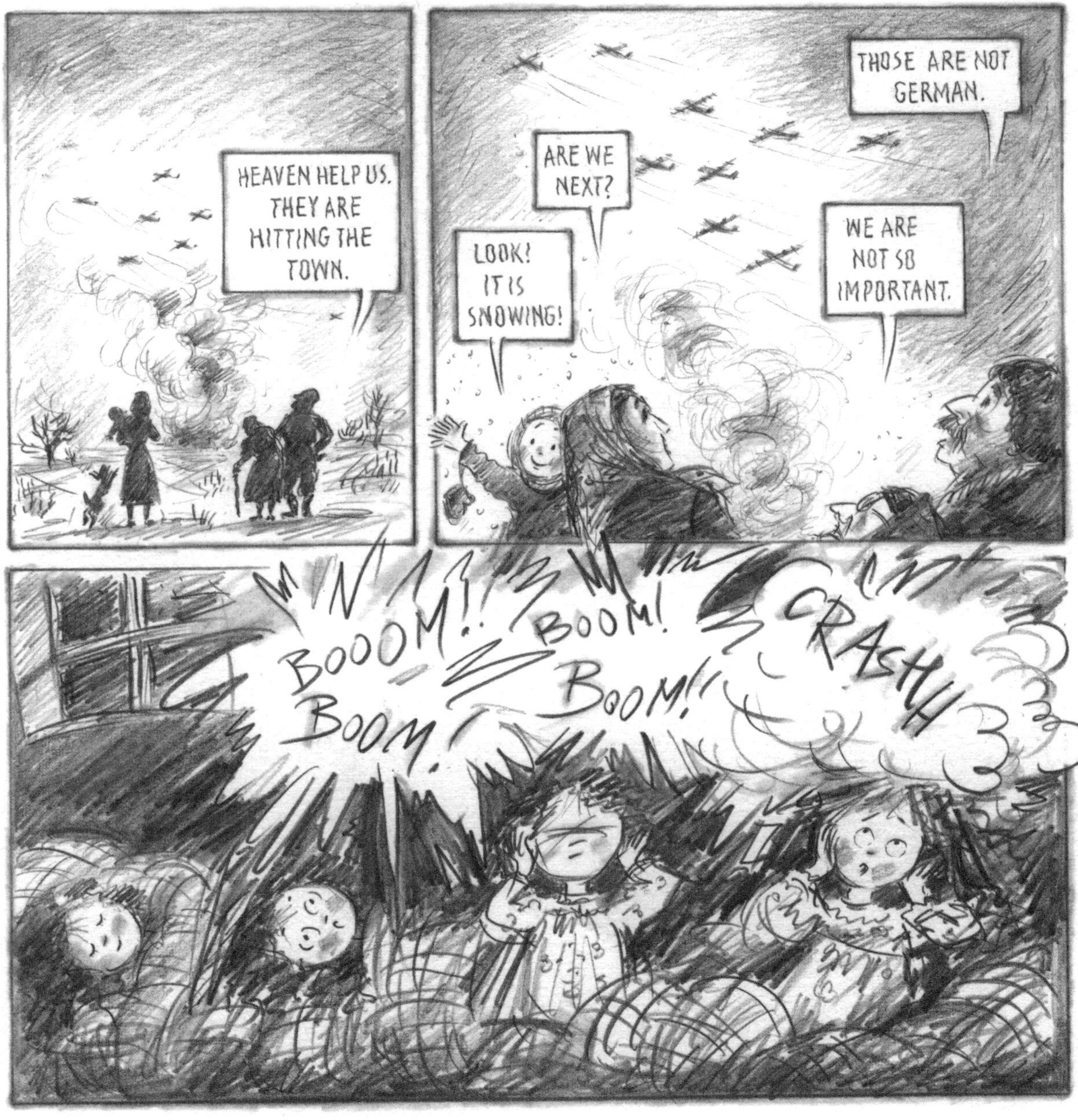
HEAVEN HELP US. THEY ARE HITTING THE TOWN.
LOOK! IT IS SNOWING!
ARE WE NEXT?
THOSE ARE NOT GERMAN.
WE ARE NOT SO IMPORTANT.
BOOOM!! BOOM!
BOOM! BOOM!
CRASHH

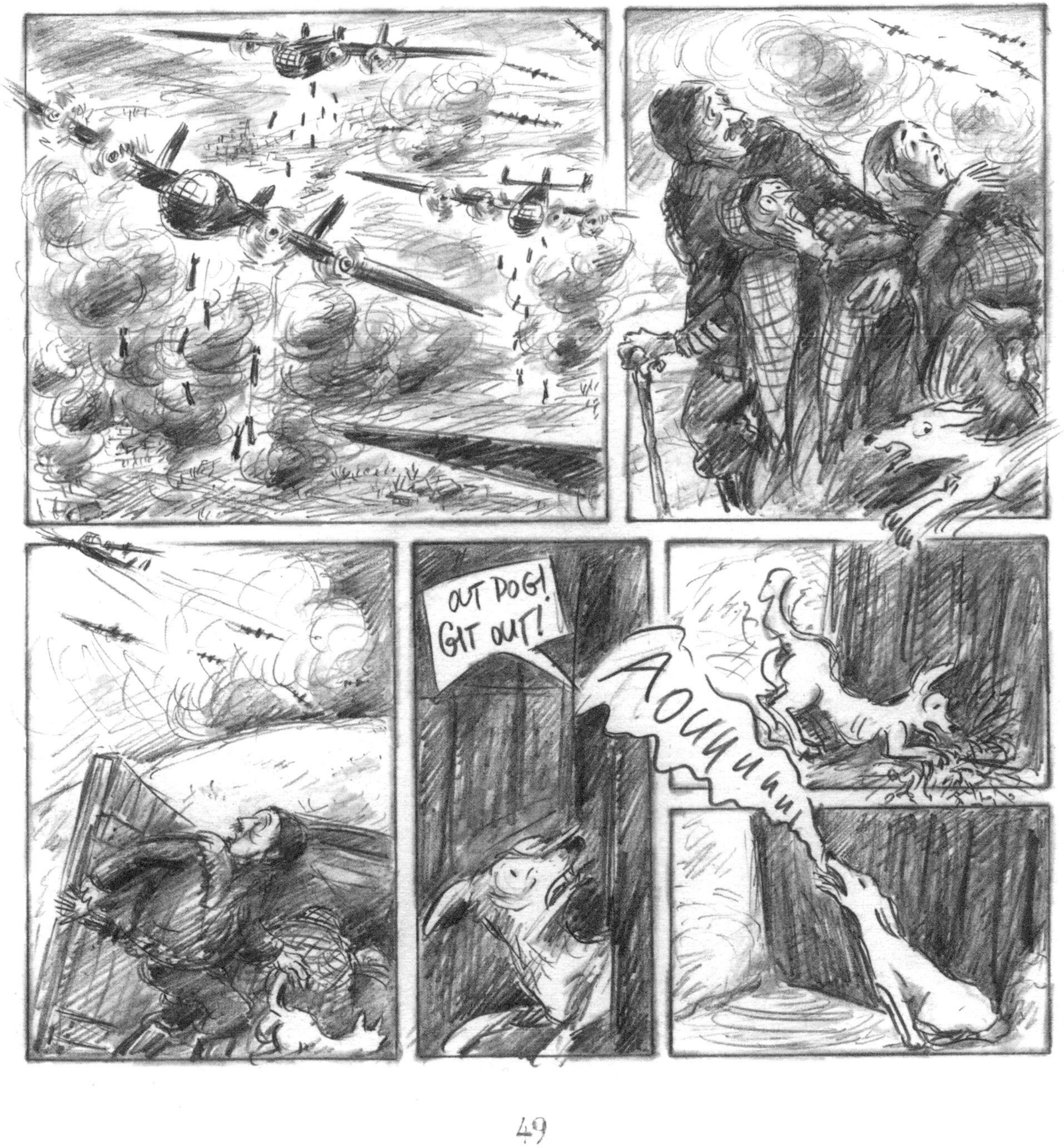
OUT DOG! GIT OUT!
AOUUUUUU

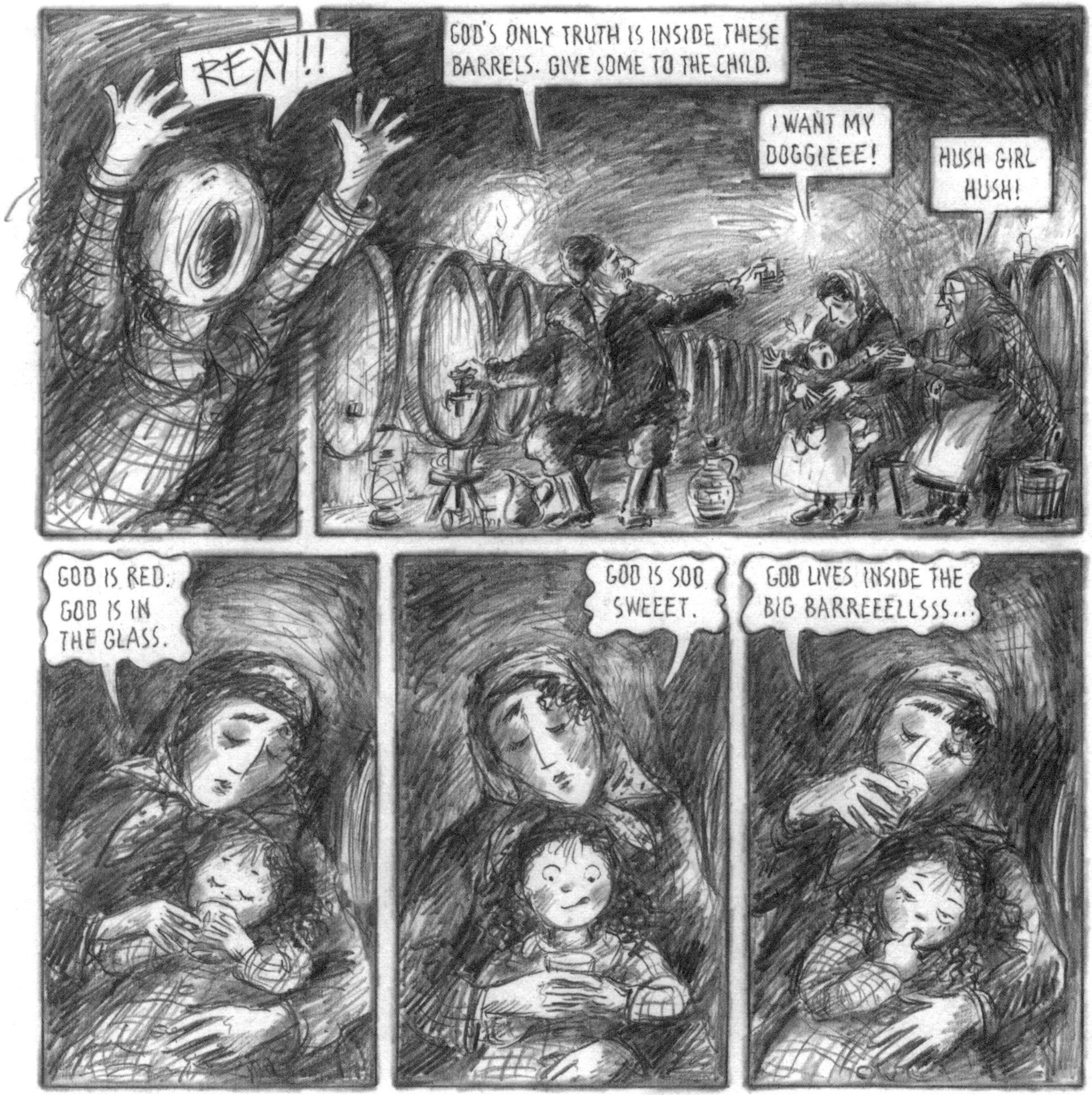
REXY!!
GOD'S ONLY TRUTH IS INSIDE THESE BARRELS. GIVE SOME TO THE CHILD.
I WANT MY DOGGIEEE!
HUSH GIRL HUSH!
GOD IS RED. GOD IS IN THE GLASS.
GOD IS SOO SWEEET.
GOD LIVES INSIDE THE BIG BARREEELLSSS...

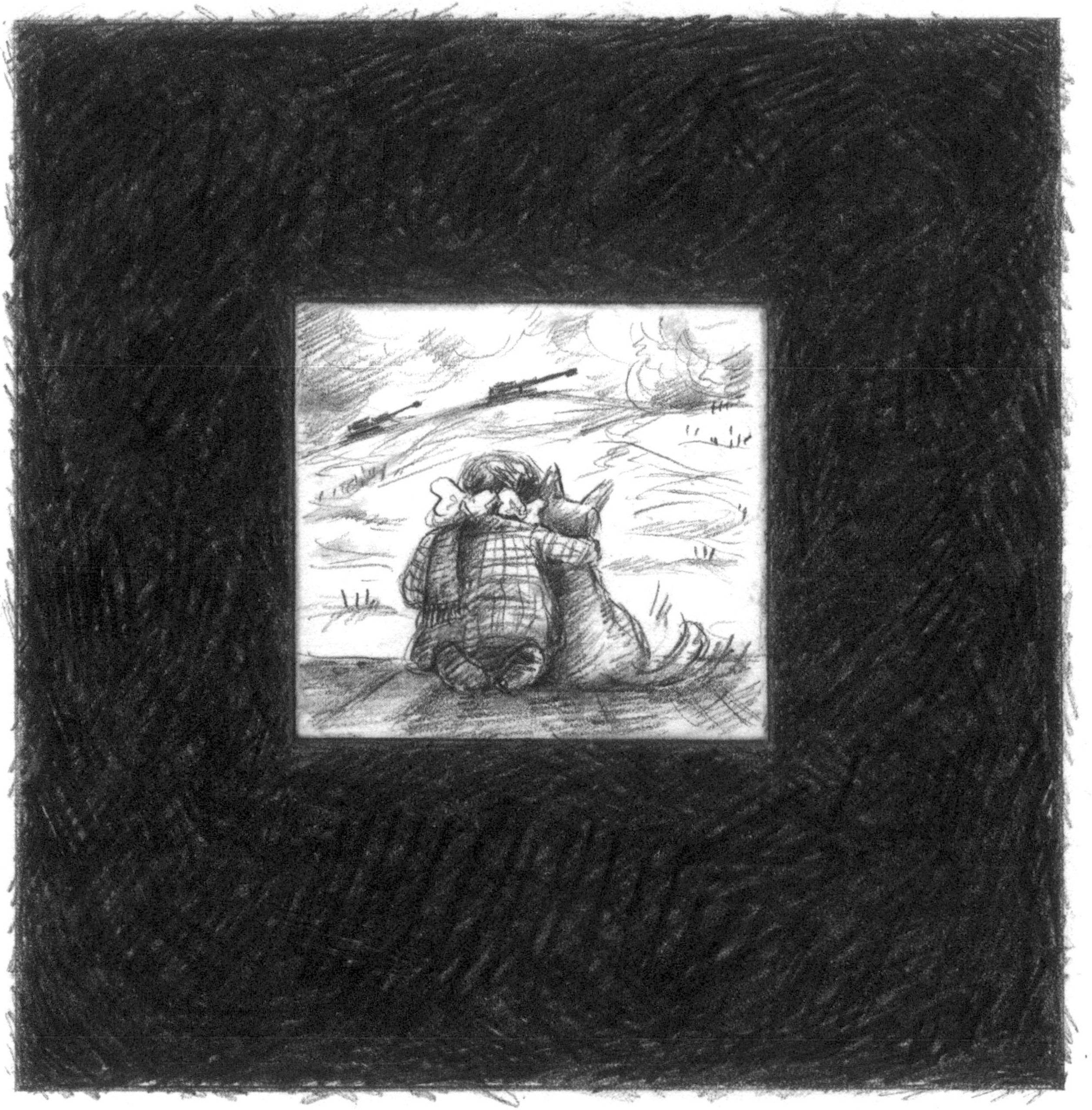

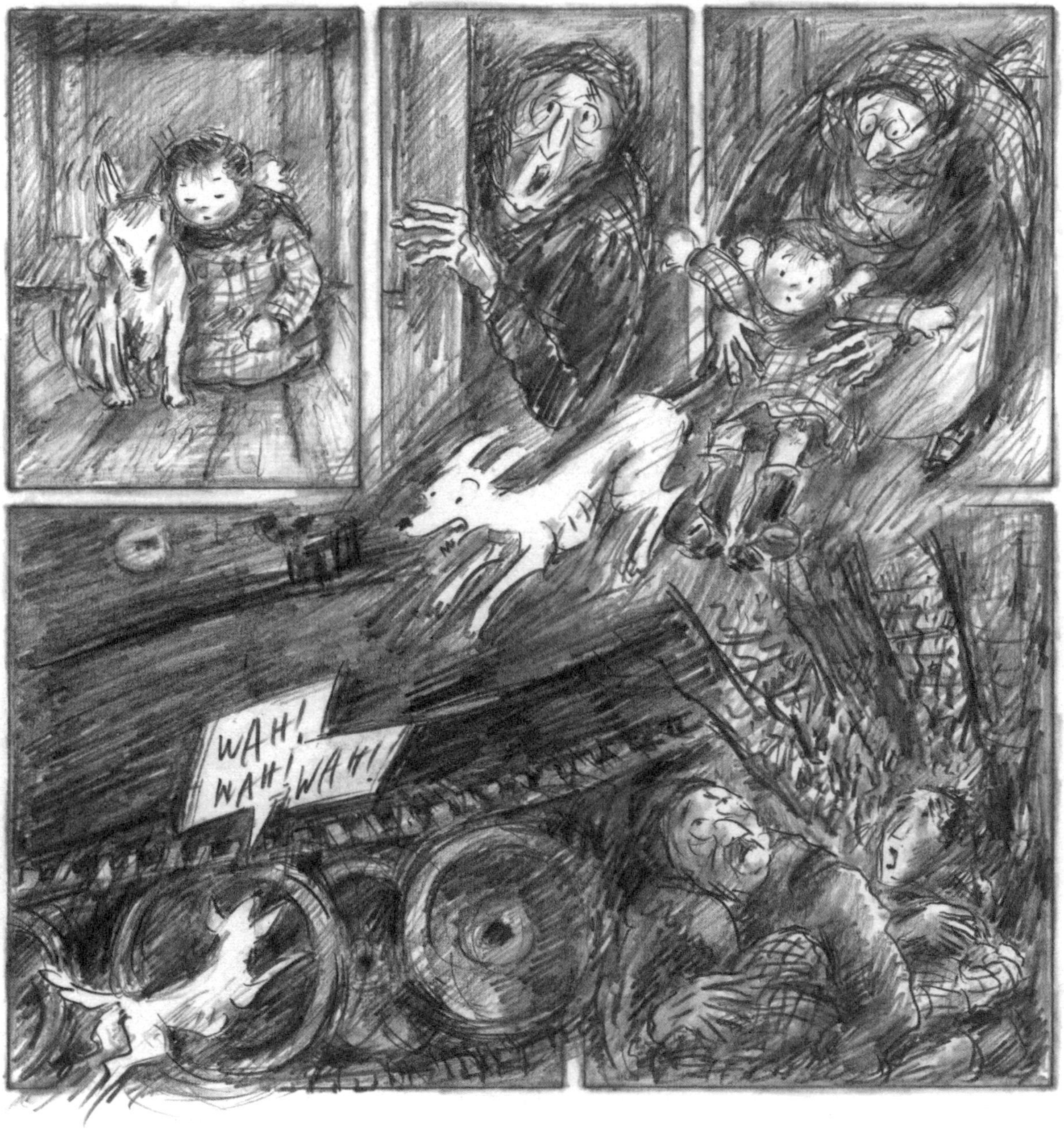
WAH!
WAH!
WAH!

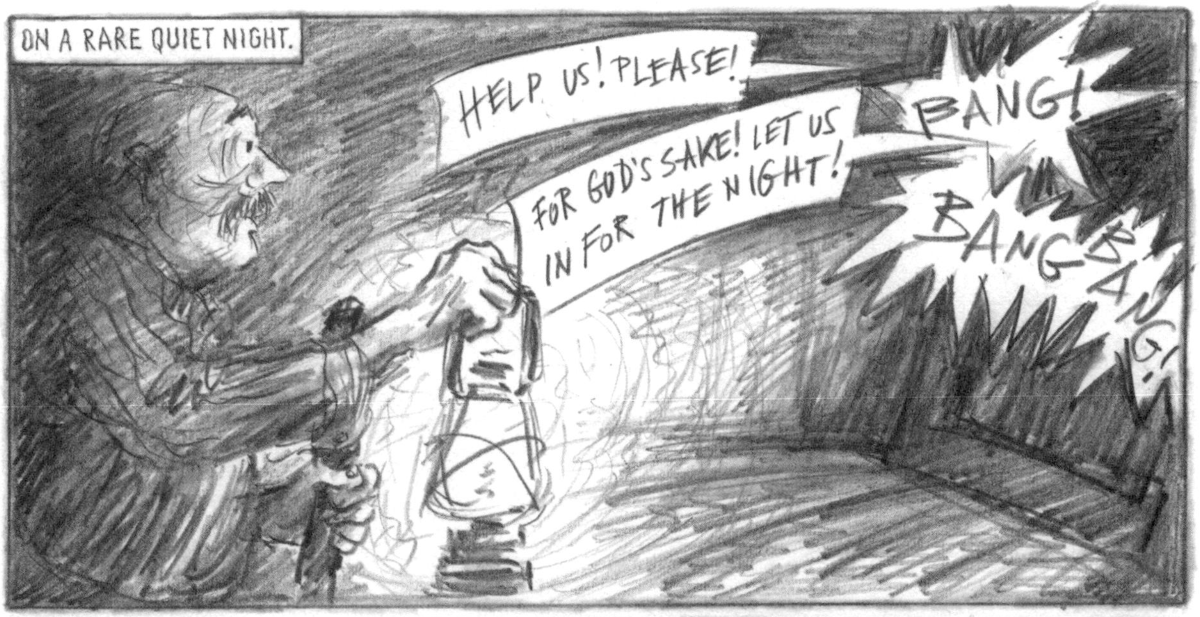
ON A RARE QUIET NIGHT.
HELP US! PLEASE!
FOR GOD'S SAKE! LET US IN FOR THE NIGHT!
BANG!
BANG
BANG!

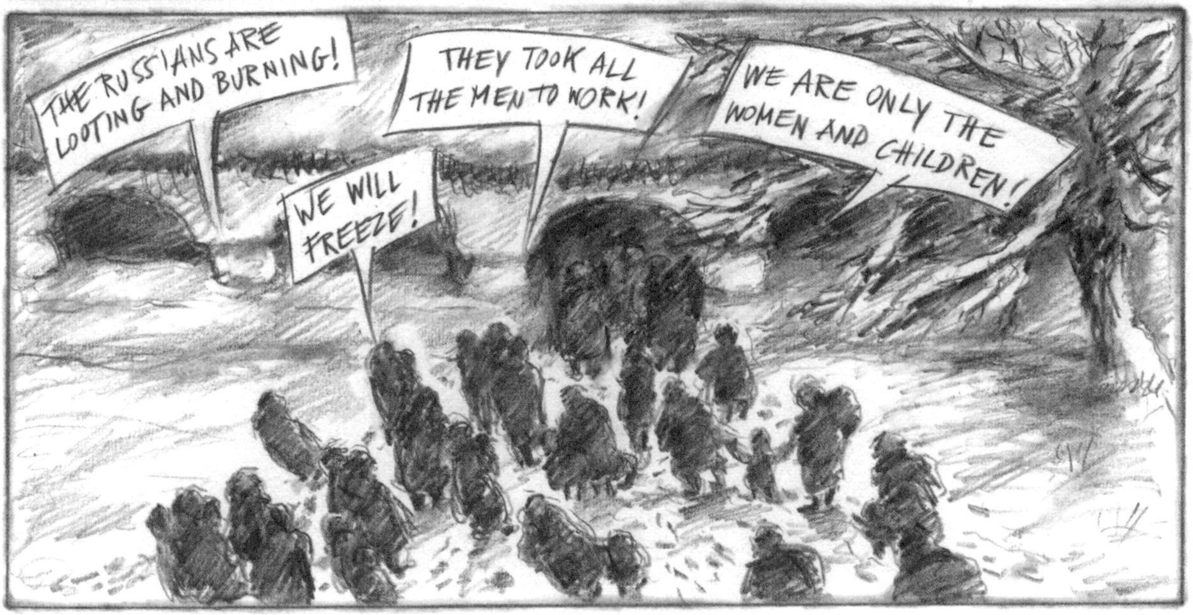
THE RUSSIANS ARE LOOTING AND BURNING!
WE WILL FREEZE!
THEY TOOK ALL THE MEN TO WORK!
WE ARE ONLY THE WOMEN AND CHILDREN!

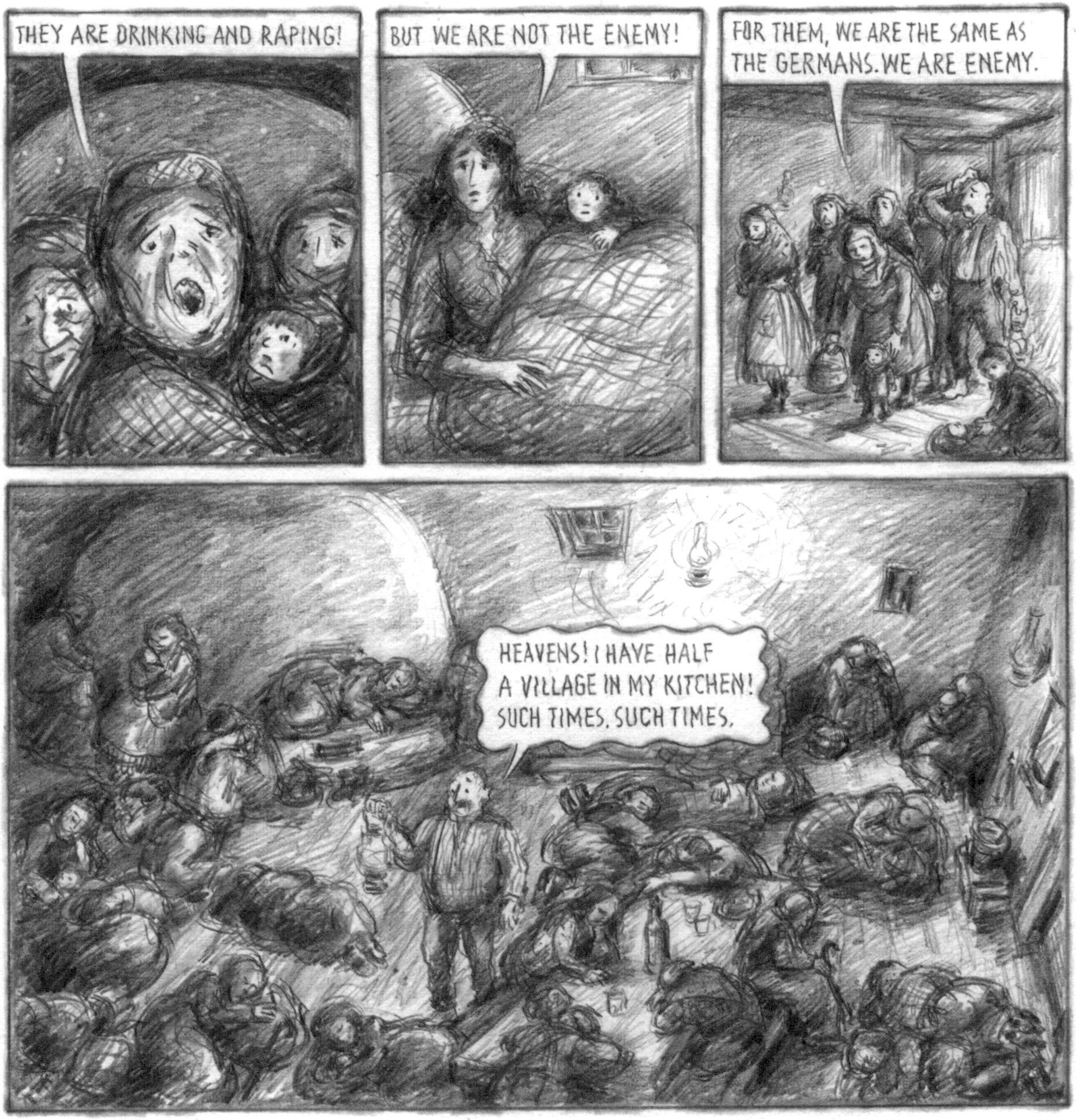
THEY ARE DRINKING AND RAPING!
BUT WE ARE NOT THE ENEMY!
FOR THEM, WE ARE THE SAME AS THE GERMANS. WE ARE ENEMY.
HEAVENS! I HAVE HALF A VILLAGE IN MY KITCHEN! SUCH TIMES. SUCH TIMES.

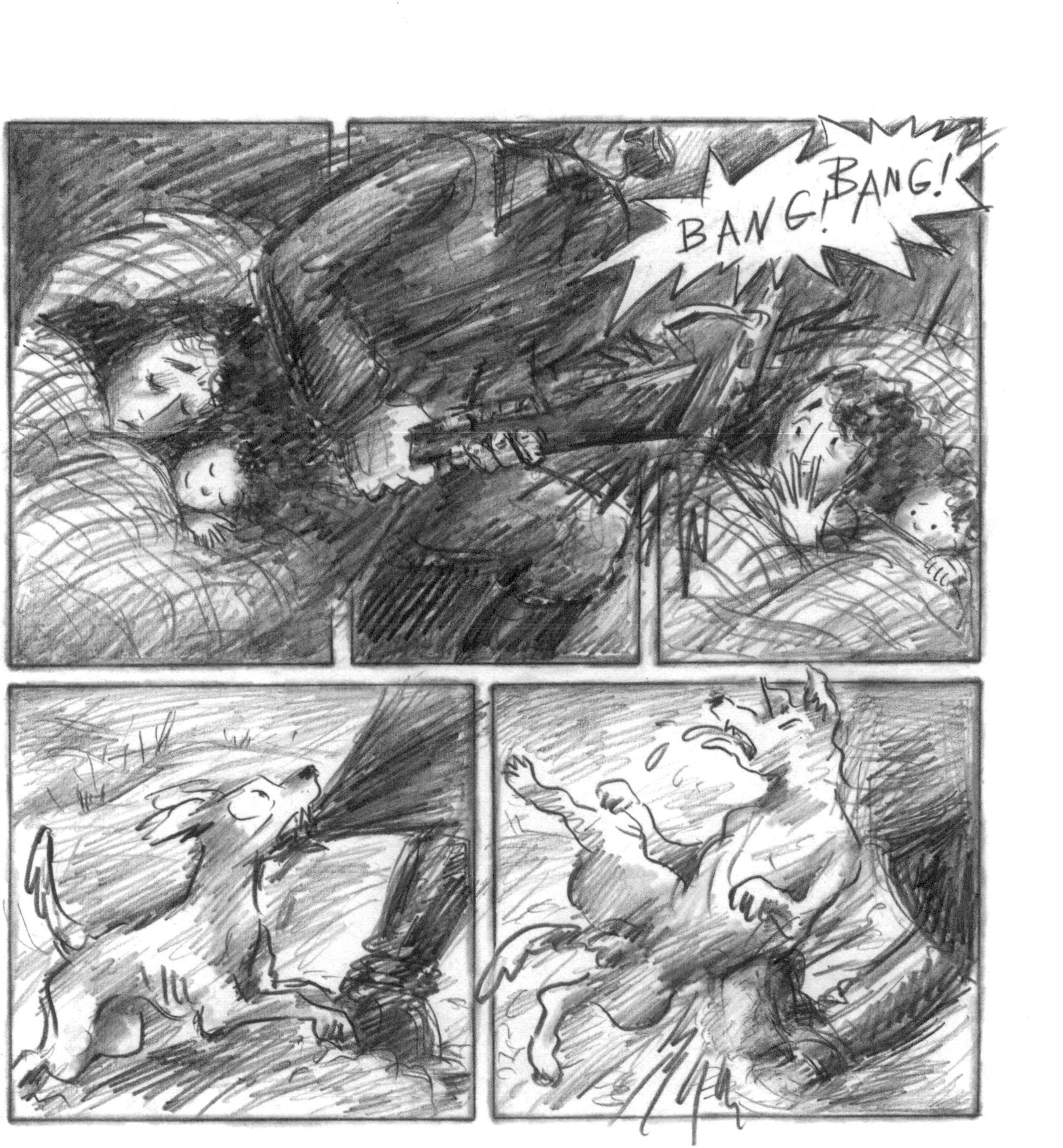
BANG! BANG!

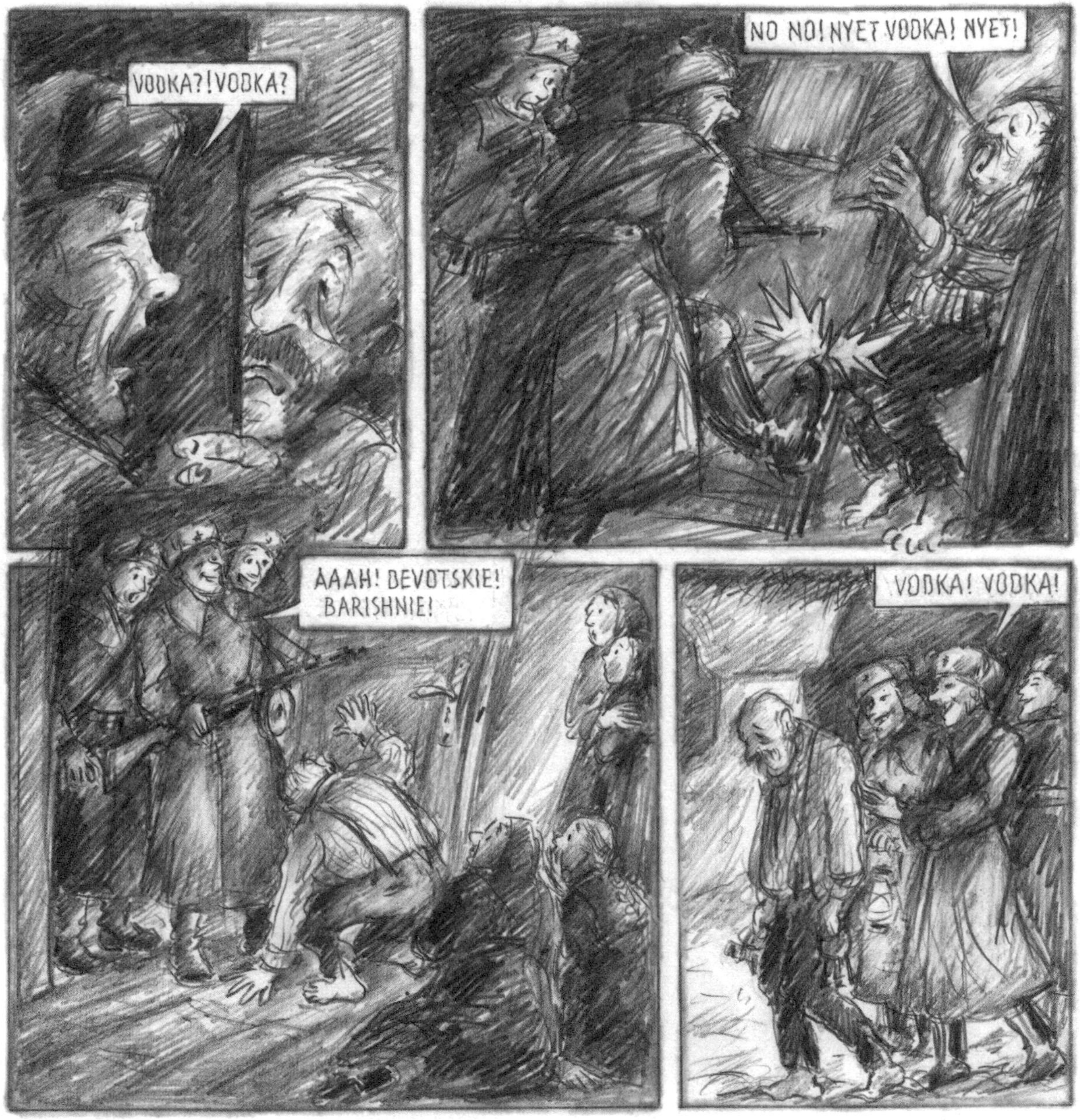
VODKA?! VODKA?
NO NO! NYET VODKA! NYET!
AAAH! DEVOTSKIE! BARISHNIE!
VODKA! VODKA!

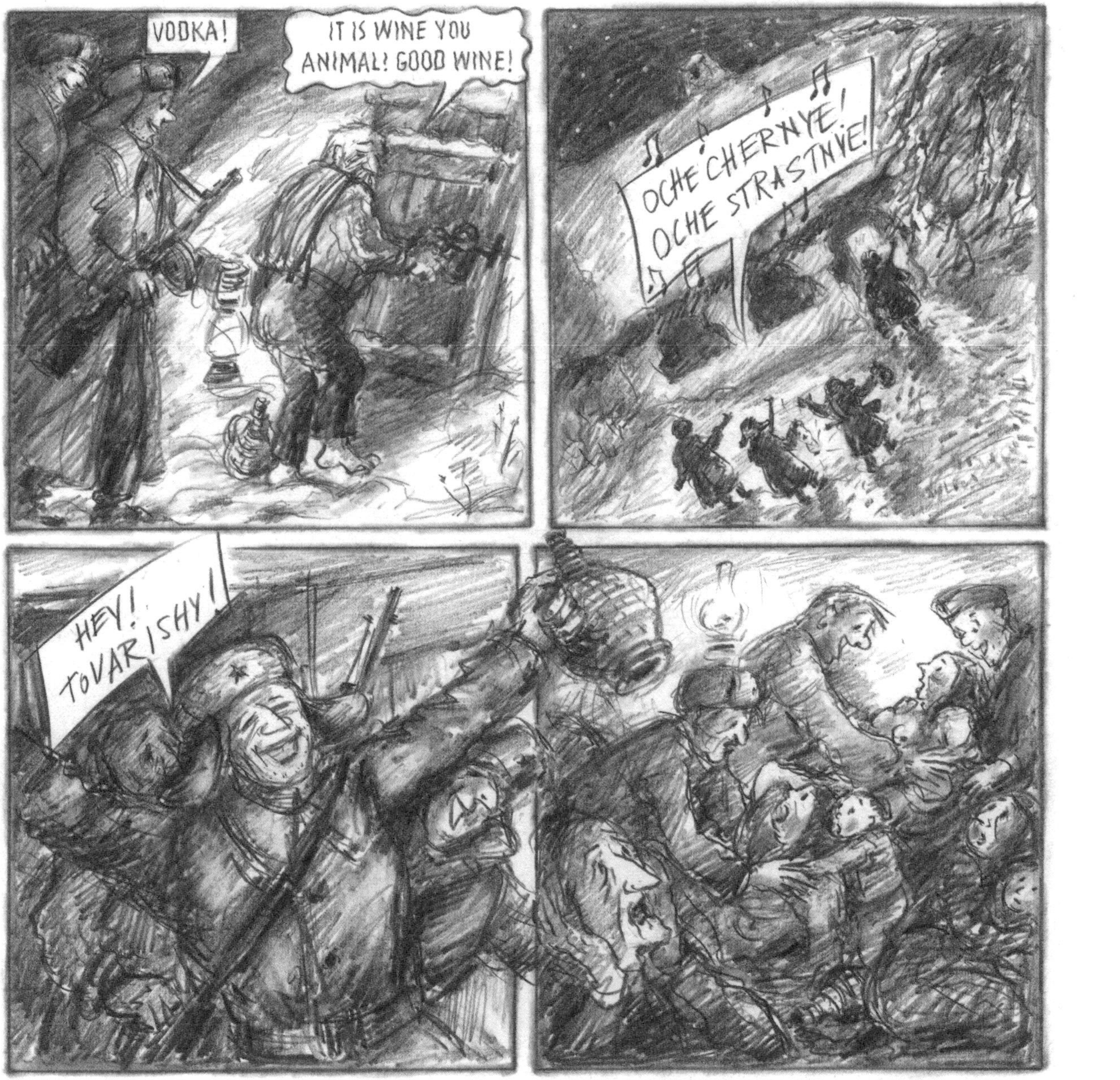
VODKA!
IT IS WINE YOU ANIMAL! GOOD WINE!
OCHE CHERNYE! OCHE STRASTNYE!
HEY! TOVARISHY!

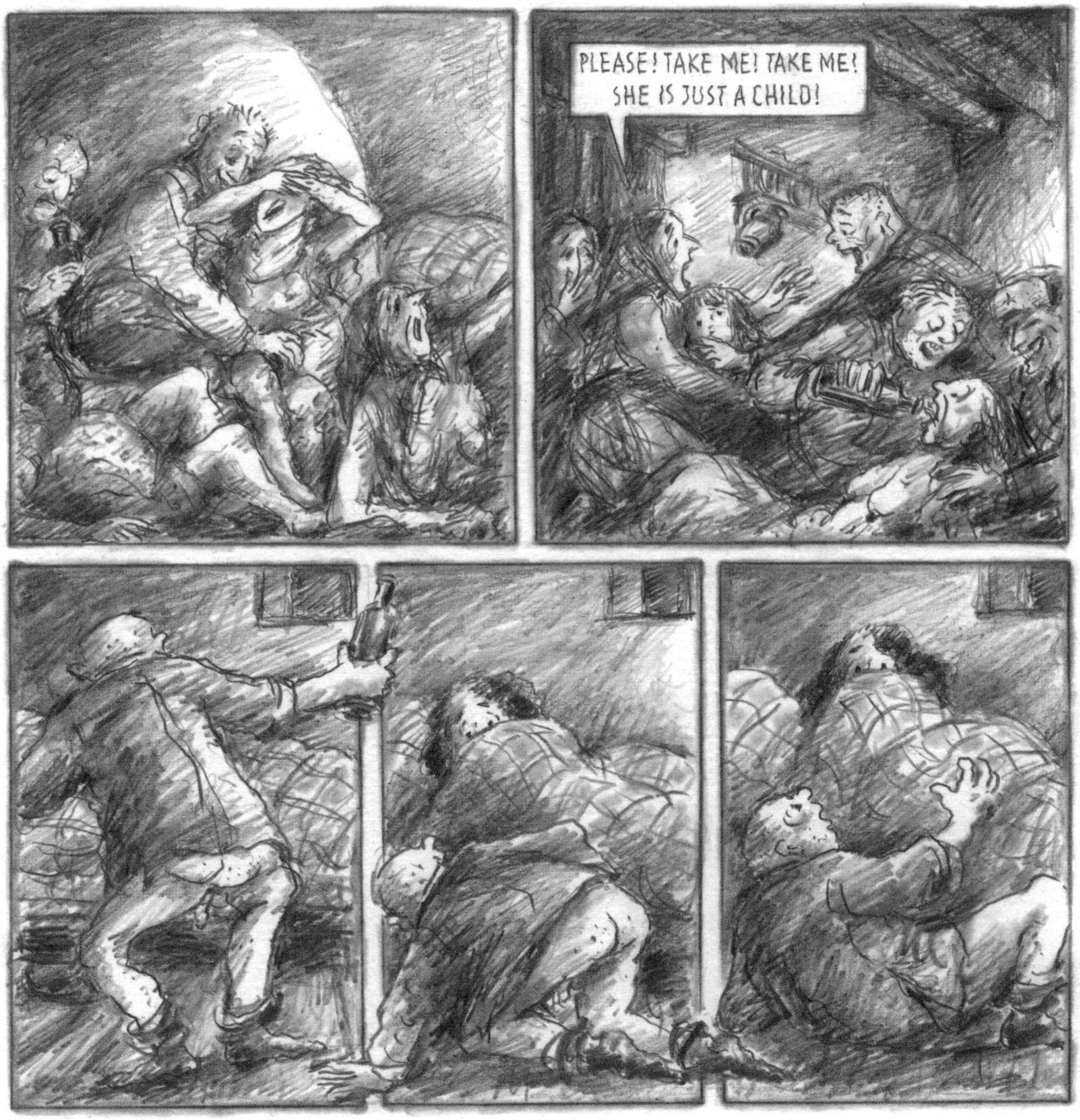
PLEASE! TAKE ME! TAKE ME! SHE IS JUST A CHILD!

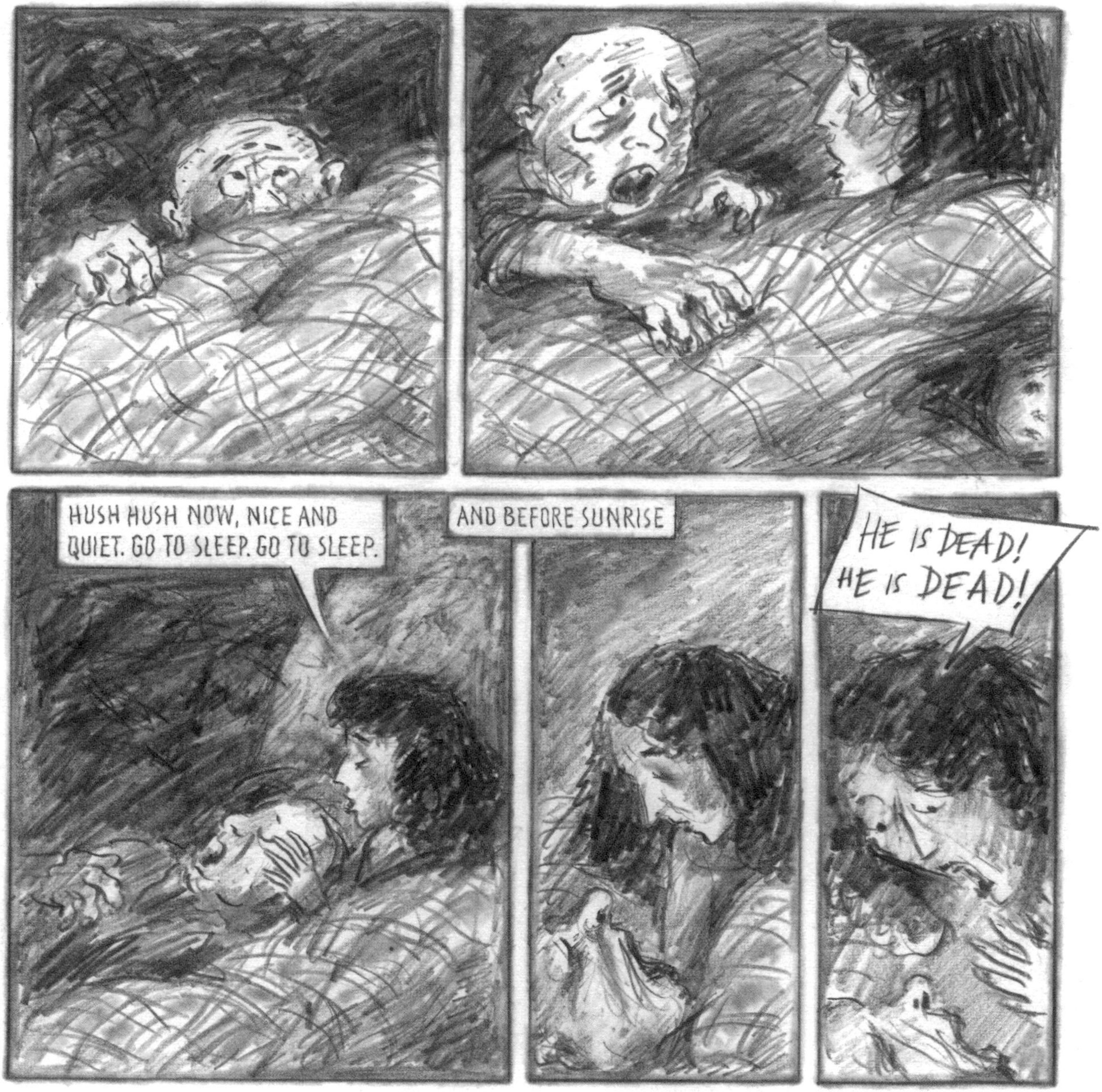
HUSH HUSH NOW, NICE AND QUIET. GO TO SLEEP. GO TO SLEEP.
AND BEFORE SUNRISE
HE IS DEAD! HE IS DEAD!

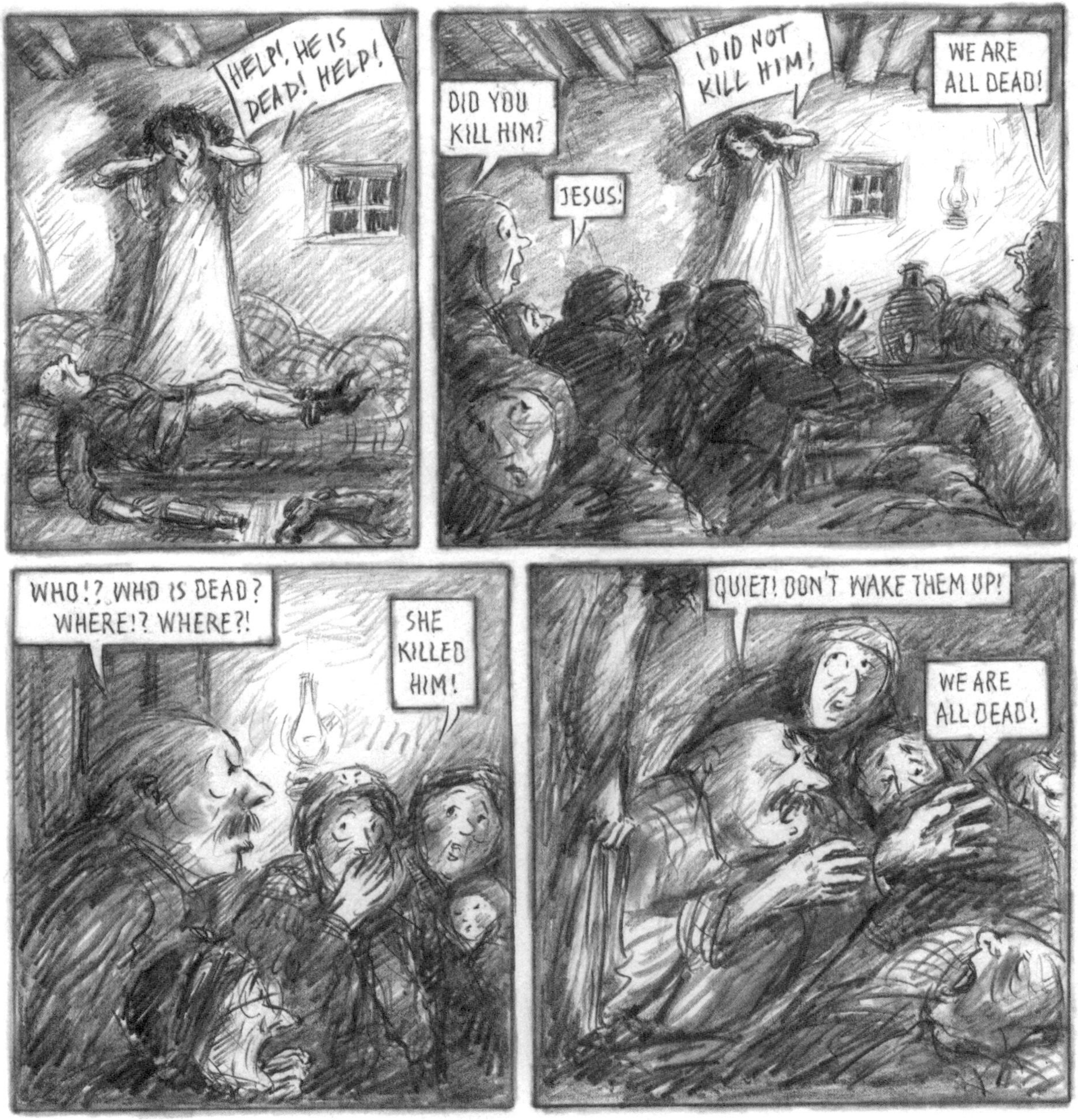
HELP!, HE IS DEAD! HELP!
DID YOU KILL HIM?
JESUS!
I DID NOT KILL HIM!
WE ARE ALL DEAD!
WHO!? WHO IS DEAD? WHERE!? WHERE?!
SHE KILLED HIM!
QUIET! DON'T WAKE THEM UP!
WE ARE ALL DEAD!

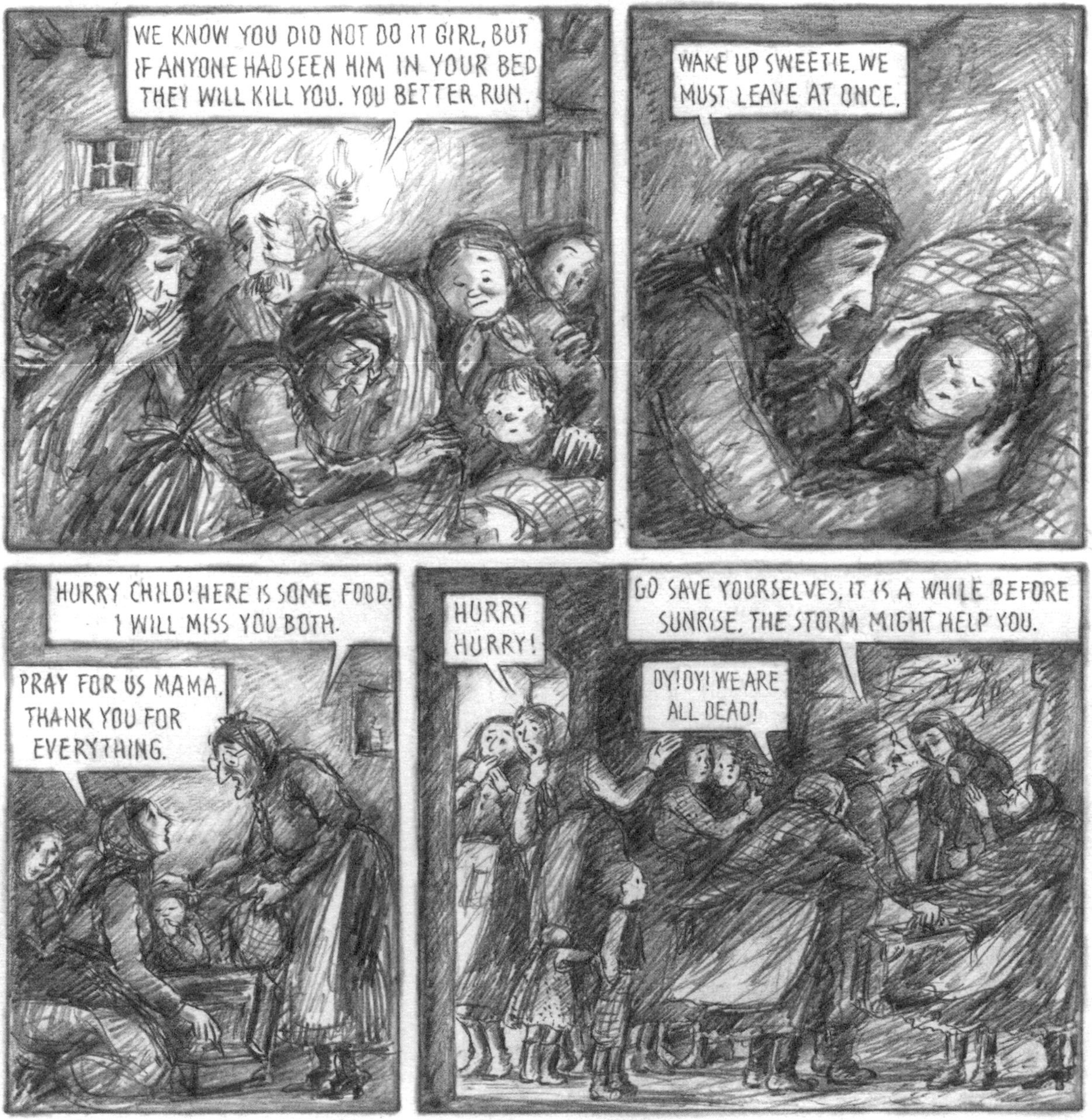
WE KNOW YOU DID NOT DO IT GIRL, BUT IF ANYONE HAD SEEN HIM IN YOUR BED THEY WILL KILL YOU. YOU BETTER RUN.
WAKE UP SWEETIE. WE MUST LEAVE AT ONCE.
HURRY CHILD! HERE IS SOME FOOD. I WILL MISS YOU BOTH.
PRAY FOR US MAMA. THANK YOU FOR EVERYTHING.
HURRY HURRY!
GO SAVE YOURSELVES. IT IS A WHILE BEFORE SUNRISE. THE STORM MIGHT HELP YOU.
OY! OY! WE ARE ALL DEAD!

WE WON'T MAKE IT THIS WAY. YOU ARE TOO HEAVY. I WILL PULL YOU. SIT DOWN. GO BACK DOGGIE!
THOSE TREES. THE ORCHARD. IF I CAN MAKE IT AND HIDE..

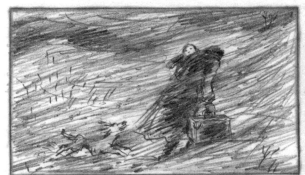

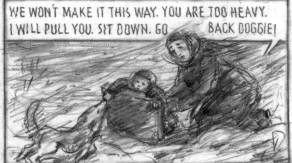

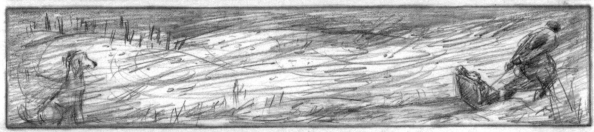

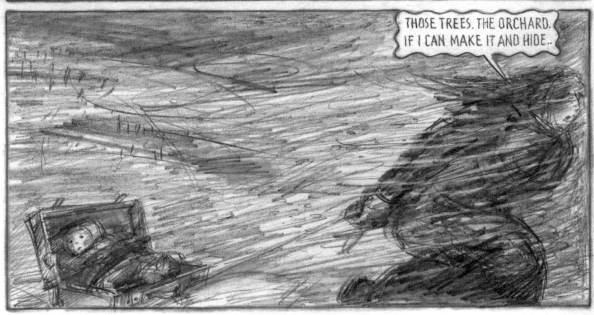

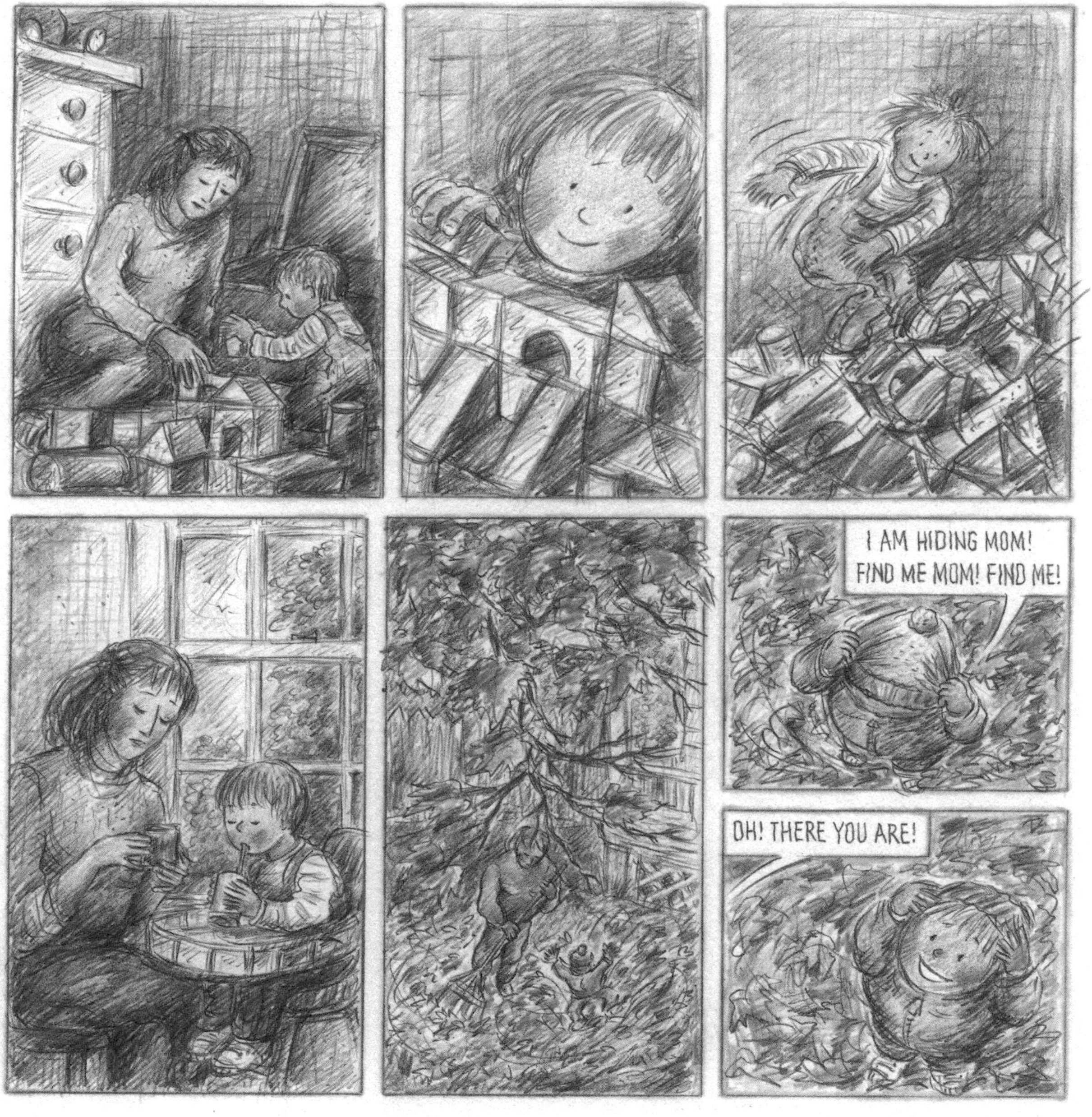
I AM HIDING MOM! FIND ME MOM! FIND ME!
OH! THERE YOU ARE!

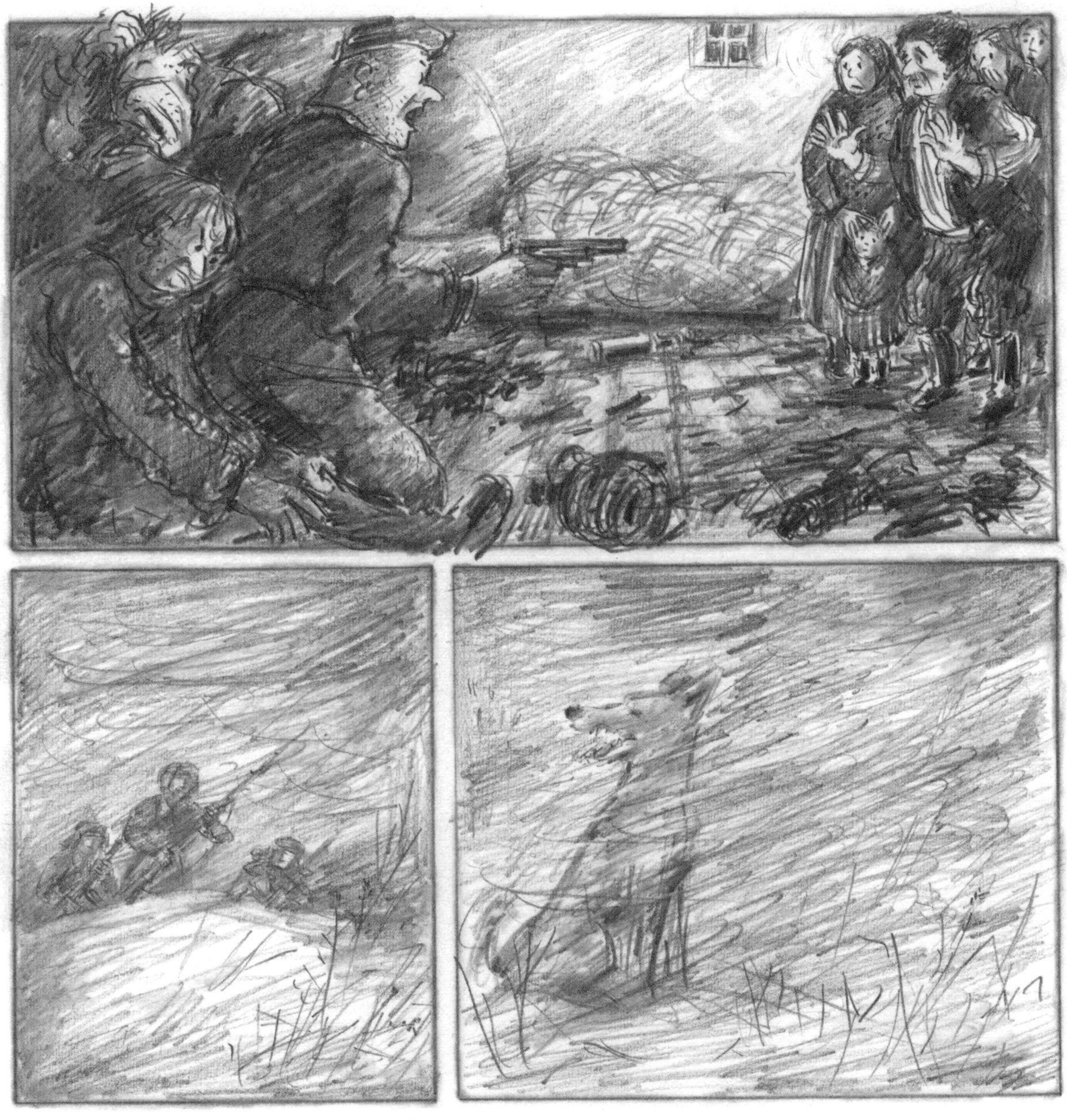

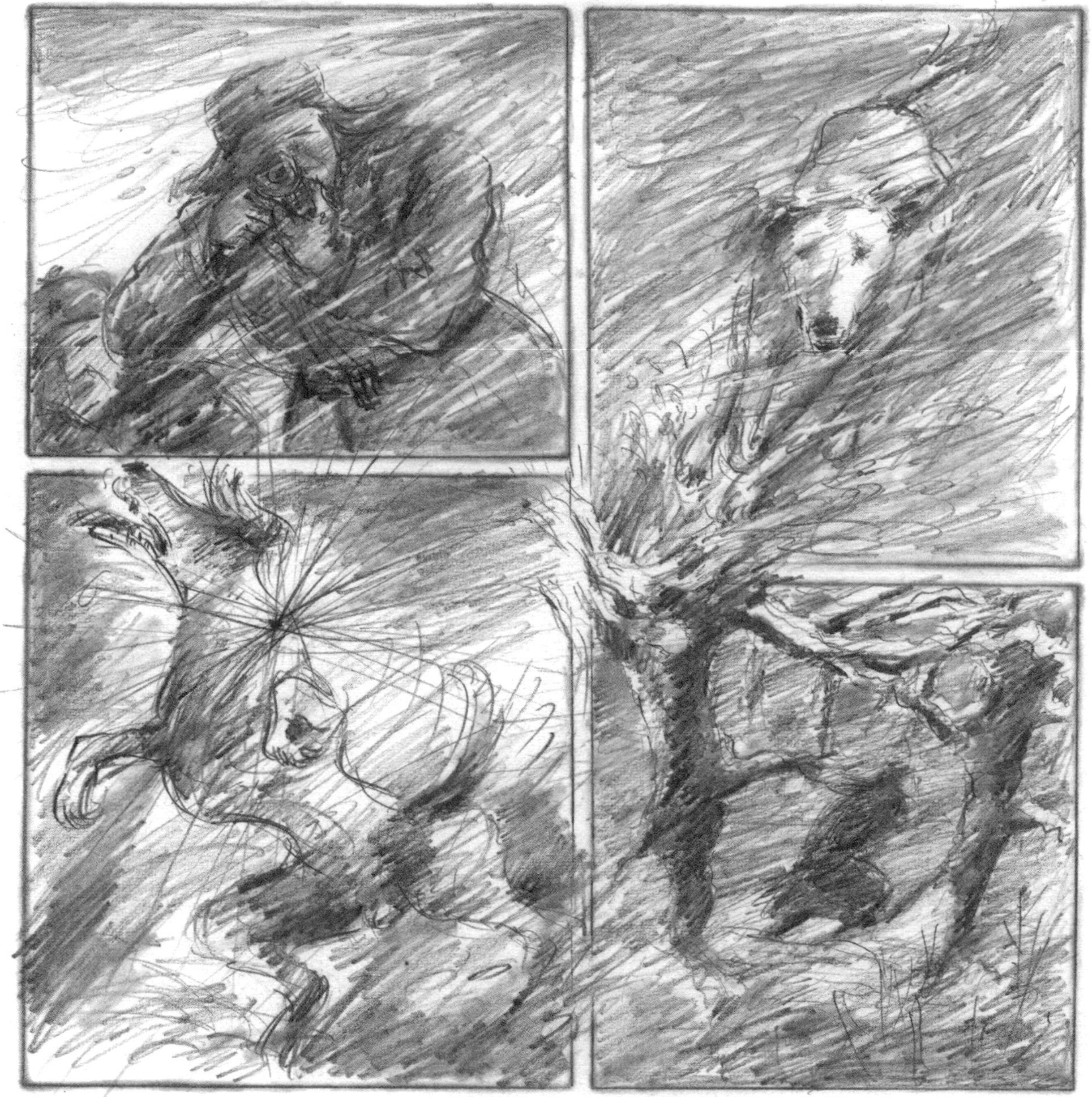

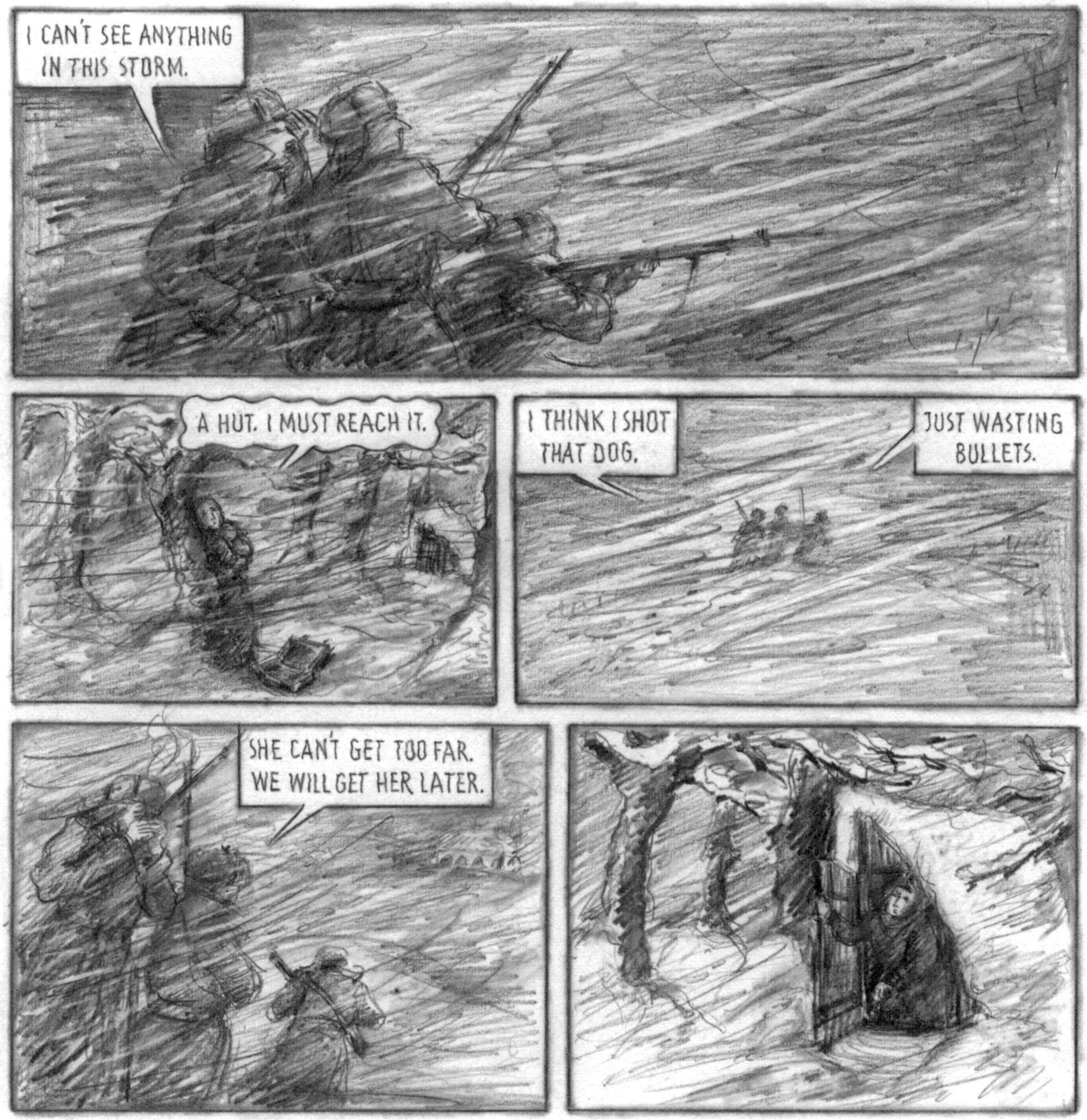
I CAN'T SEE ANYTHING IN THIS STORM.
A HUT. I MUST REACH IT.
I THINK I SHOT THAT DOG.
JUST WASTING BULLETS.
SHE CAN'T GET TOO FAR. WE WILL GET HER LATER.

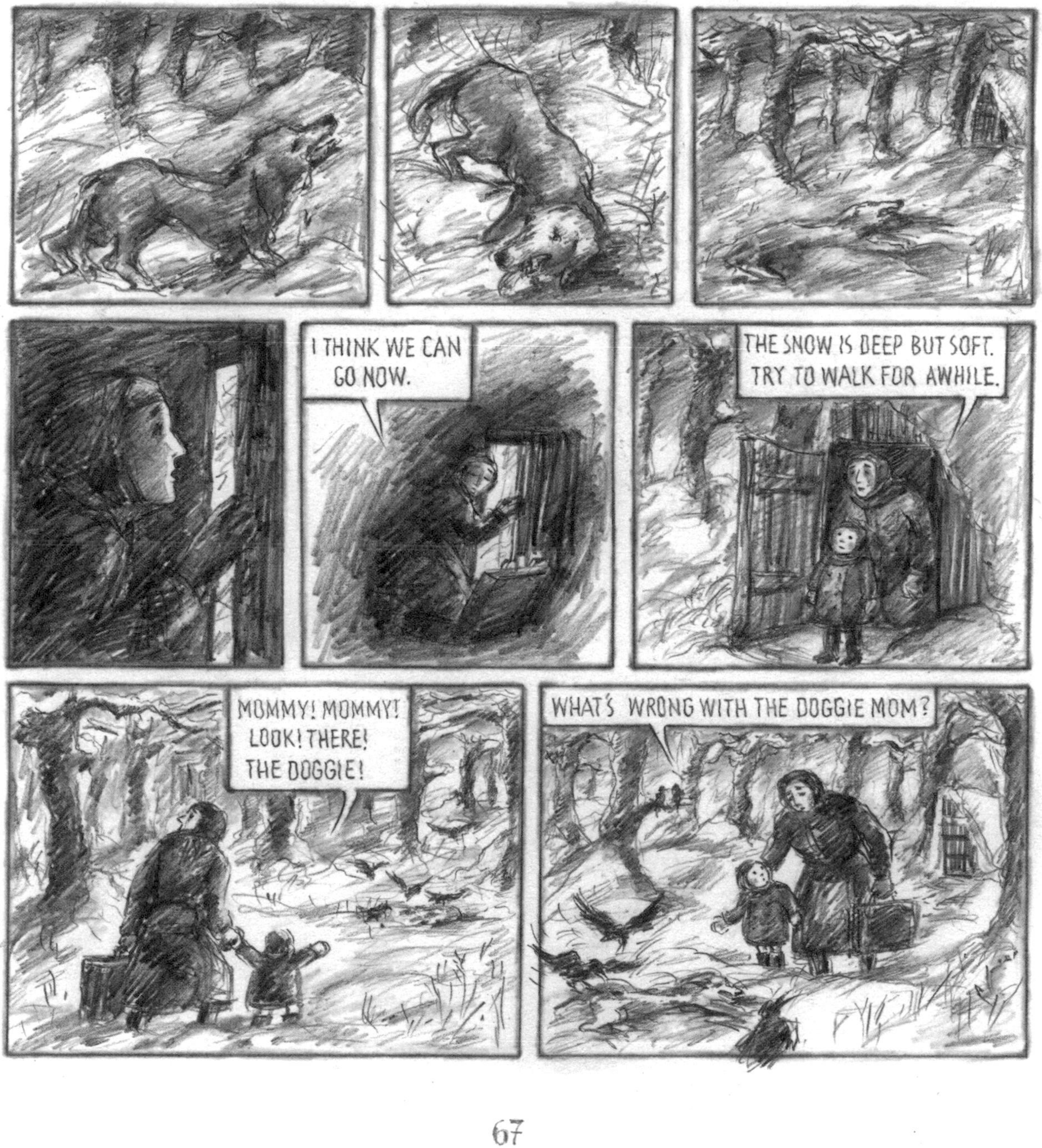
I THINK WE CAN GO NOW.
THE SNOW IS DEEP BUT SOFT. TRY TO WALK FOR AWHILE.
MOMMY! MOMMY! LOOK! THERE! THE DOGGIE!
WHAT'S WRONG WITH THE DOGGIE MOM?

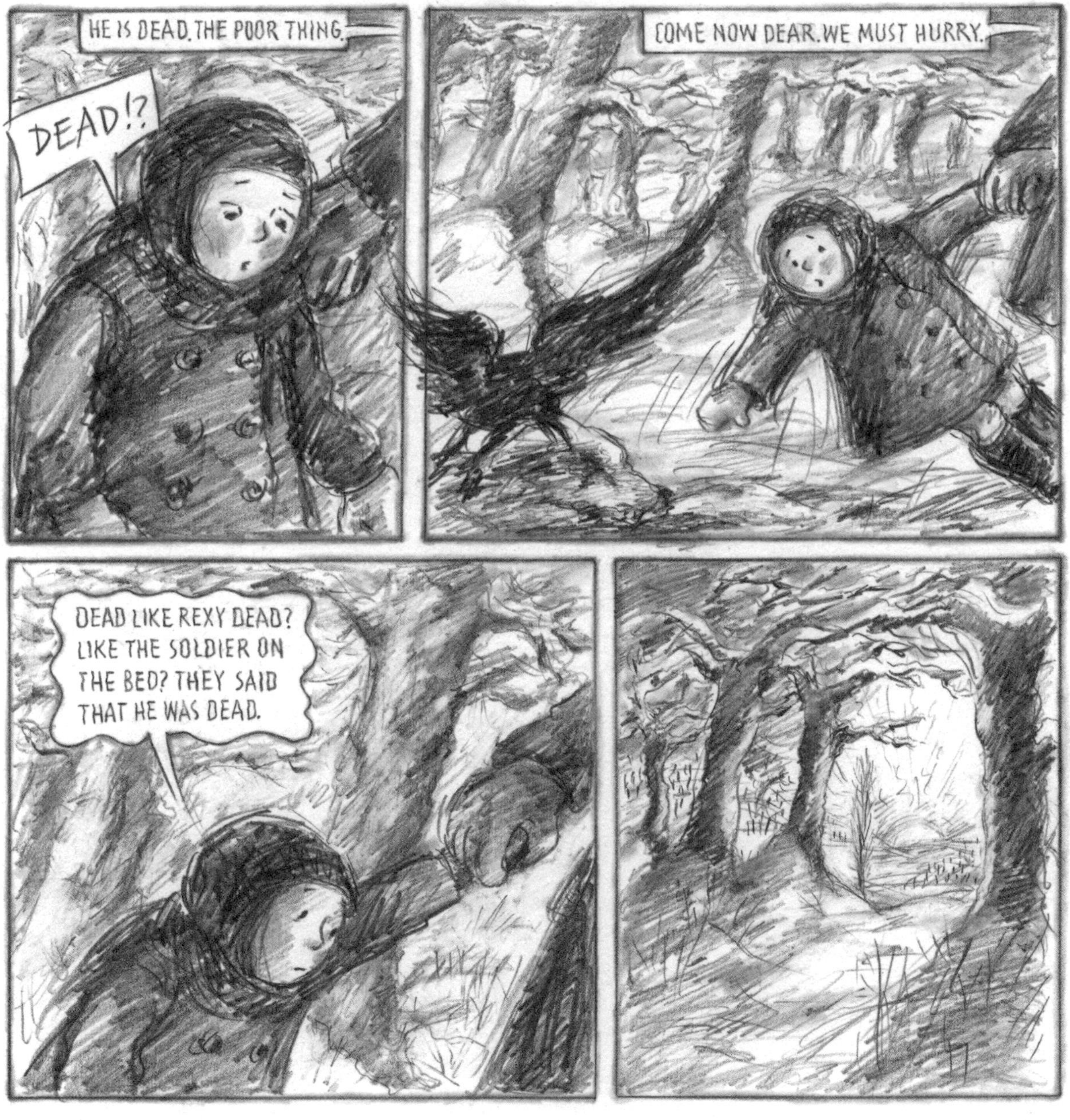
HE IS DEAD. THE POOR THING.
DEAD!?
COME NOW DEAR. WE MUST HURRY.
DEAD LIKE REXY DEAD? LIKE THE SOLDIER ON THE BED? THEY SAID THAT HE WAS DEAD.

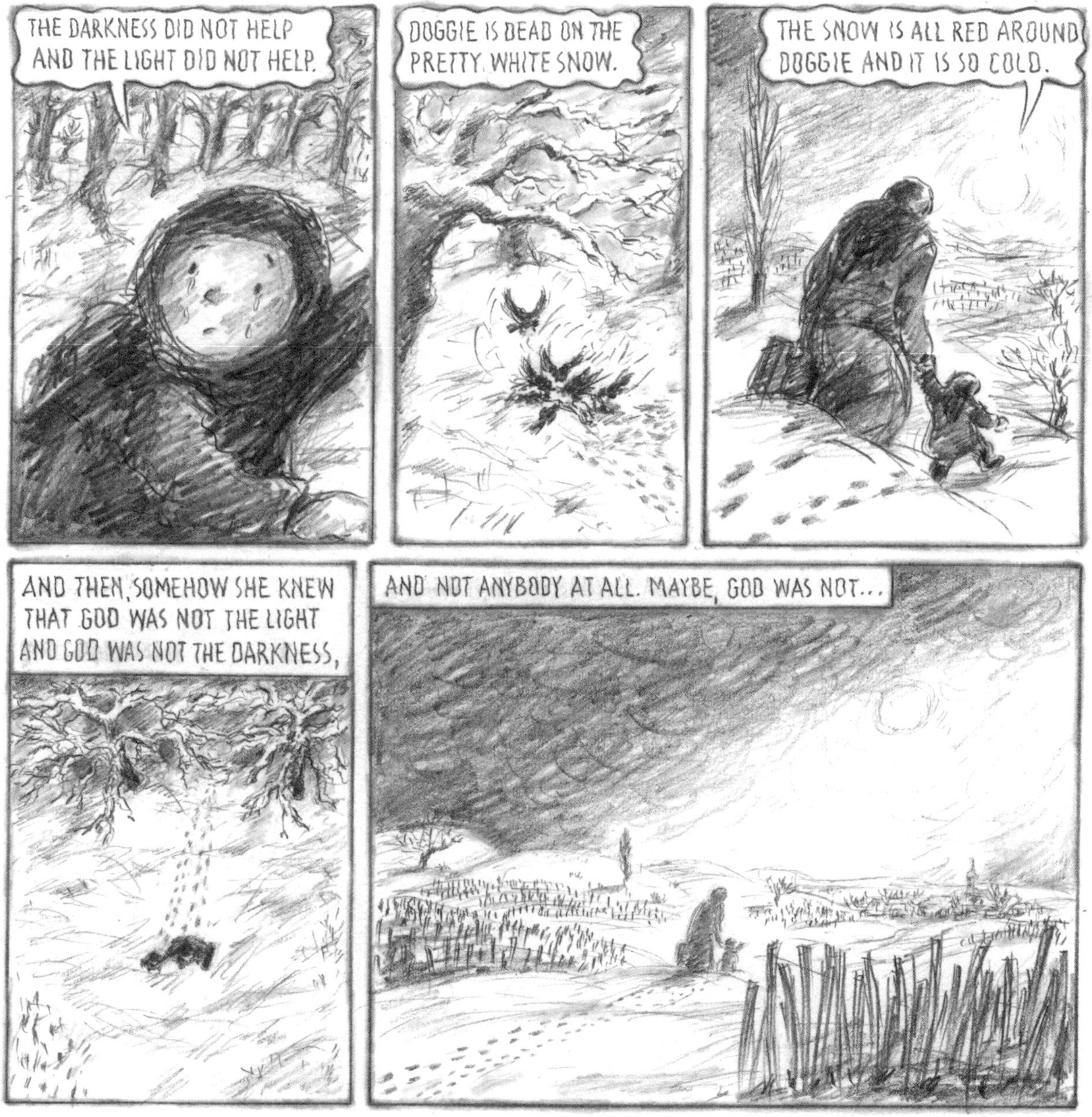
THE DARKNESS DID NOT HELP AND THE LIGHT DID NOT HELP.
DOGGIE IS DEAD ON THE PRETTY, WHITE SNOW.
THE SNOW IS ALL RED AROUND DOGGIE AND IT IS SO COLD.
AND THEN, SOMEHOW SHE KNEW THAT GOD WAS NOT THE LIGHT AND GOD WAS NOT THE DARKNESS,
AND NOT ANYBODY AT ALL. MAYBE, GOD WAS NOT...

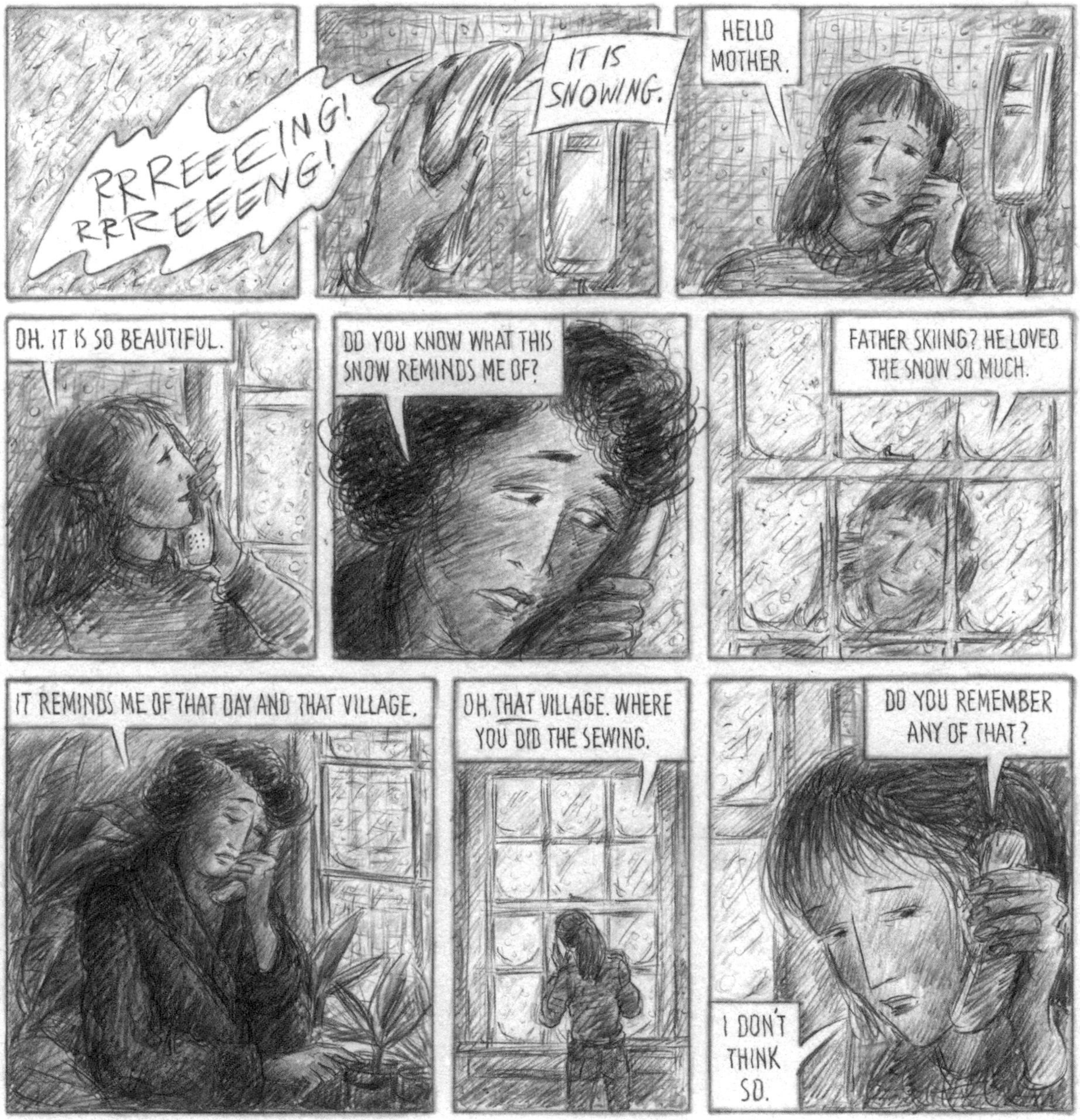
RRREEEING!
RRREEENG!
IT IS SNOWING.
HELLO MOTHER.
OH. IT IS SO BEAUTIFUL.
DO YOU KNOW WHAT THIS SNOW REMINDS ME OF?
FATHER SKIING? HE LOVED THE SNOW SO MUCH.
IT REMINDS ME OF THAT DAY AND THAT VILLAGE.
OH, THAT VILLAGE. WHERE YOU DID THE SEWING.
DO YOU REMEMBER ANY OF THAT?
I DON'T THINK SO.

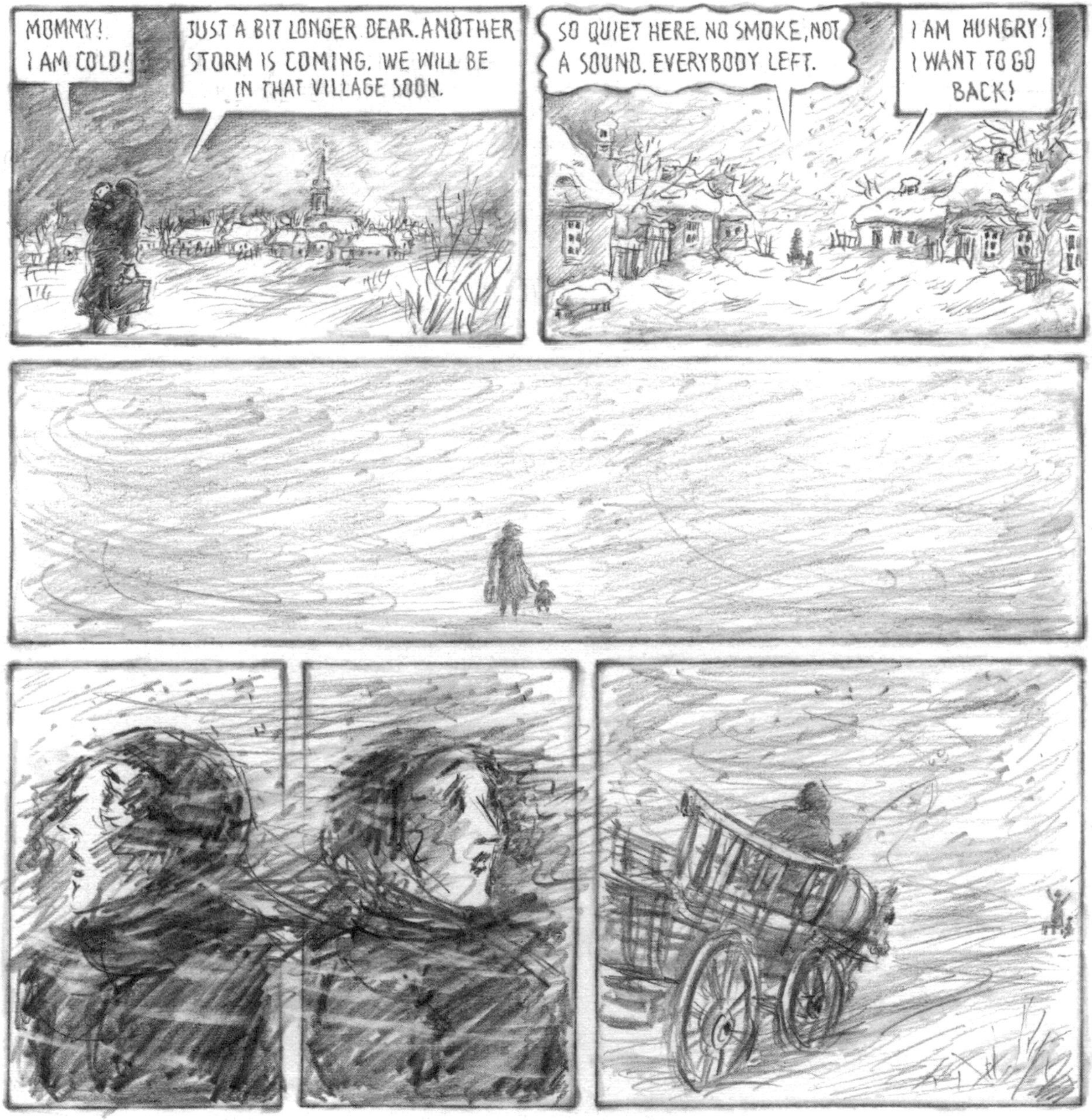
MOMMY! I AM COLD!
JUST A BIT LONGER DEAR. ANOTHER STORM IS COMING. WE WILL BE IN THAT VILLAGE SOON.
SO QUIET HERE. NO SMOKE, NOT A SOUND. EVERYBODY LEFT.
I AM HUNGRY! I WANT TO GO BACK!

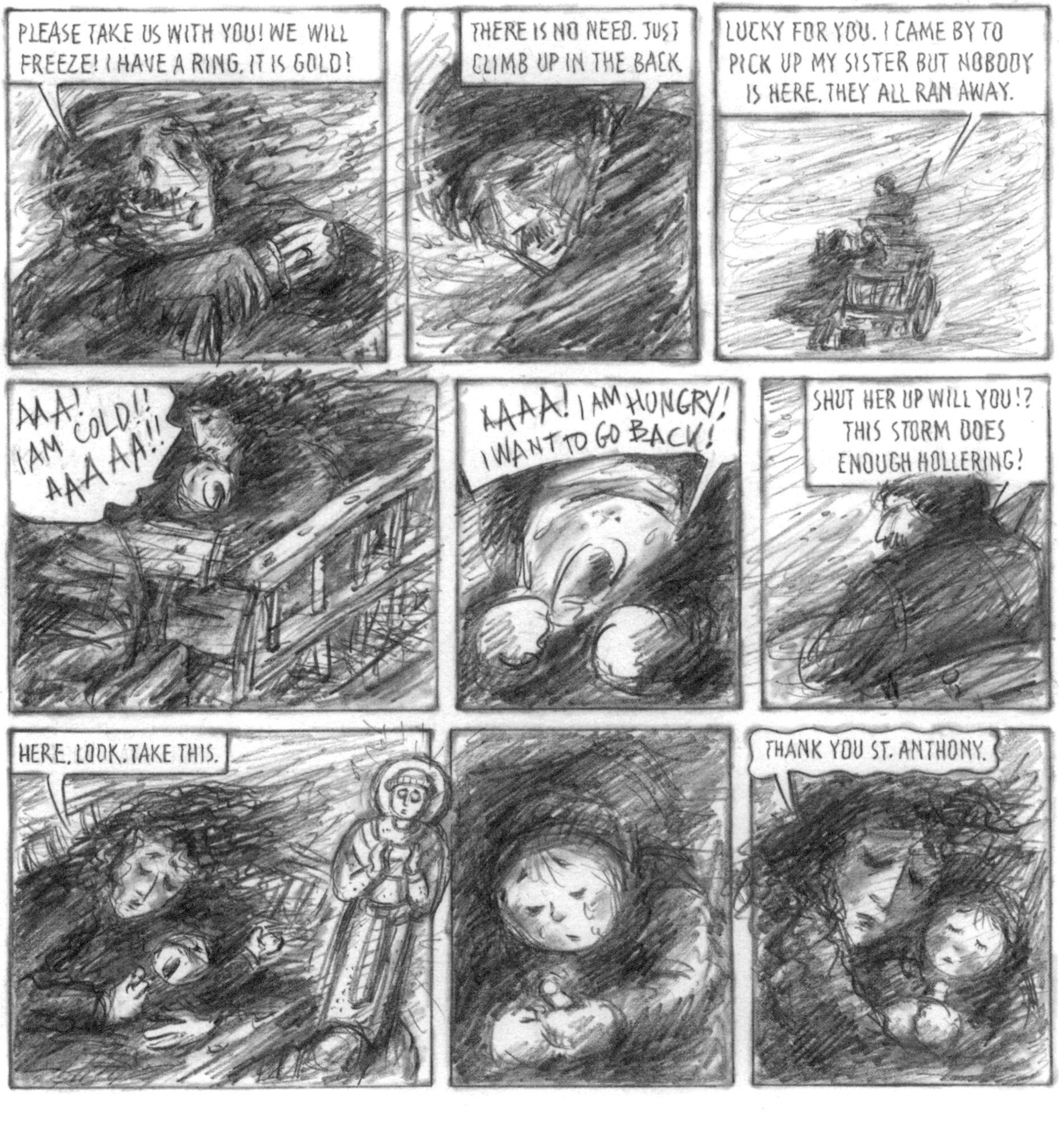
PLEASE TAKE US WITH YOU! WE WILL FREEZE! I HAVE A RING. IT IS GOLD!
THERE IS NO NEED. JUST CLIMB UP IN THE BACK.
LUCKY FOR YOU. I CAME BY TO PICK UP MY SISTER BUT NOBODY IS HERE. THEY ALL RAN AWAY.
AAA! I AM COLD!! AAAAA!!
AAAA! I AM HUNGRY! I WANT TO GO BACK!
SHUT HER UP WILL YOU!? THIS STORM DOES ENOUGH HOLLERING!
HERE. LOOK. TAKE THIS.
THANK YOU ST. ANTHONY.

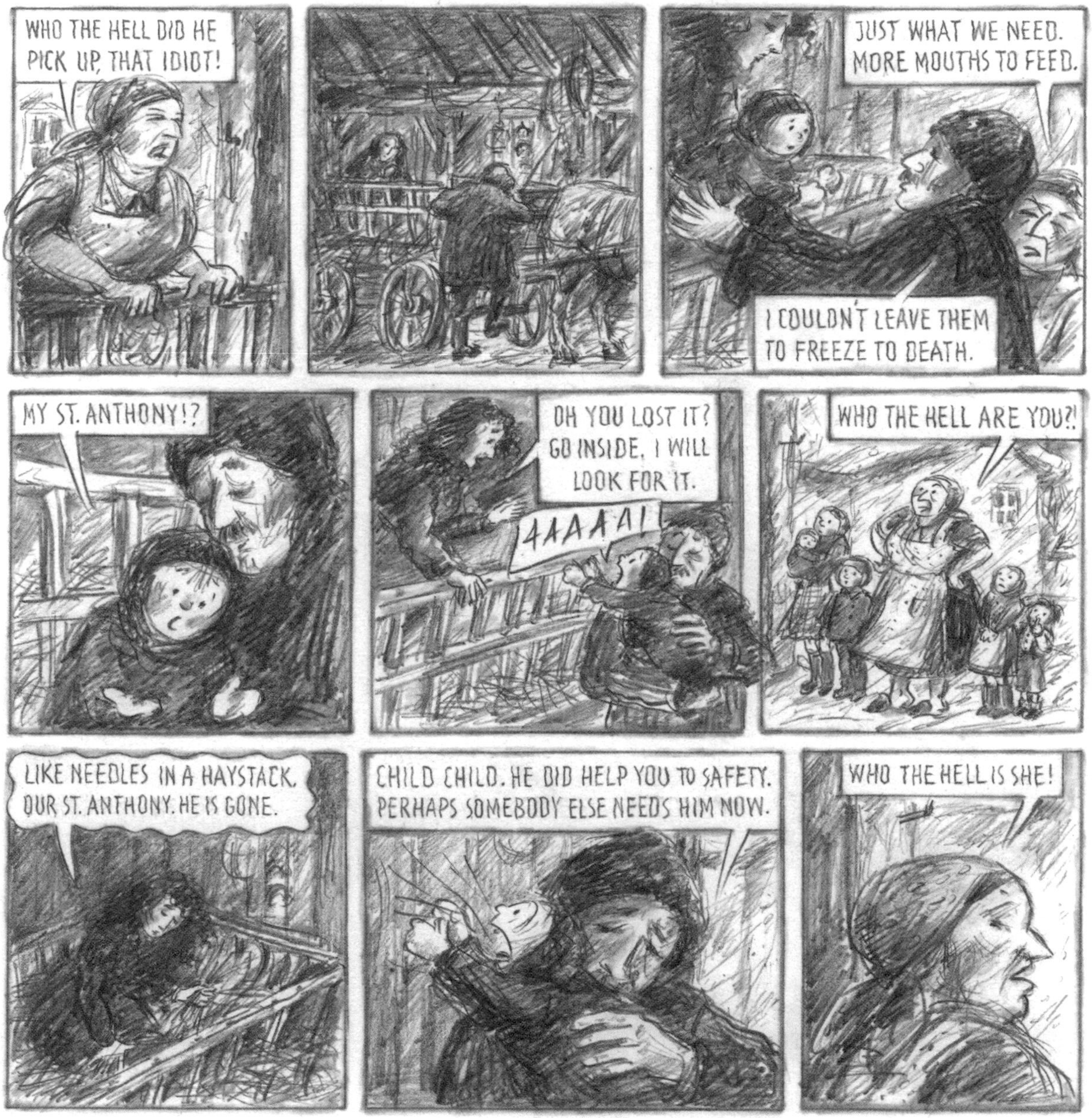
WHO THE HELL DID HE PICK UP, THAT IDIOT!
JUST WHAT WE NEED. MORE MOUTHS TO FEED.
I COULDN'T LEAVE THEM TO FREEZE TO DEATH.
MY ST. ANTHONY!?
OH YOU LOST IT? GO INSIDE, I WILL LOOK FOR IT.
AAAAA!
WHO THE HELL ARE YOU?!
LIKE NEEDLES IN A HAYSTACK. OUR ST. ANTHONY. HE IS GONE.
CHILD CHILD. HE DID HELP YOU TO SAFETY. PERHAPS SOMEBODY ELSE NEEDS HIM NOW.
WHO THE HELL IS SHE!

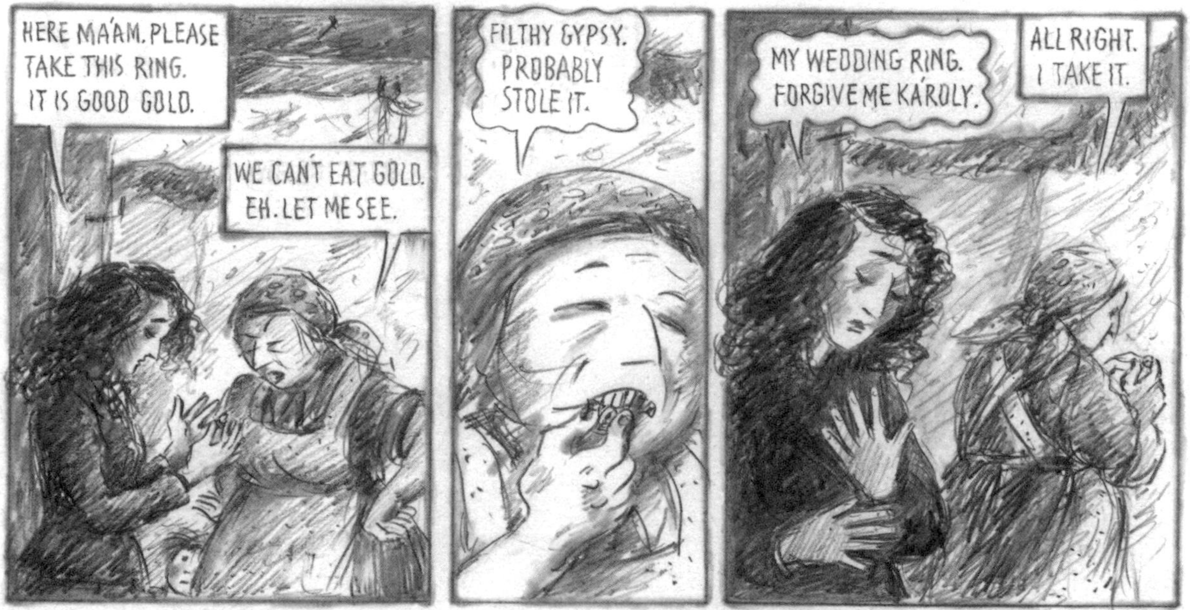
HERE MA'AM. PLEASE TAKE THIS RING. IT IS GOOD GOLD.
WE CAN'T EAT GOLD. EH. LET ME SEE.
FILTHY GYPSY. PROBABLY STOLE IT.
MY WEDDING RING. FORGIVE ME KÁROLY.
ALL RIGHT. I TAKE IT.

SPRING WAS NOT FAR BUT WINTER HELD FAST. THE BATTLES RAGED ALL AROUND.

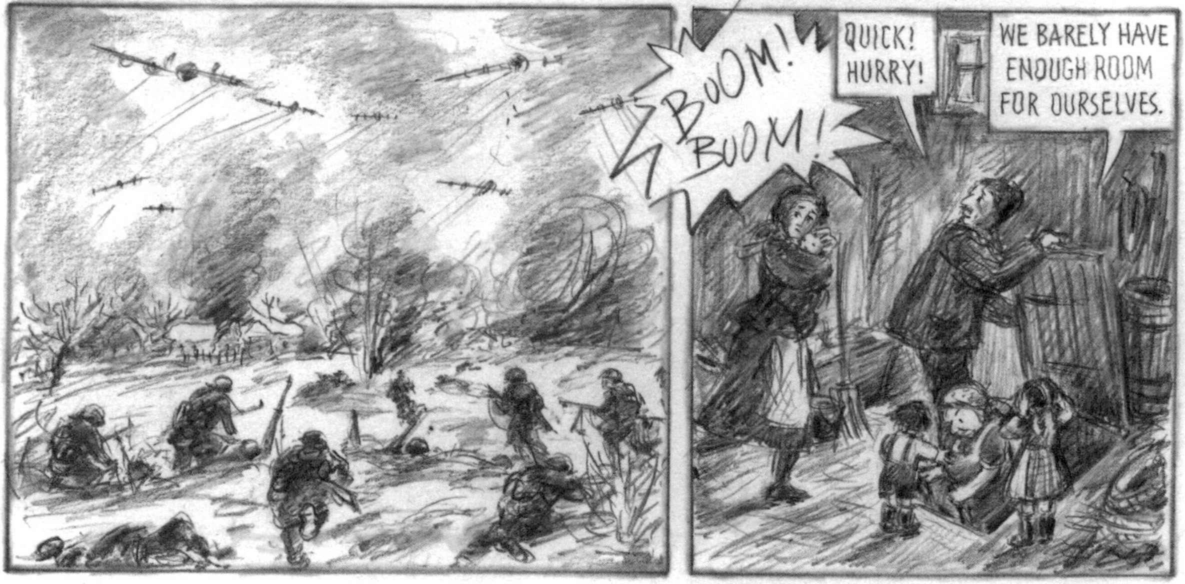
BOOM! BOOM!
QUICK! HURRY!
WE BARELY HAVE ENOUGH ROOM FOR OURSELVES.

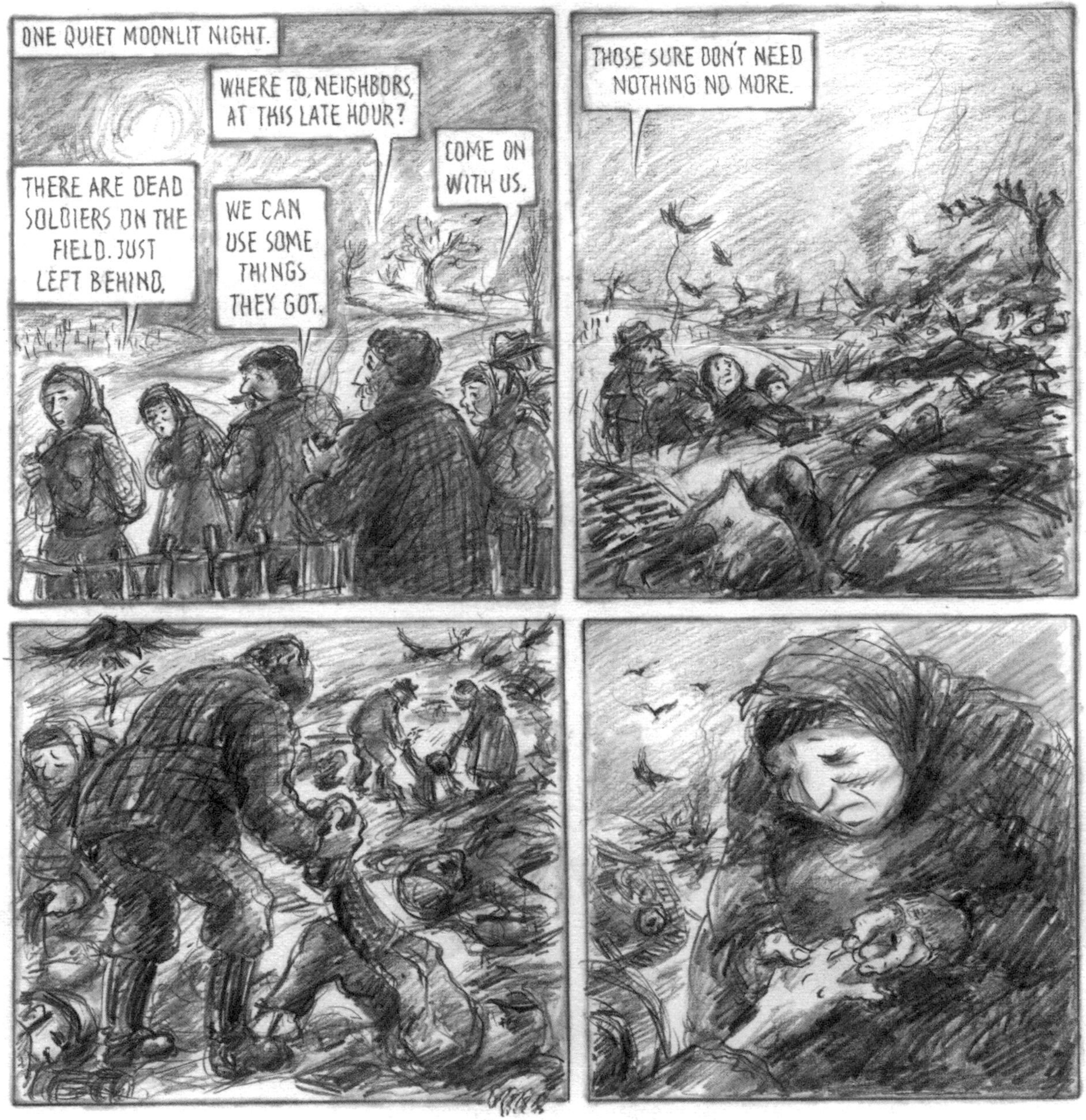
ONE QUIET MOONLIT NIGHT.
WHERE TO, NEIGHBORS, AT THIS LATE HOUR?
COME ON WITH US.
THERE ARE DEAD SOLDIERS ON THE FIELD. JUST LEFT BEHIND.
WE CAN USE SOME THINGS THEY GOT.
THOSE SURE DON'T NEED NOTHING NO MORE.

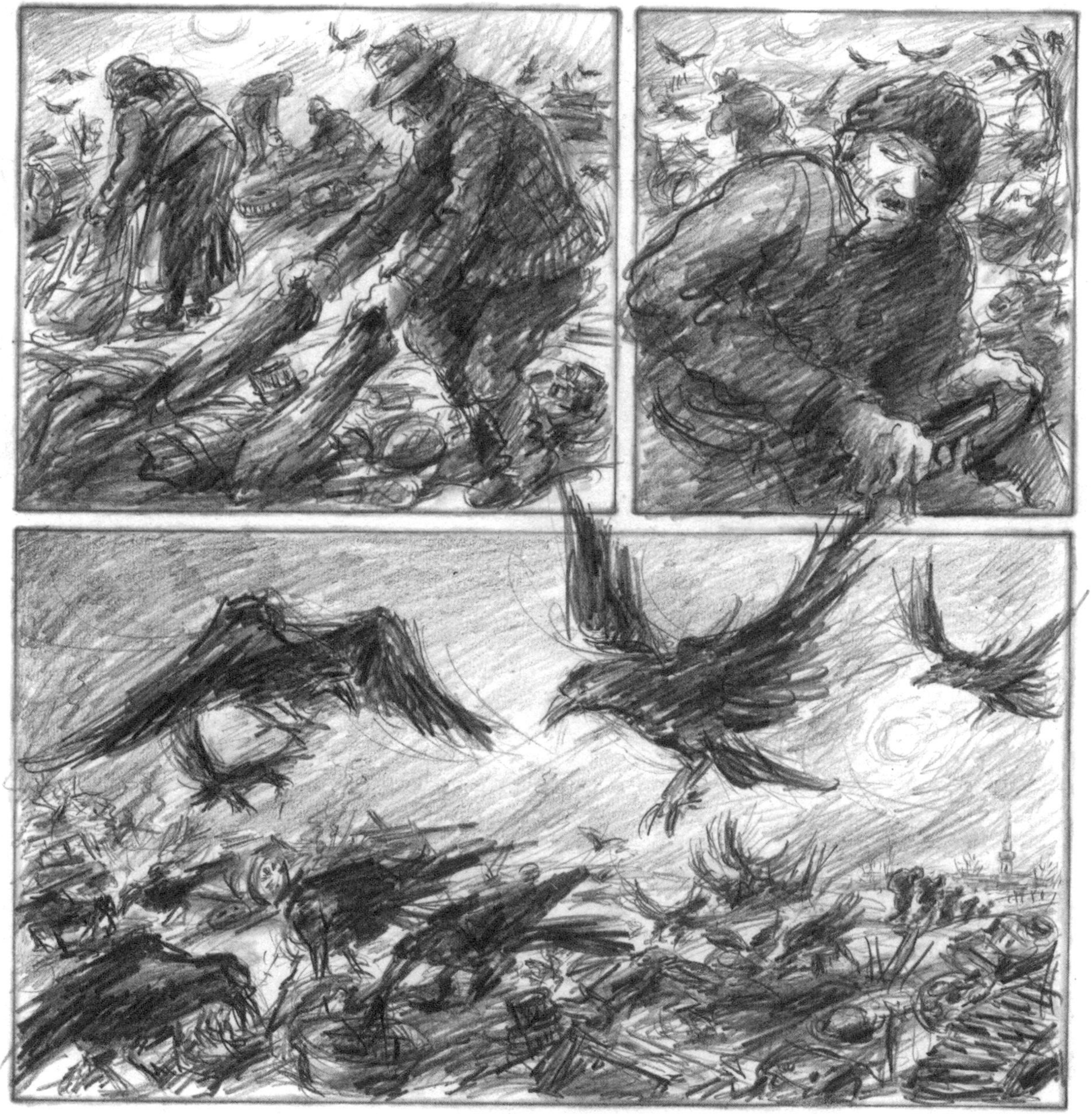

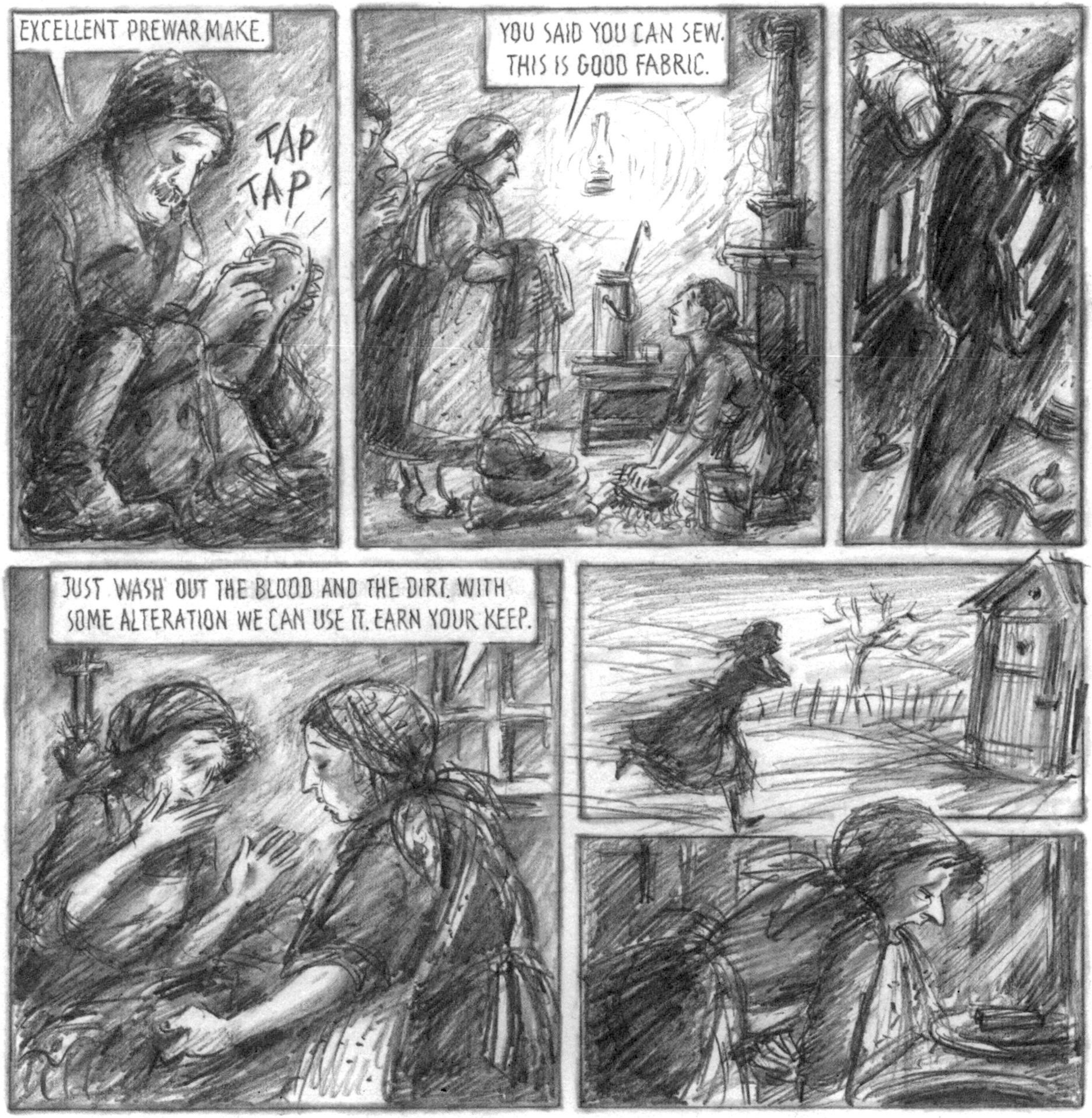
EXCELLENT PREWAR MAKE.
TAP TAP
YOU SAID YOU CAN SEW. THIS IS GOOD FABRIC.
JUST WASH OUT THE BLOOD AND THE DIRT. WITH SOME ALTERATION WE CAN USE IT. EARN YOUR KEEP.

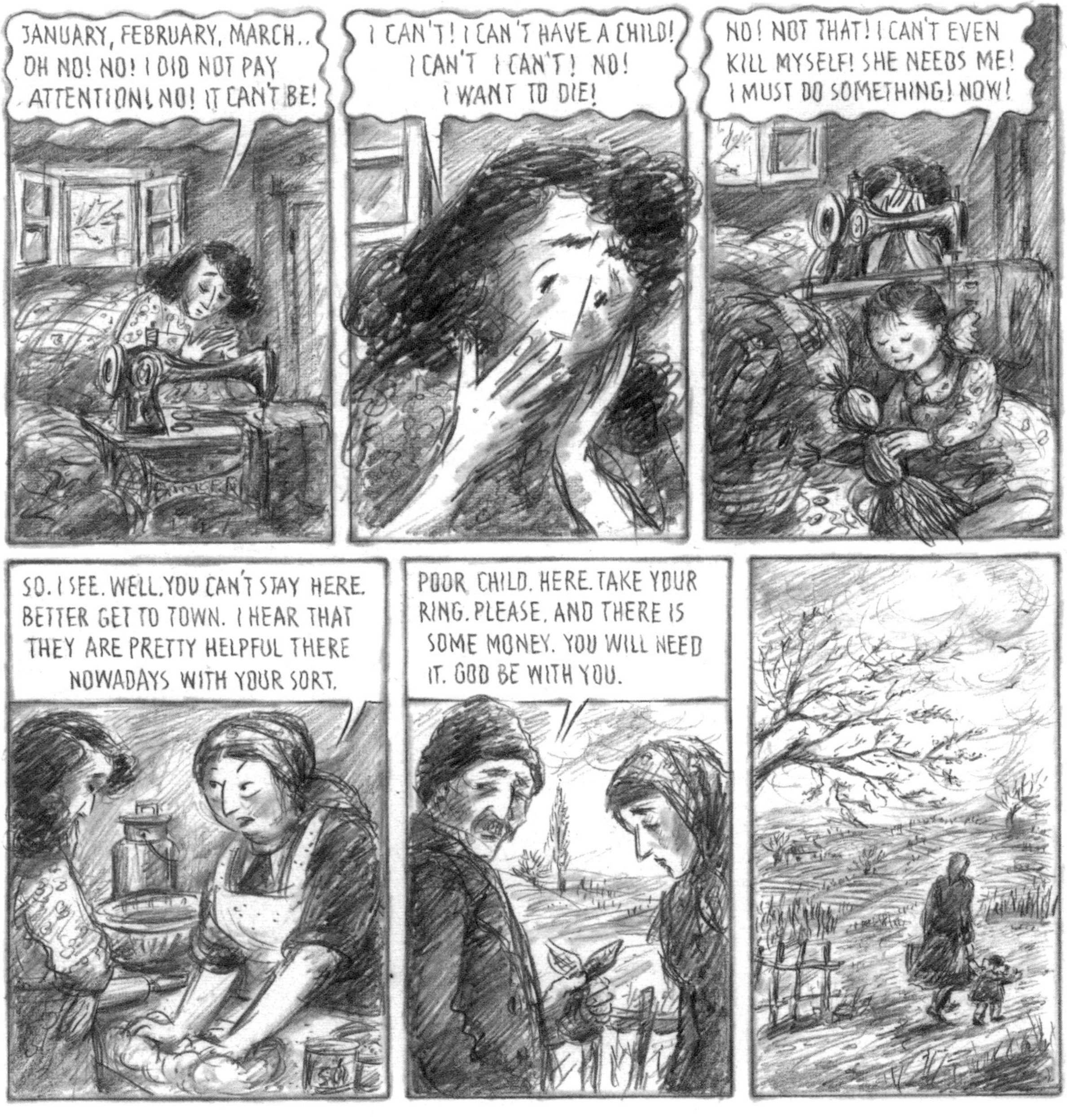
JANUARY, FEBRUARY, MARCH.. OH NO! NO! I DID NOT PAY ATTENTION! NO! IT CAN'T BE!
I CAN'T! I CAN'T HAVE A CHILD! I CAN'T I CAN'T! NO! I WANT TO DIE!
NO! NOT THAT! I CAN'T EVEN KILL MYSELF! SHE NEEDS ME! I MUST DO SOMETHING! NOW!
SO. I SEE. WELL. YOU CAN'T STAY HERE. BETTER GET TO TOWN. I HEAR THAT THEY ARE PRETTY HELPFUL THERE NOWADAYS WITH YOUR SORT.
POOR CHILD. HERE. TAKE YOUR RING. PLEASE. AND THERE IS SOME MONEY. YOU WILL NEED IT. GOD BE WITH YOU.

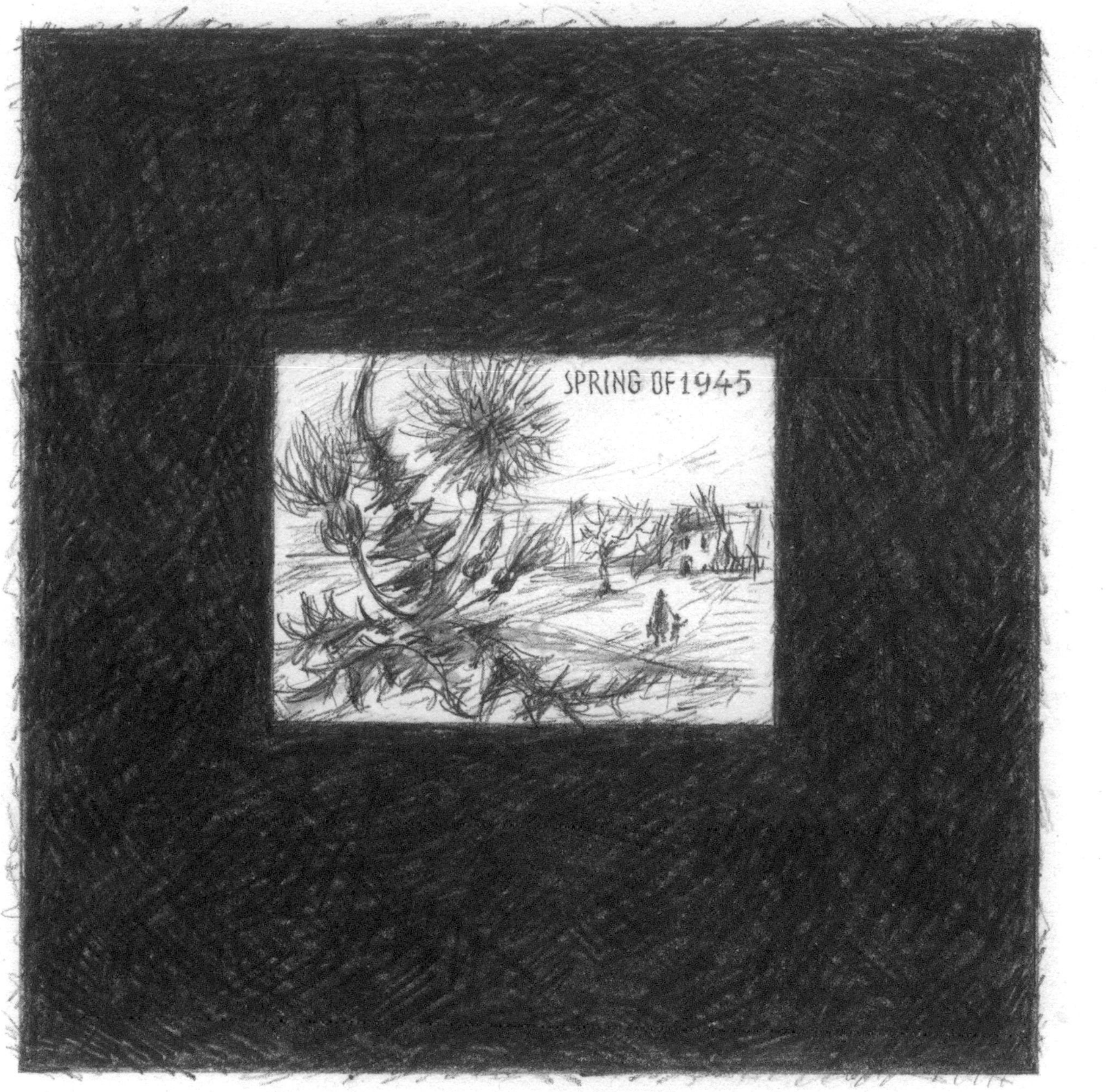
SPRING OF 1945

A SMALL COUNTRY STATION.

A RUSSIAN GUARD! TOO LATE TO LEAVE NOW. BESIDES, WHERE WOULD I GO?

THIS MIGHT BE THE RIGHT TIME TO START USING OUR REAL NAME.

ESTHER LEVY. DOCUMENTS LOST.

ESTHER LEVY? A JEW! ALIVE! RIGHT HERE? HARD TO BELIEVE.

SORRY, NO TRAINS UNTIL MAYBE AFTER MIDNIGHT.

I CAN'T UNDERSTAND A WORD HE IS SAYING.

NYET TRAIN. NYET CHU-CHU. NYET.

SHE IS SCARED OF ME. TERRIFIED.. WAIT.

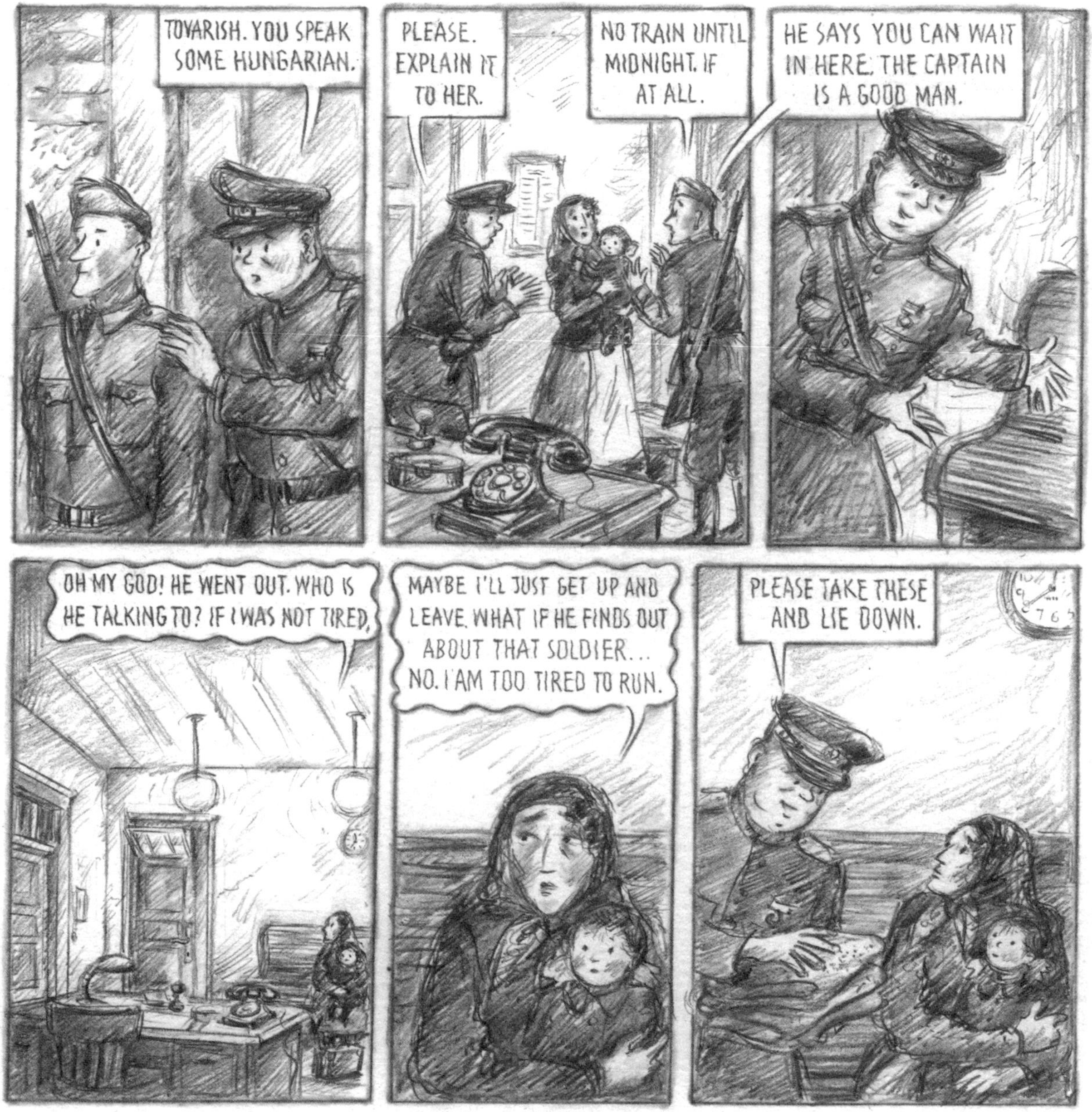
TOVARISH. YOU SPEAK SOME HUNGARIAN.
PLEASE. EXPLAIN IT TO HER.
NO TRAIN UNTIL MIDNIGHT. IF AT ALL.
HE SAYS YOU CAN WAIT IN HERE. THE CAPTAIN IS A GOOD MAN.
OH MY GOD! HE WENT OUT. WHO IS HE TALKING TO? IF I WAS NOT TIRED,
MAYBE I'LL JUST GET UP AND LEAVE. WHAT IF HE FINDS OUT ABOUT THAT SOLDIER... NO. I AM TOO TIRED TO RUN.
PLEASE TAKE THESE AND LIE DOWN.

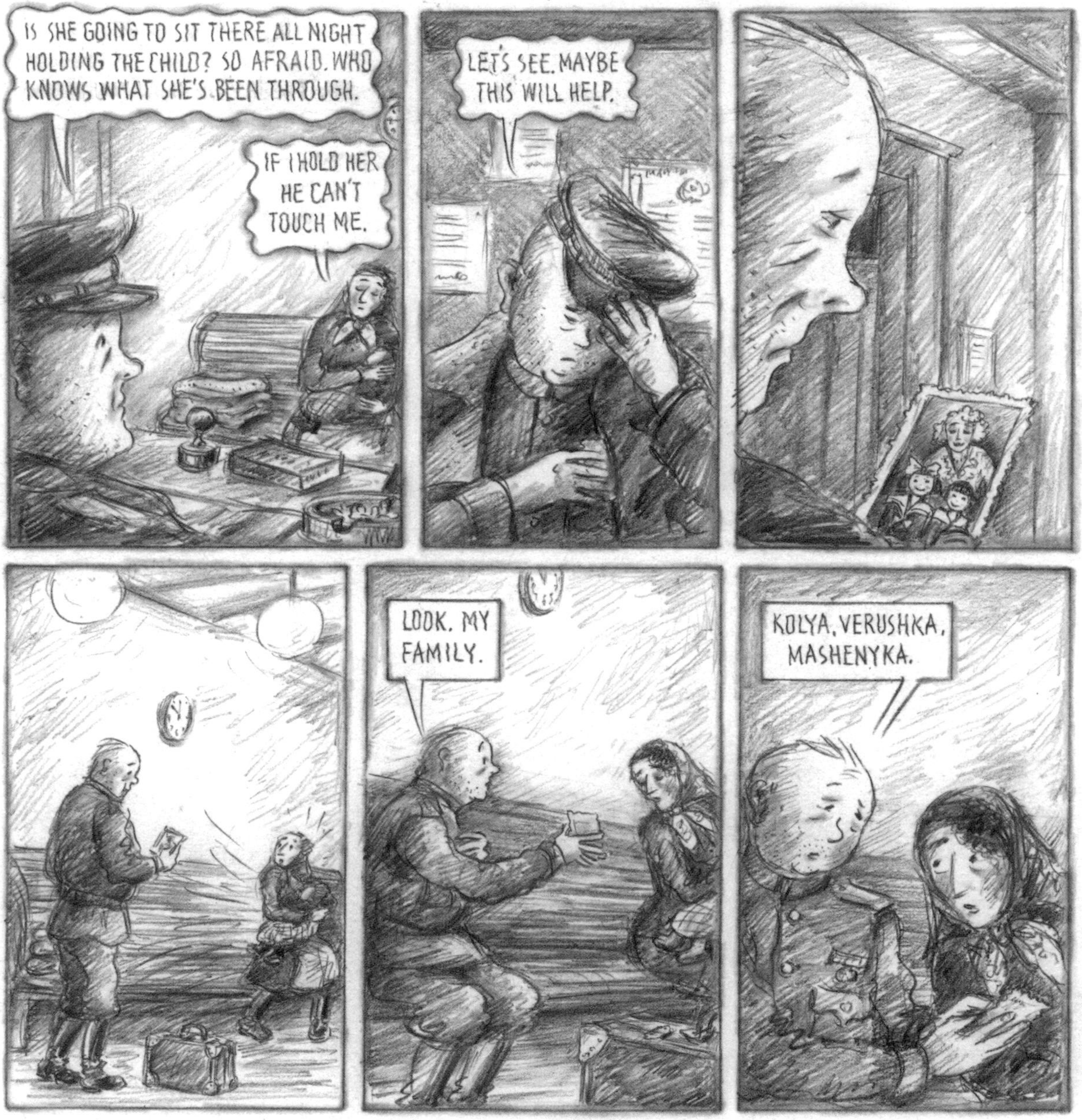
IS SHE GOING TO SIT THERE ALL NIGHT HOLDING THE CHILD? SO AFRAID. WHO KNOWS WHAT SHE'S BEEN THROUGH.
IF I HOLD HER HE CAN'T TOUCH ME.
LET'S SEE. MAYBE THIS WILL HELP.
LOOK. MY FAMILY.
KOLYA, VERUSHKA, MASHENYKA.

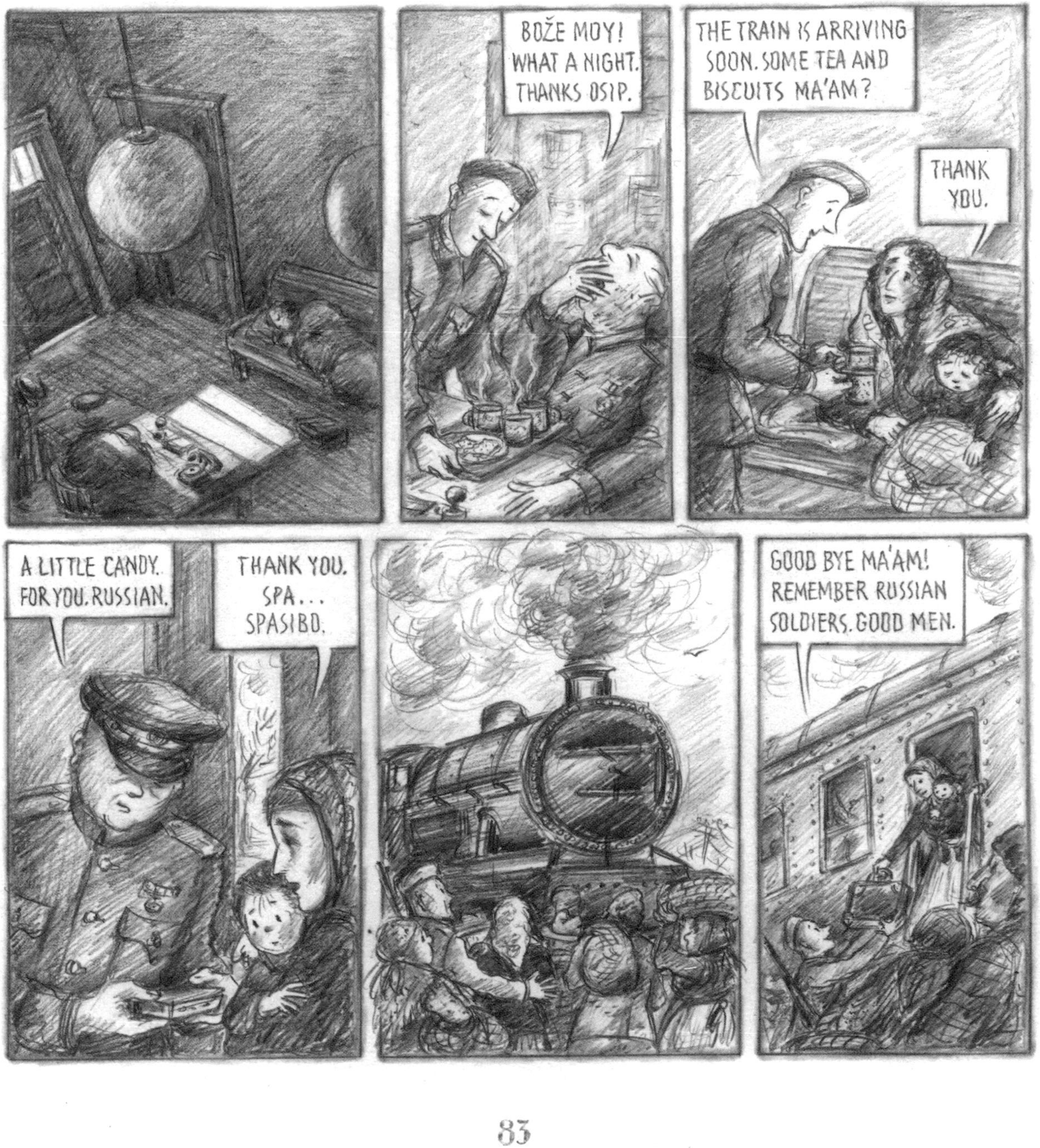
BOŽE MOY! WHAT A NIGHT. THANKS OSIP.
THE TRAIN IS ARRIVING SOON. SOME TEA AND BISCUITS MA'AM?
THANK YOU.
A LITTLE CANDY. FOR YOU. RUSSIAN.
THANK YOU. SPA... SPASIBO.
GOOD BYE MA'AM! REMEMBER RUSSIAN SOLDIERS. GOOD MEN.

HEBREW SCHOOL, WHY WOULD HE HAVE TO GO TO HEBREW SCHOOL?

ALL THE JEWISH KIDS AROUND HERE GO TO HEBREW SCHOOL..

TO BE WITH OUR OWN KIND.

YOU MEAN TO SEPARATE. AGAIN. US, THEM.

HE MUST LEARN THE BIBLE AND THE PRAYERS THE WAY I DID.

AND SO DID I. I PRAYED AND I PRAYED AND THEN,

GOD, HE TURNED OUT TO BE RESIDING IN A WINE BARREL.

IN THE TOWN OF BOROSVÁR.

A REFUGEE'S AID CENTER.

PLEASE, FOLKS, PLEASE! EVERYBODY WILL GET IN! ONE BY ONE! ONE BY ONE!

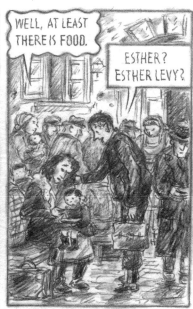

WELL, AT LEAST THERE IS FOOD.

ESTHER? ESTHER LEVY?

ZOLTÁN?

NO. DAVID. DAVID BLAU. WE MET IN BUDAPEST. FRIEND OF THE WEISSES.

I AM FROM THIS TOWN. THE BREWERY. THAT WAS US. MY PARENTS ARE ... GONE. ALL MY FAMILY.

I CAN'T START UP THE BREWERY YET SO I WORK FOR THE AGENCY. LET ME HELP YOU REGISTER.

85

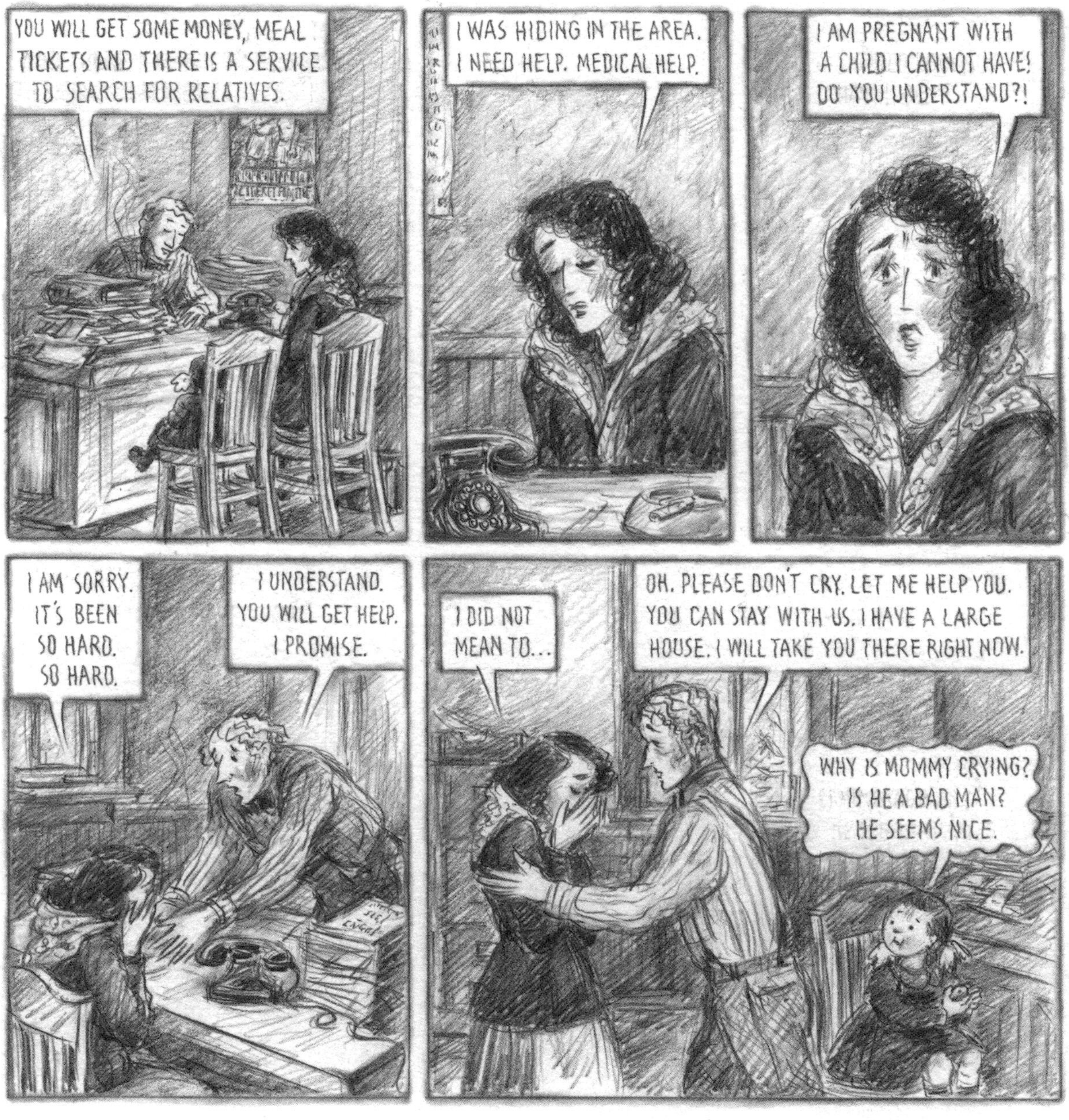
YOU WILL GET SOME MONEY, MEAL TICKETS AND THERE IS A SERVICE TO SEARCH FOR RELATIVES.
I WAS HIDING IN THE AREA. I NEED HELP. MEDICAL HELP.
I AM PREGNANT WITH A CHILD I CANNOT HAVE! DO YOU UNDERSTAND?!
I AM SORRY. IT'S BEEN SO HARD. SO HARD.
I UNDERSTAND. YOU WILL GET HELP. I PROMISE.
I DID NOT MEAN TO...
OH. PLEASE DON'T CRY. LET ME HELP YOU. YOU CAN STAY WITH US. I HAVE A LARGE HOUSE. I WILL TAKE YOU THERE RIGHT NOW.
WHY IS MOMMY CRYING? IS HE A BAD MAN? HE SEEMS NICE.

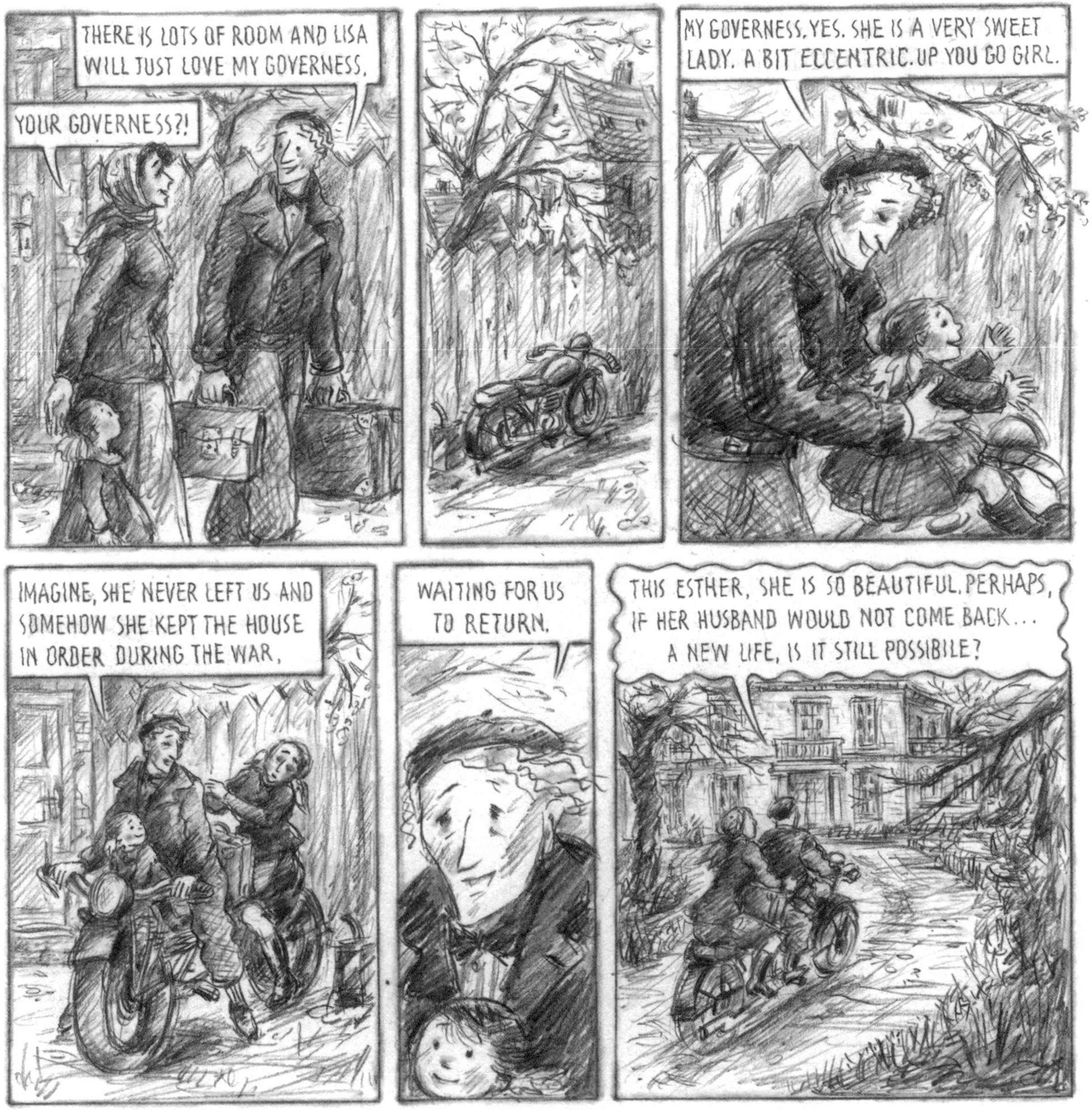
THERE IS LOTS OF ROOM AND LISA WILL JUST LOVE MY GOVERNESS.
YOUR GOVERNESS?!
MY GOVERNESS, YES. SHE IS A VERY SWEET LADY. A BIT ECCENTRIC. UP YOU GO GIRL.
IMAGINE, SHE NEVER LEFT US AND SOMEHOW SHE KEPT THE HOUSE IN ORDER DURING THE WAR,
WAITING FOR US TO RETURN.
THIS ESTHER, SHE IS SO BEAUTIFUL. PERHAPS, IF HER HUSBAND WOULD NOT COME BACK... A NEW LIFE, IS IT STILL POSSIBILE?

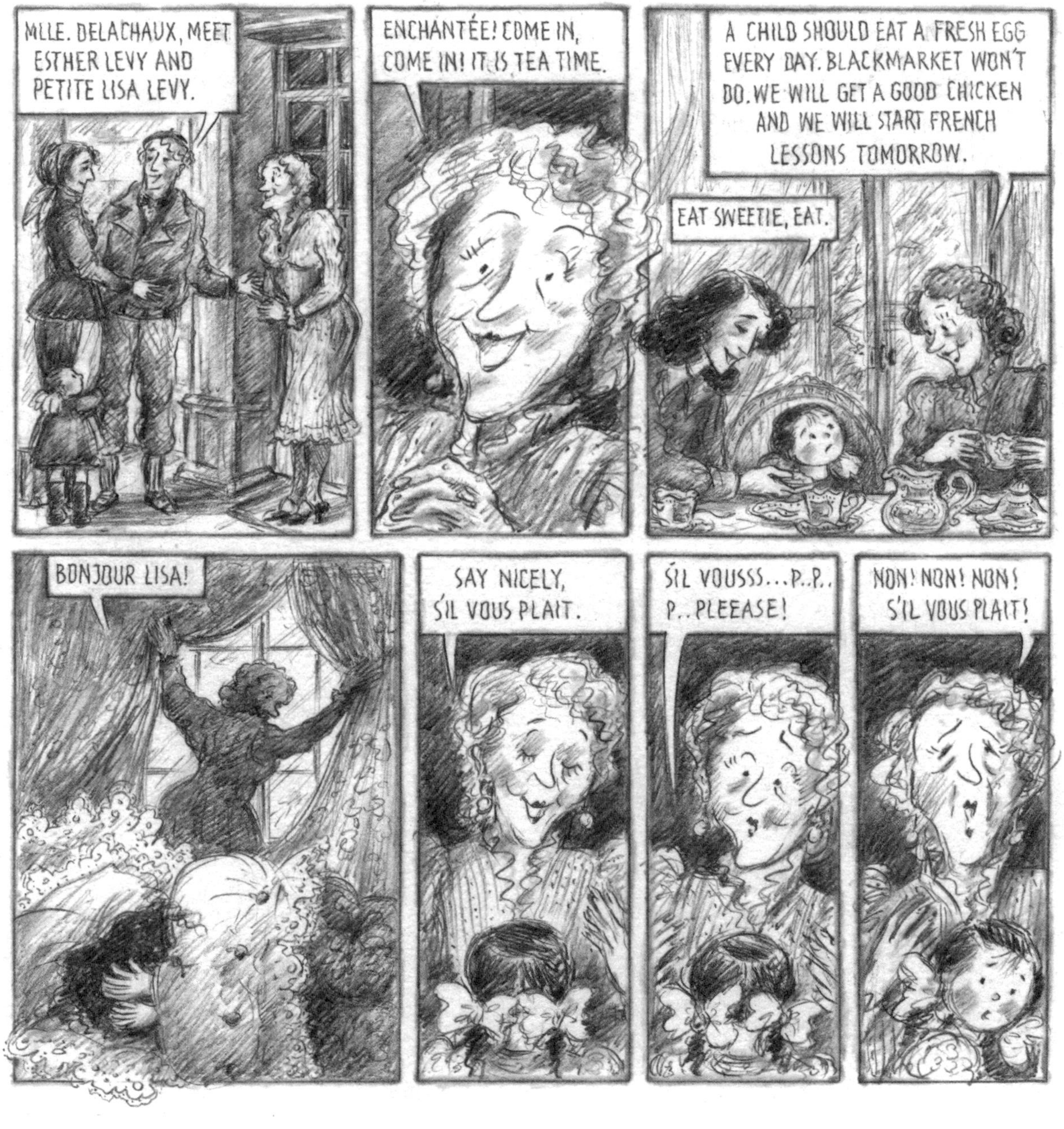
MLLE. DELACHAUX, MEET ESTHER LEVY AND PETITE LISA LEVY.
ENCHANTÉE! COME IN, COME IN! IT IS TEA TIME.
A CHILD SHOULD EAT A FRESH EGG EVERY DAY. BLACKMARKET WON'T DO. WE WILL GET A GOOD CHICKEN AND WE WILL START FRENCH LESSONS TOMORROW.
EAT SWEETIE, EAT.
BONJOUR LISA!
SAY NICELY, S'IL VOUS PLAIT.
S'IL VOUSSS...P..P.. P..PLEEASE!
NON! NON! NON! S'IL VOUS PLAIT!

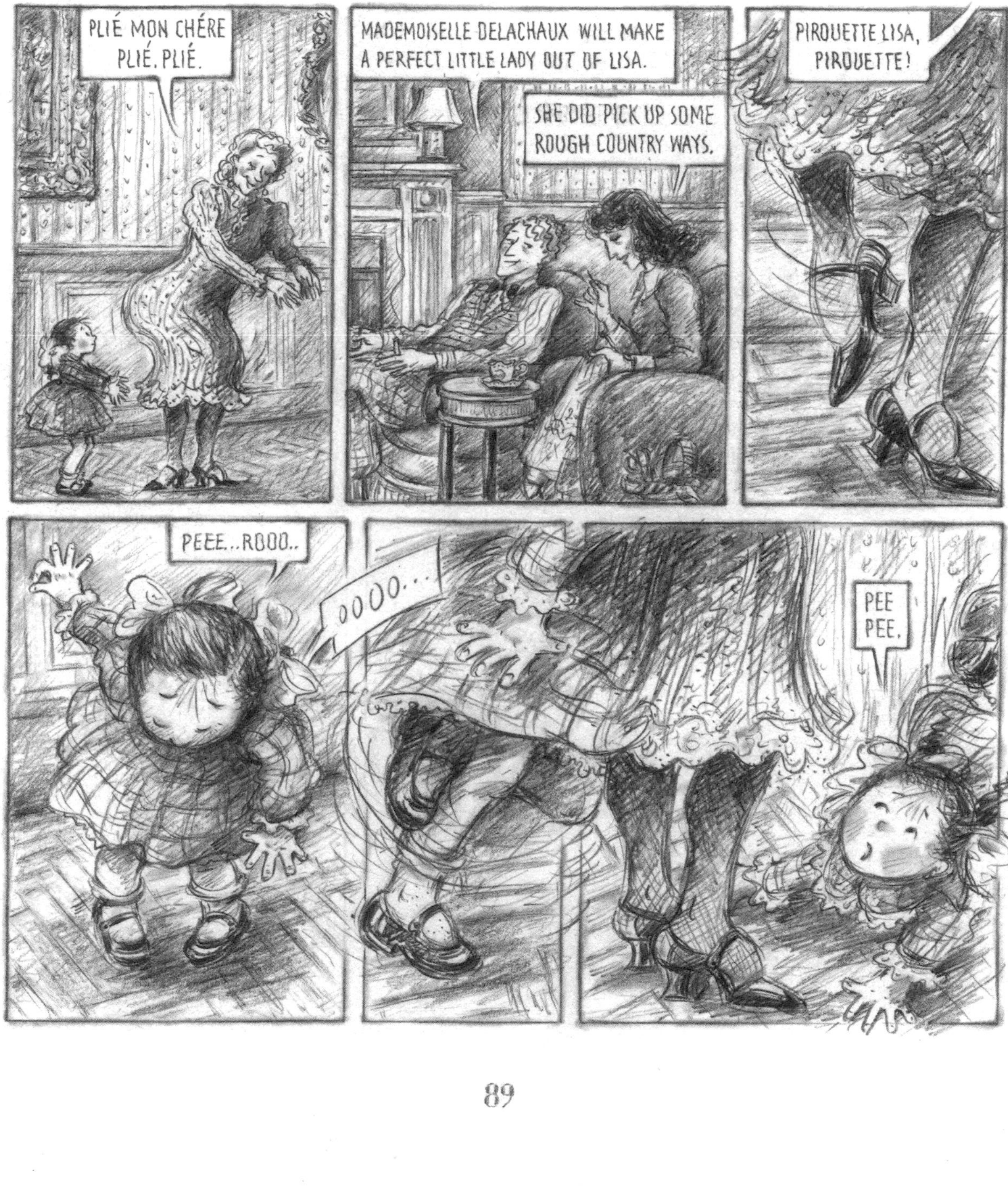

PLIÉ MON CHÉRE PLIÉ. PLIÉ.
MADEMOISELLE DELACHAUX WILL MAKE A PERFECT LITTLE LADY OUT OF LISA.
SHE DID PICK UP SOME ROUGH COUNTRY WAYS.
PIROUETTE LISA, PIROUETTE!
PEEE...ROOO..
OOOO...
PEE PEE.

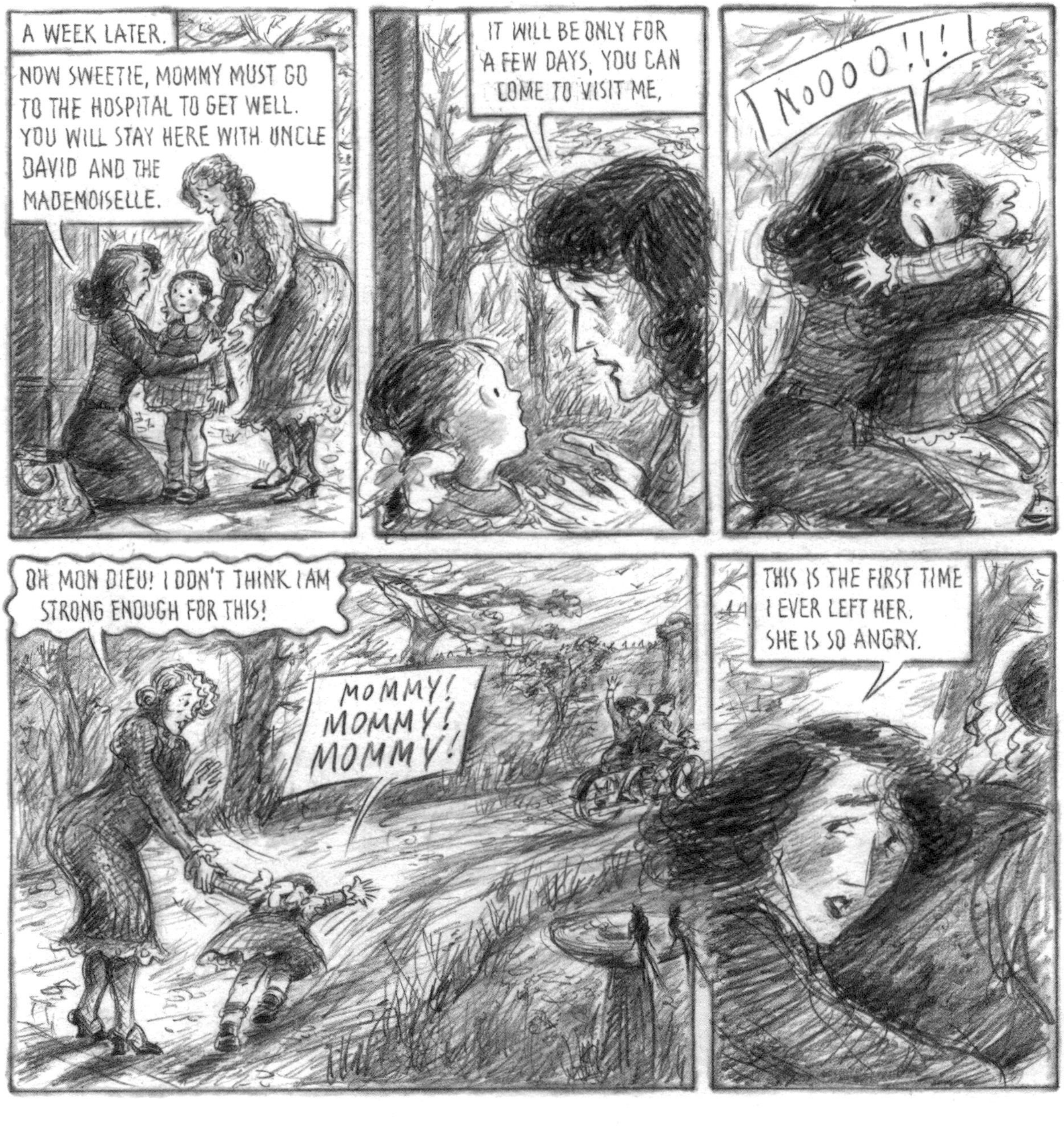
A WEEK LATER.
NOW SWEETIE, MOMMY MUST GO TO THE HOSPITAL TO GET WELL. YOU WILL STAY HERE WITH UNCLE DAVID AND THE MADEMOISELLE.
IT WILL BE ONLY FOR A FEW DAYS, YOU CAN COME TO VISIT ME,
NoOOO!!!
OH MON DIEU! I DON'T THINK I AM STRONG ENOUGH FOR THIS!
MOMMY! MOMMY! MOMMY!
THIS IS THE FIRST TIME I EVER LEFT HER. SHE IS SO ANGRY.

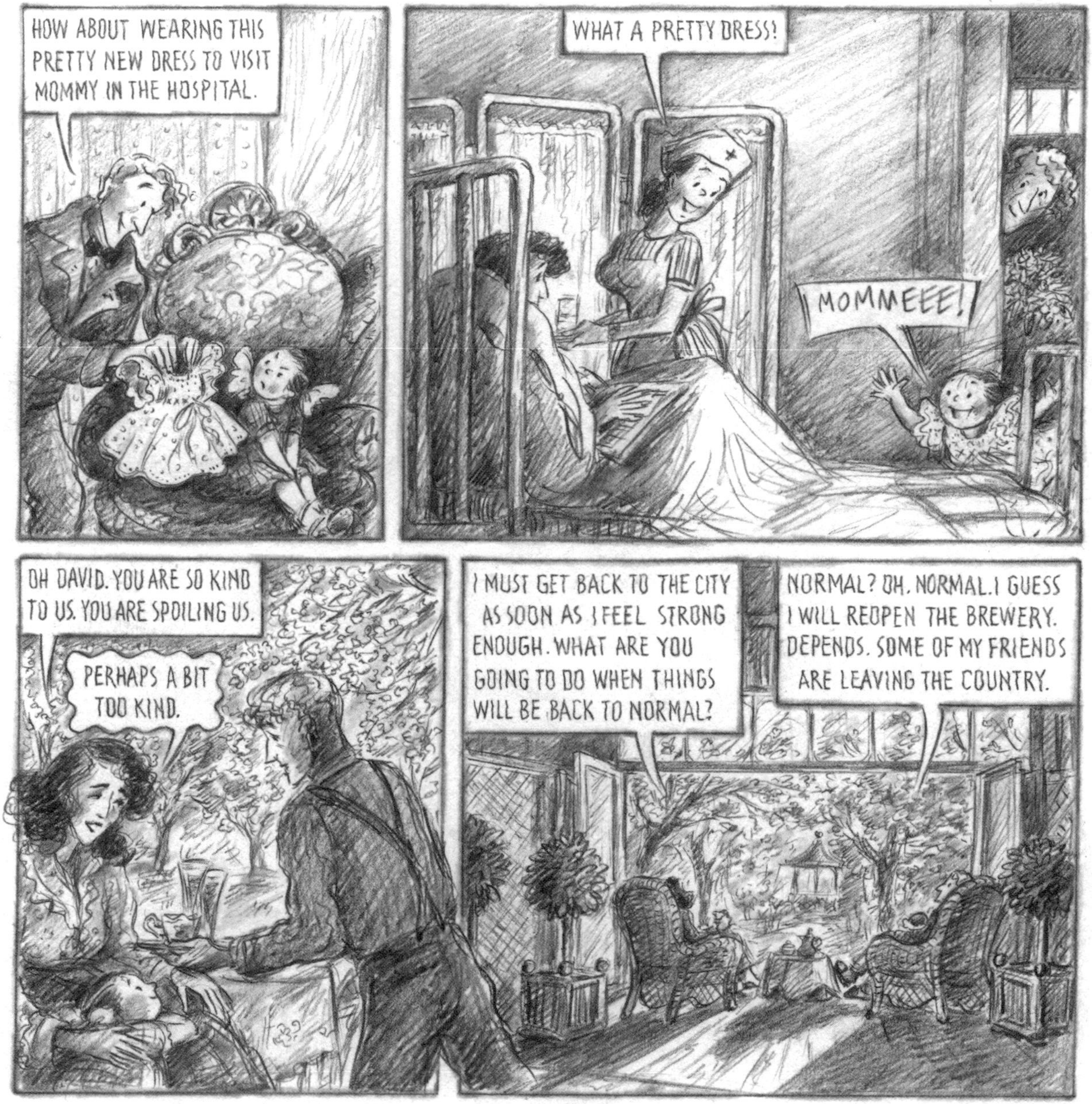
HOW ABOUT WEARING THIS PRETTY NEW DRESS TO VISIT MOMMY IN THE HOSPITAL.
WHAT A PRETTY DRESS!
MOMMEEE!
OH DAVID. YOU ARE SO KIND TO US. YOU ARE SPOILING US.
PERHAPS A BIT TOO KIND.
I MUST GET BACK TO THE CITY AS SOON AS I FEEL STRONG ENOUGH. WHAT ARE YOU GOING TO DO WHEN THINGS WILL BE BACK TO NORMAL?
NORMAL? OH, NORMAL. I GUESS I WILL REOPEN THE BREWERY. DEPENDS. SOME OF MY FRIENDS ARE LEAVING THE COUNTRY.

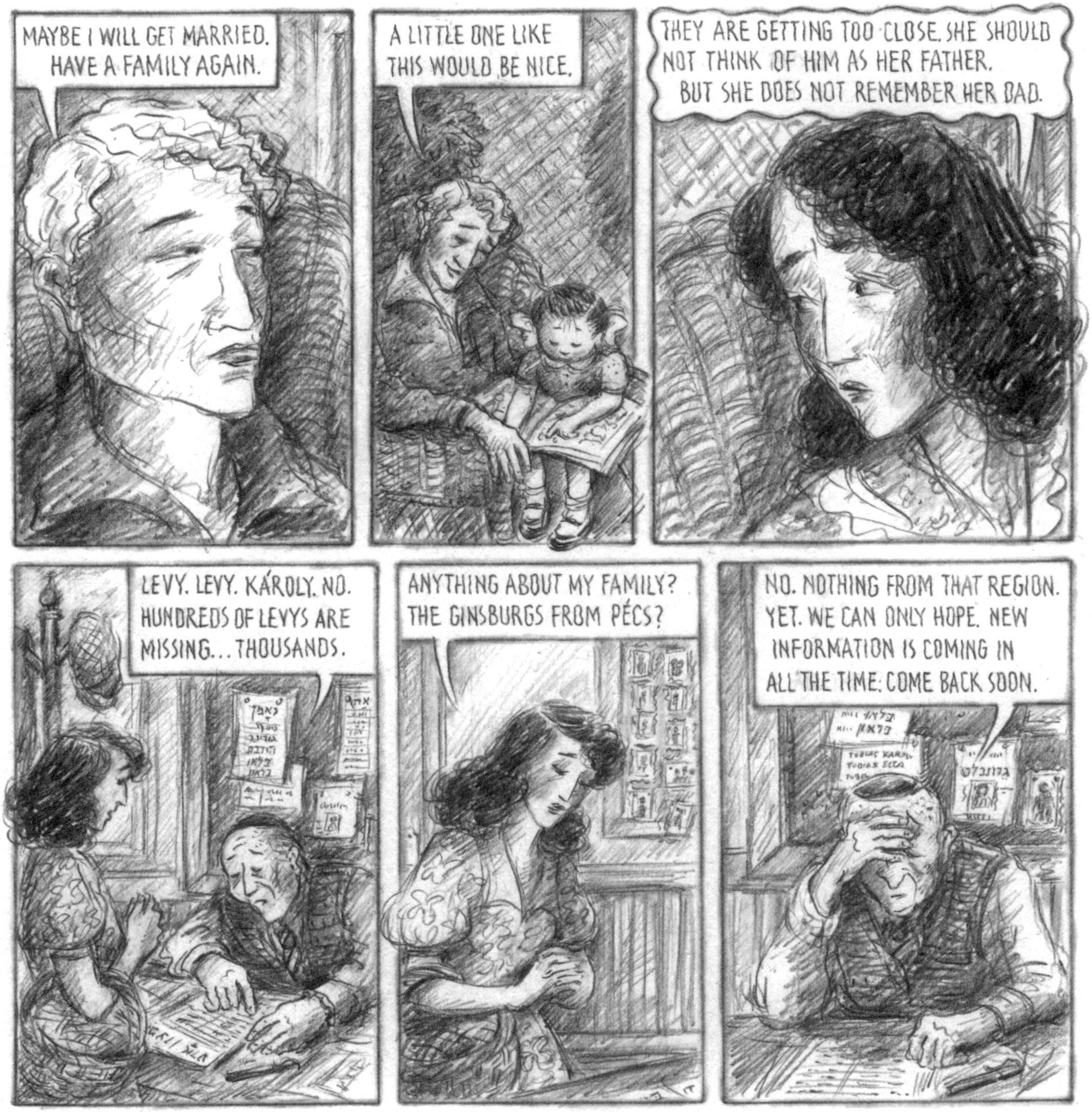
MAYBE I WILL GET MARRIED. HAVE A FAMILY AGAIN.
A LITTLE ONE LIKE THIS WOULD BE NICE.
THEY ARE GETTING TOO CLOSE. SHE SHOULD NOT THINK OF HIM AS HER FATHER. BUT SHE DOES NOT REMEMBER HER DAD.
LEVY. LEVY. KÁROLY. NO. HUNDREDS OF LEVYS ARE MISSING... THOUSANDS.
ANYTHING ABOUT MY FAMILY? THE GINSBURGS FROM PÉCS?
NO. NOTHING FROM THAT REGION. YET. WE CAN ONLY HOPE. NEW INFORMATION IS COMING IN ALL THE TIME. COME BACK SOON.

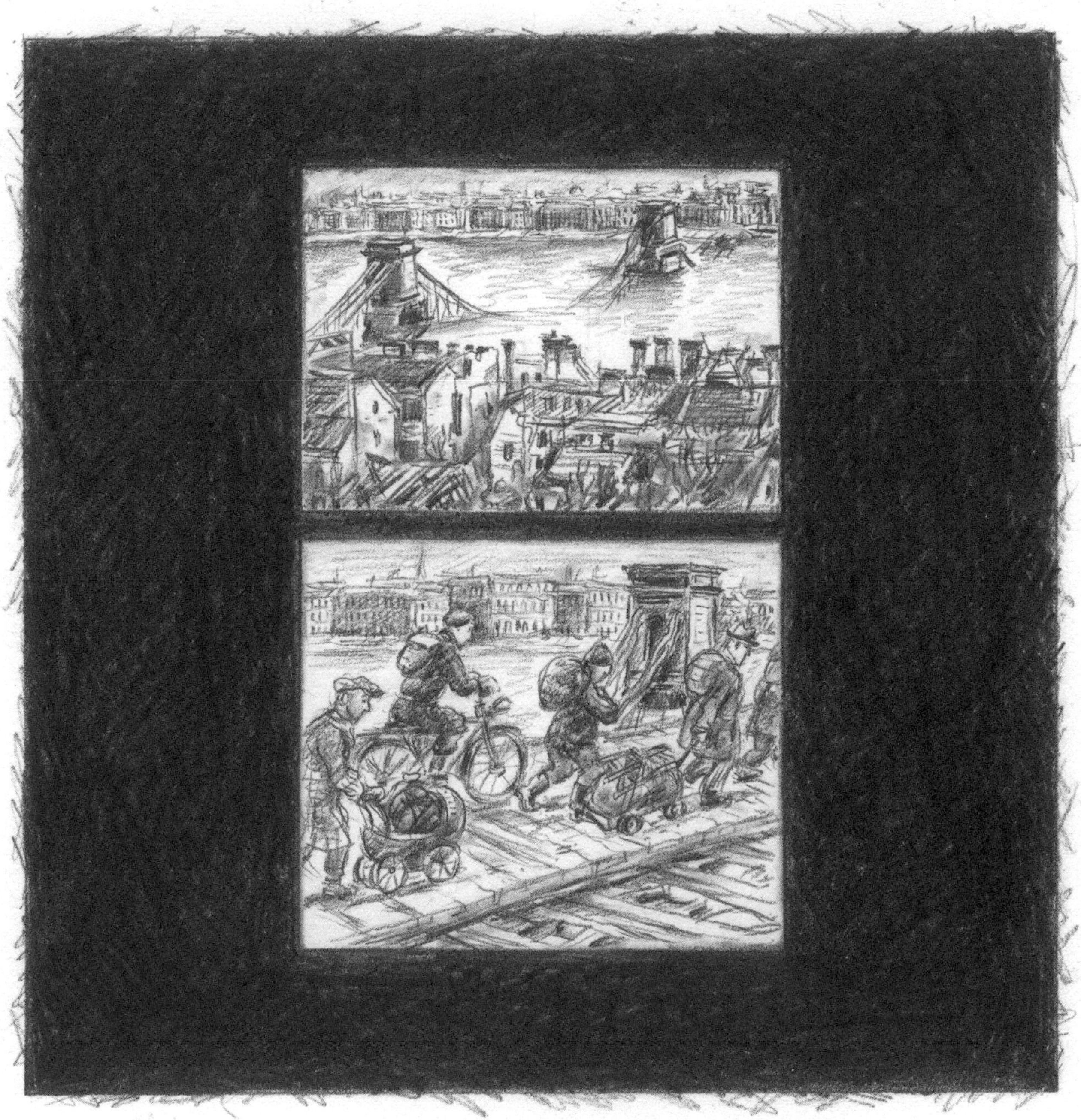

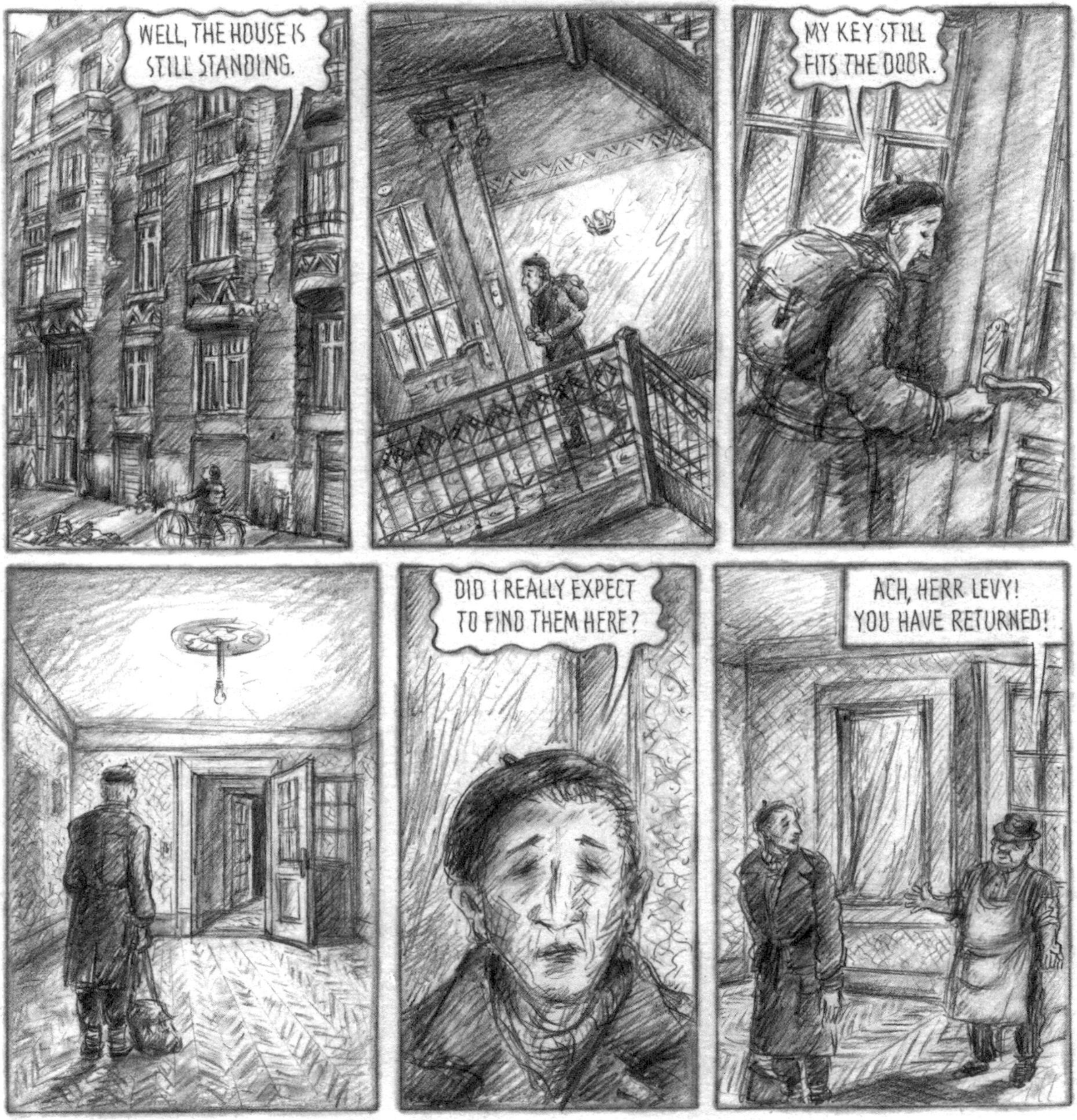
WELL, THE HOUSE IS STILL STANDING.
MY KEY STILL FITS THE DOOR.
DID I REALLY EXPECT TO FIND THEM HERE?
ACH, HERR LEVY! YOU HAVE RETURNED!

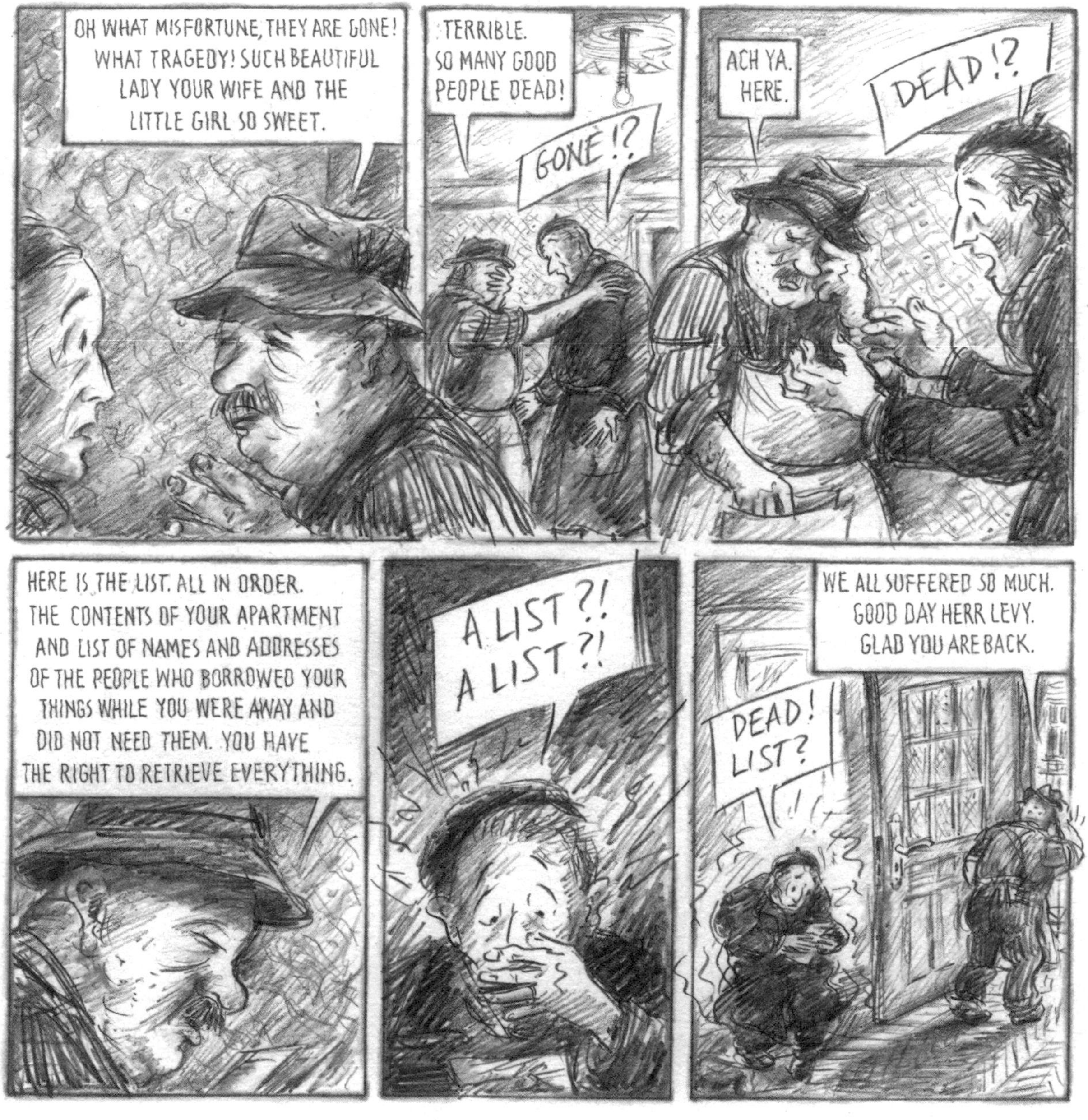
OH WHAT MISFORTUNE, THEY ARE GONE! WHAT TRAGEDY! SUCH BEAUTIFUL LADY YOUR WIFE AND THE LITTLE GIRL SO SWEET.
TERRIBLE. SO MANY GOOD PEOPLE DEAD!
GONE!?
ACH YA. HERE.
DEAD!?
HERE IS THE LIST. ALL IN ORDER. THE CONTENTS OF YOUR APARTMENT AND LIST OF NAMES AND ADDRESSES OF THE PEOPLE WHO BORROWED YOUR THINGS WHILE YOU WERE AWAY AND DID NOT NEED THEM. YOU HAVE THE RIGHT TO RETRIEVE EVERYTHING.
A LIST?! A LIST?!
WE ALL SUFFERED SO MUCH. GOOD DAY HERR LEVY. GLAD YOU ARE BACK.
DEAD! LIST?

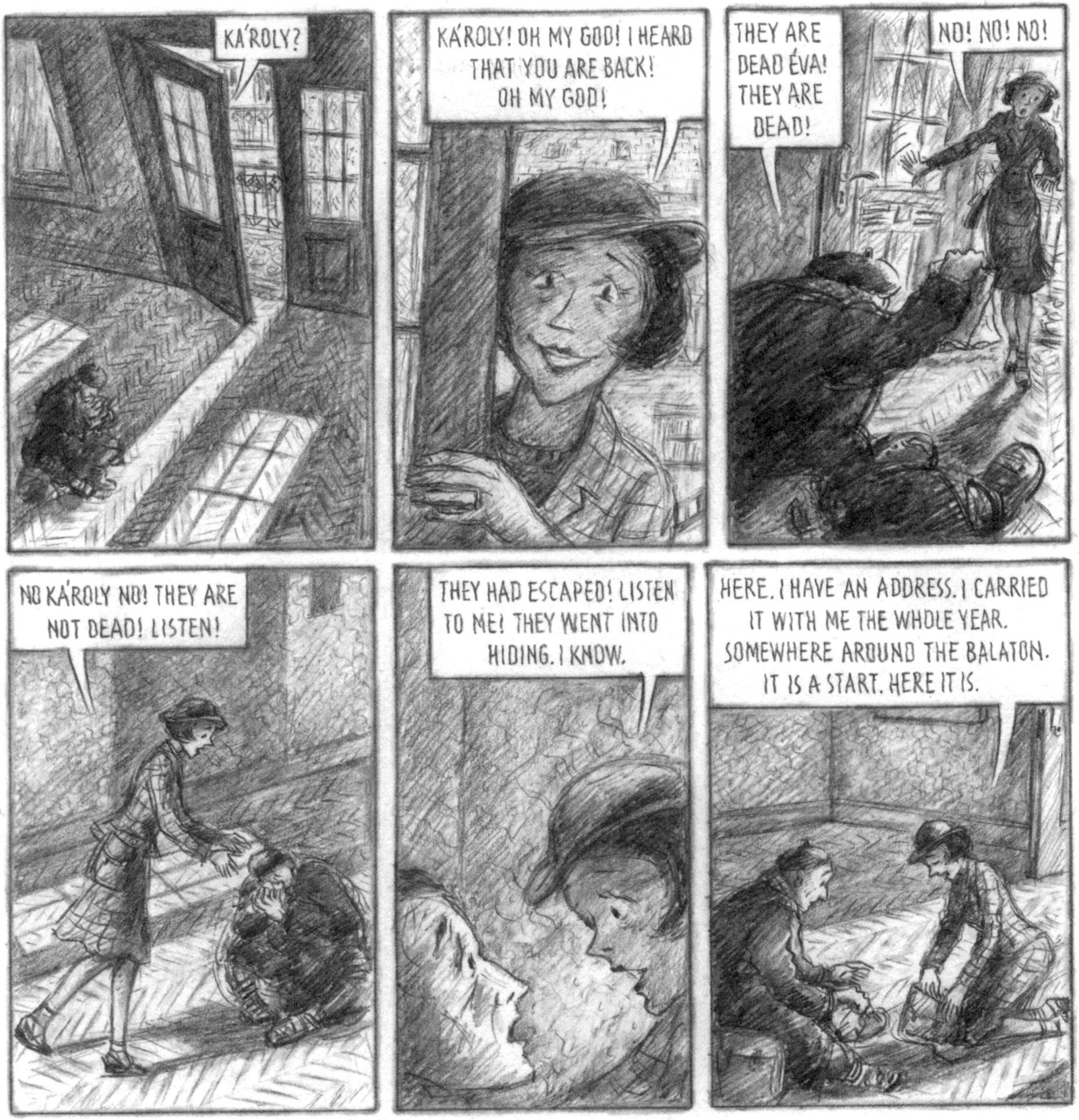
KÁROLY?
KÁROLY! OH MY GOD! I HEARD THAT YOU ARE BACK! OH MY GOD!
THEY ARE DEAD ÉVA! THEY ARE DEAD!
NO! NO! NO!
NO KÁROLY NO! THEY ARE NOT DEAD! LISTEN!
THEY HAD ESCAPED! LISTEN TO ME! THEY WENT INTO HIDING. I KNOW.
HERE. I HAVE AN ADDRESS. I CARRIED IT WITH ME THE WHOLE YEAR. SOMEWHERE AROUND THE BALATON. IT IS A START. HERE IT IS.

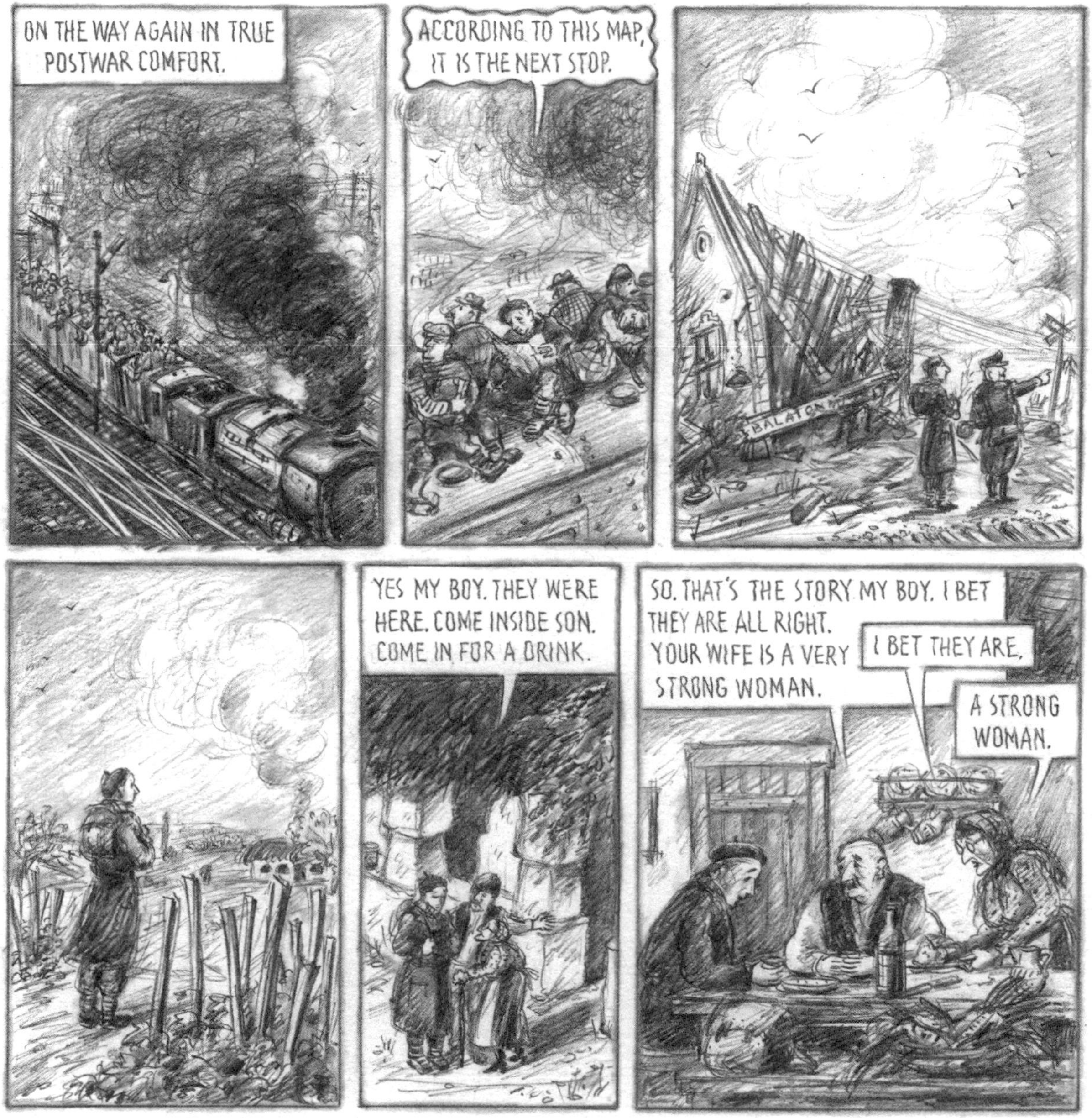
ON THE WAY AGAIN IN TRUE POSTWAR COMFORT.
ACCORDING TO THIS MAP, IT IS THE NEXT STOP.
BALATON
YES MY BOY. THEY WERE HERE. COME INSIDE SON. COME IN FOR A DRINK.
SO. THAT'S THE STORY MY BOY. I BET THEY ARE ALL RIGHT. YOUR WIFE IS A VERY STRONG WOMAN.
I BET THEY ARE.
A STRONG WOMAN.

WELL, I WILL BE OFF. THANK YOU BOTH FOR YOUR KINDNESS.
I MUST HURRY NOW AND CONTINUE MY SEARCH RIGHT AWAY.
STAY SON. STAY FOR THE NIGHT. WHERE WOULD YOU GO IN THE DARK. AND IT LOOKS LIKE YOU ARE NOT USED TO DRINKING WINE.
HERE SONNY. NICE AND SOFT. TOMORROW. TOMORROW YOU WILL FIND THEM.
THEY SLEPT HERE IN THIS BED BUT NOW I CAN'T FIND REST OR COMFORT. SOME DAY I WILL GIVE LISA A LITTLE DOG AGAIN.
THE NEXT MORNING,

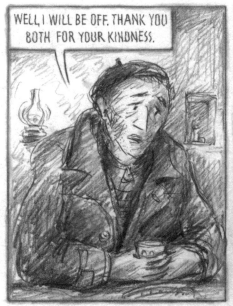

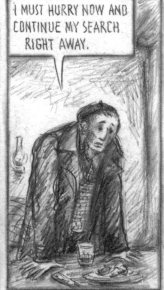

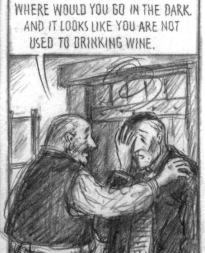

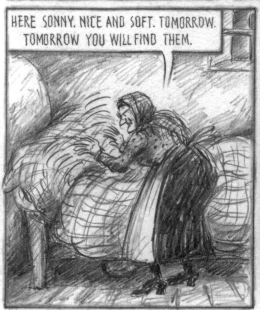

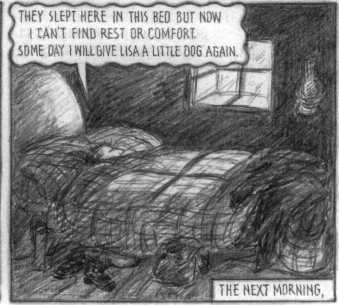

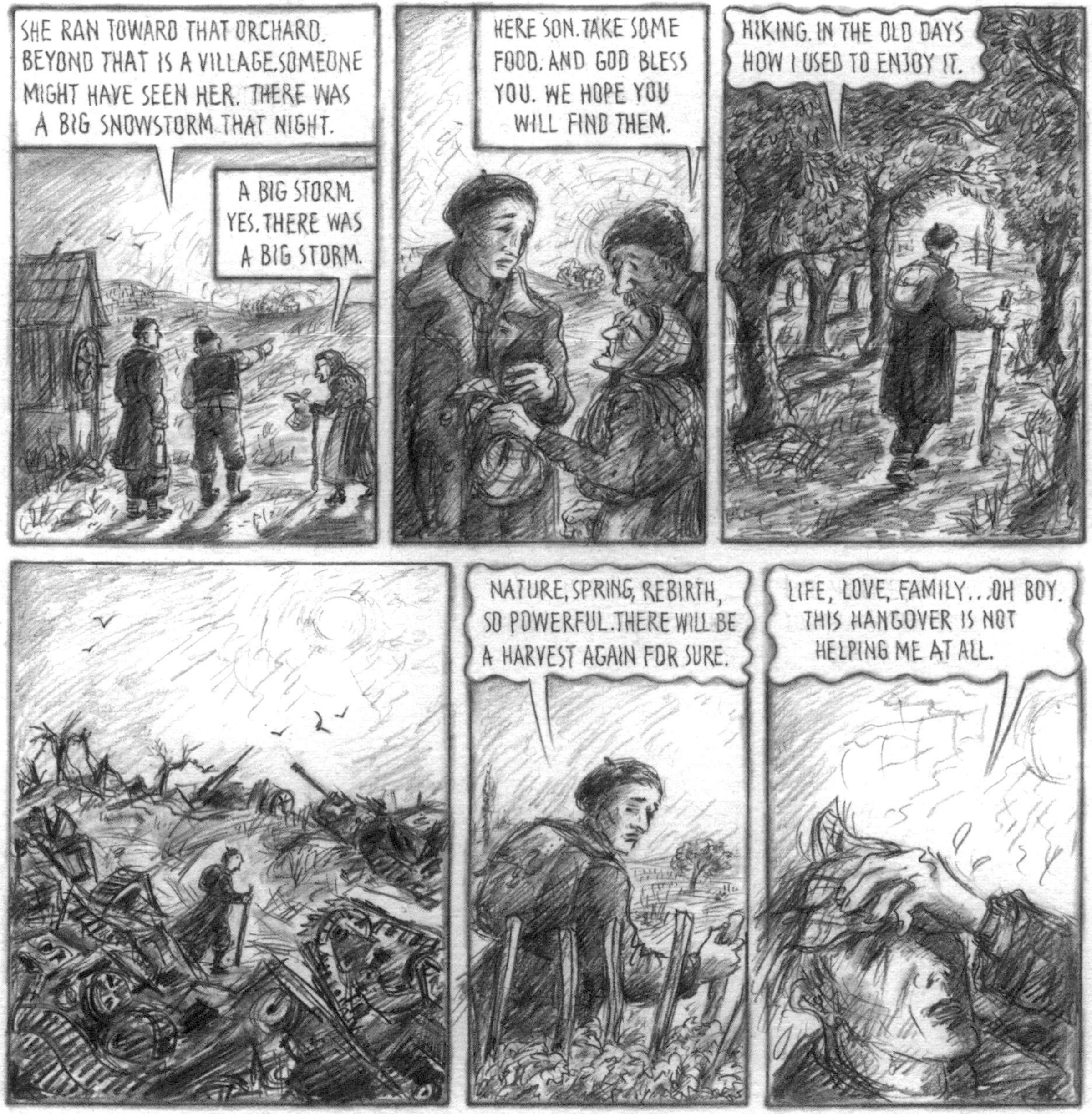
SHE RAN TOWARD THAT ORCHARD. BEYOND THAT IS A VILLAGE.SOMEONE MIGHT HAVE SEEN HER. THERE WAS A BIG SNOWSTORM THAT NIGHT.
A BIG STORM. YES. THERE WAS A BIG STORM.
HERE SON. TAKE SOME FOOD. AND GOD BLESS YOU. WE HOPE YOU WILL FIND THEM.
HIKING. IN THE OLD DAYS HOW I USED TO ENJOY IT.
NATURE, SPRING, REBIRTH, SO POWERFUL. THERE WILL BE A HARVEST AGAIN FOR SURE.
LIFE, LOVE, FAMILY... OH BOY. THIS HANGOVER IS NOT HELPING ME AT ALL.

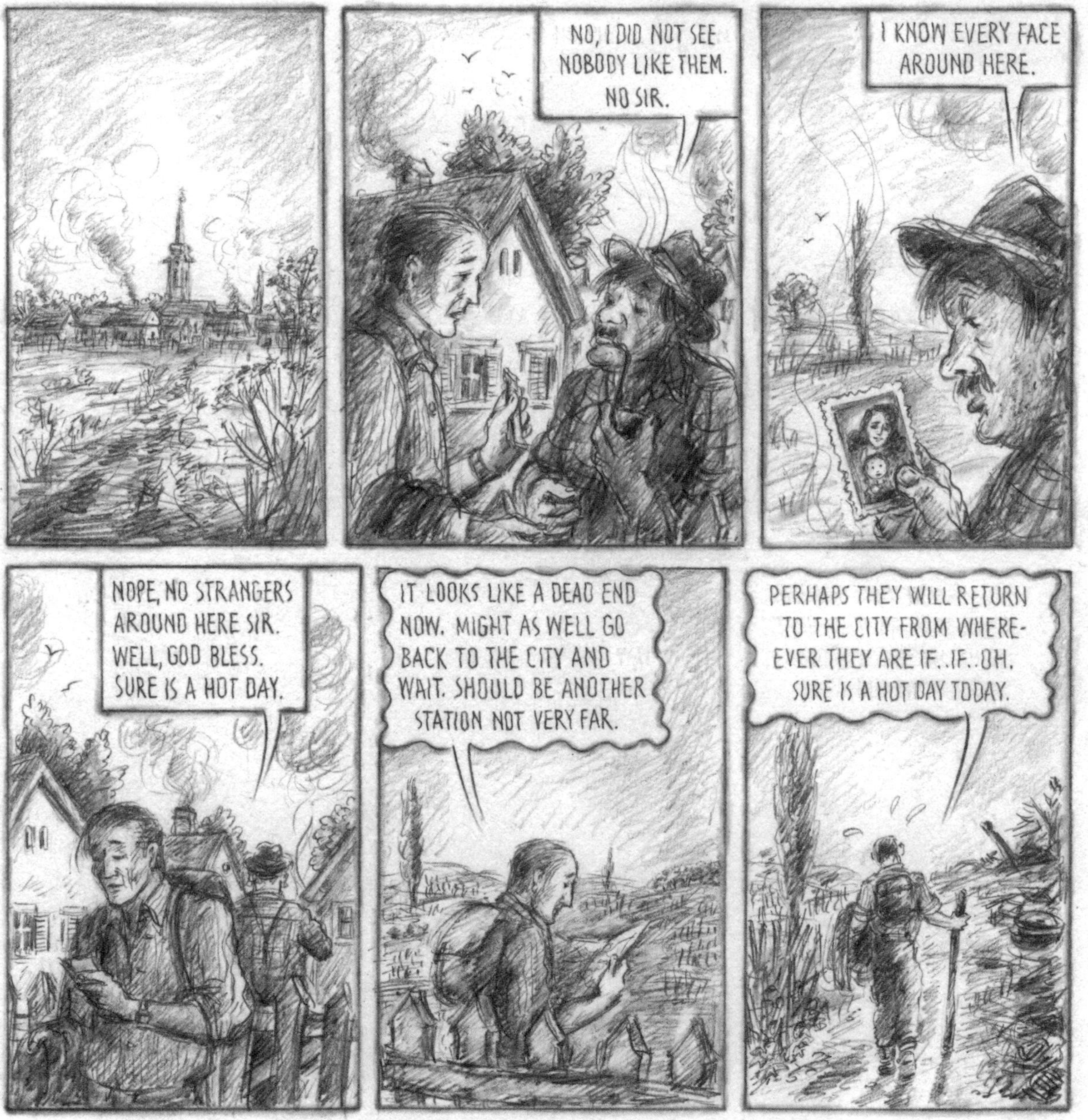
NO, I DID NOT SEE NOBODY LIKE THEM. NO SIR.
I KNOW EVERY FACE AROUND HERE.
NOPE, NO STRANGERS AROUND HERE SIR. WELL, GOD BLESS. SURE IS A HOT DAY.
IT LOOKS LIKE A DEAD END NOW. MIGHT AS WELL GO BACK TO THE CITY AND WAIT. SHOULD BE ANOTHER STATION NOT VERY FAR.
PERHAPS THEY WILL RETURN TO THE CITY FROM WHERE-EVER THEY ARE IF..IF..OH. SURE IS A HOT DAY TODAY.

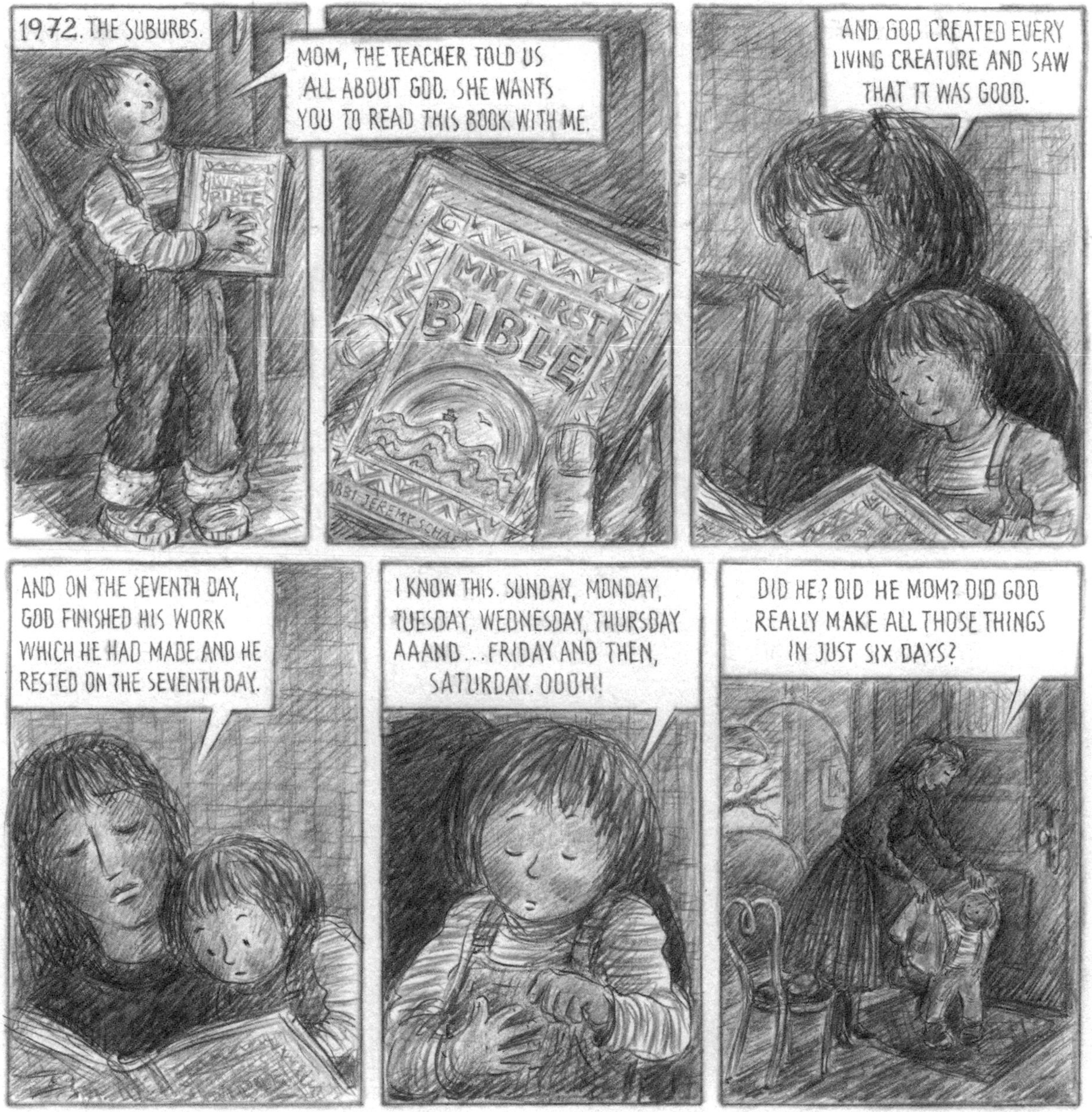
1972. THE SUBURBS.
MOM, THE TEACHER TOLD US ALL ABOUT GOD. SHE WANTS YOU TO READ THIS BOOK WITH ME.
MY FIRST BIBLE
AND GOD CREATED EVERY LIVING CREATURE AND SAW THAT IT WAS GOOD.
AND ON THE SEVENTH DAY, GOD FINISHED HIS WORK WHICH HE HAD MADE AND HE RESTED ON THE SEVENTH DAY.
I KNOW THIS. SUNDAY, MONDAY, TUESDAY, WEDNESDAY, THURSDAY AAAND...FRIDAY AND THEN, SATURDAY. OOOH!
DID HE? DID HE MOM? DID GOD REALLY MAKE ALL THOSE THINGS IN JUST SIX DAYS?

MOTHER'S ROSES, BLOOMING AGAIN AND SHE IS GONE. ANYWAY, I DECIDED NOT TO STAY IN THIS COUNTRY. THERE IS NO FUTURE FOR US HERE. MAYBE IN AMERICA OR AUSTRALIA. OR EVEN PALESTINE... ESTHER,

DO YOU THINK THE TWO OF YOU, YOU COULD BOTH COME WITH ME?

DAVID! PLEASE! I AM WAITING FOR MY HUSBAND TO RETURN!

I KNOW. I AM SORRY.

BUT IF...

DAVID!

FORGIVE ME. THESE TIMES. EVERYTHING. FORGIVE ME. PLEASE.

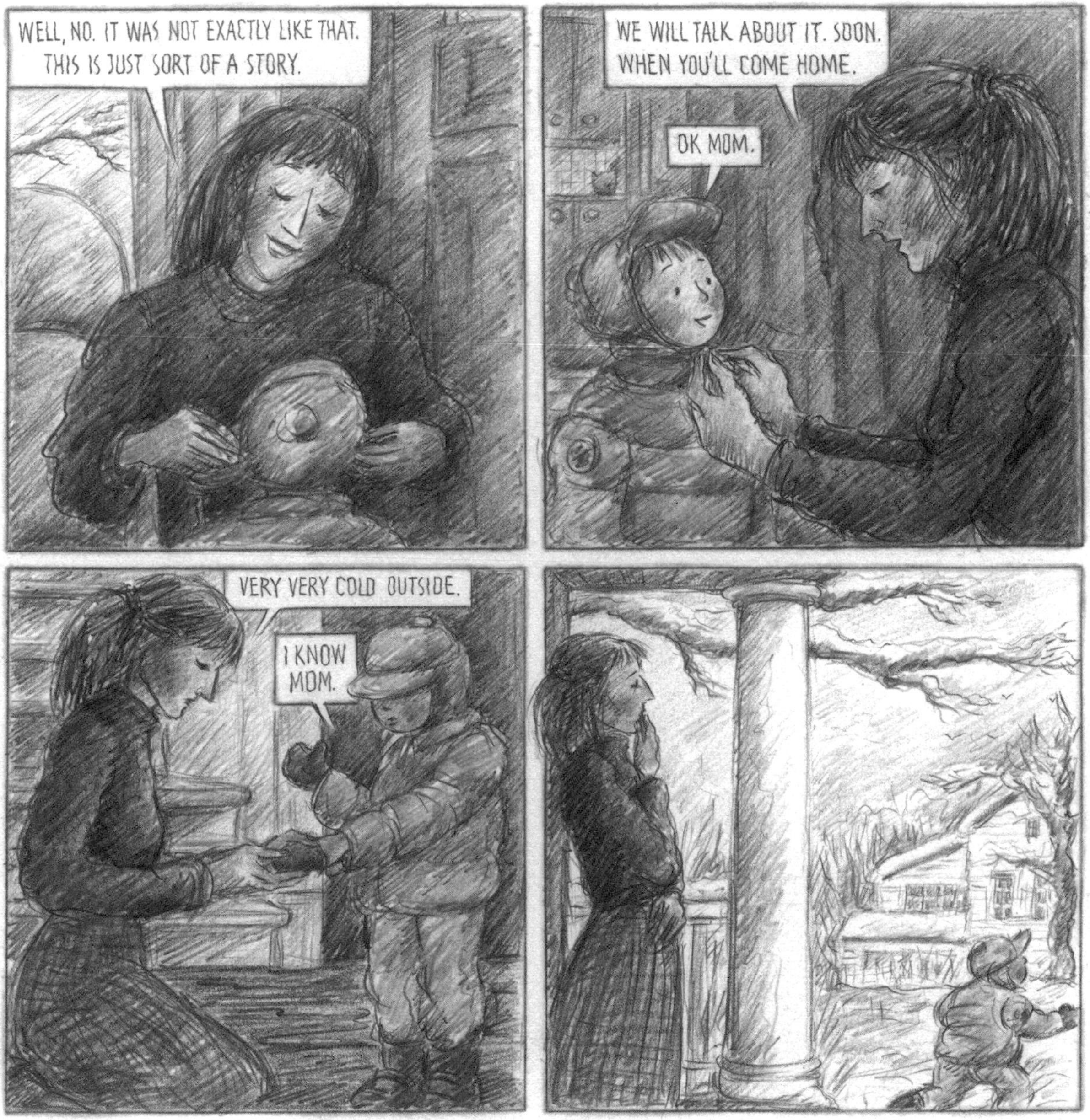
WELL, NO. IT WAS NOT EXACTLY LIKE THAT. THIS IS JUST SORT OF A STORY.
WE WILL TALK ABOUT IT. SOON. WHEN YOU'LL COME HOME.
OK MOM.
VERY VERY COLD OUTSIDE.
I KNOW MOM.

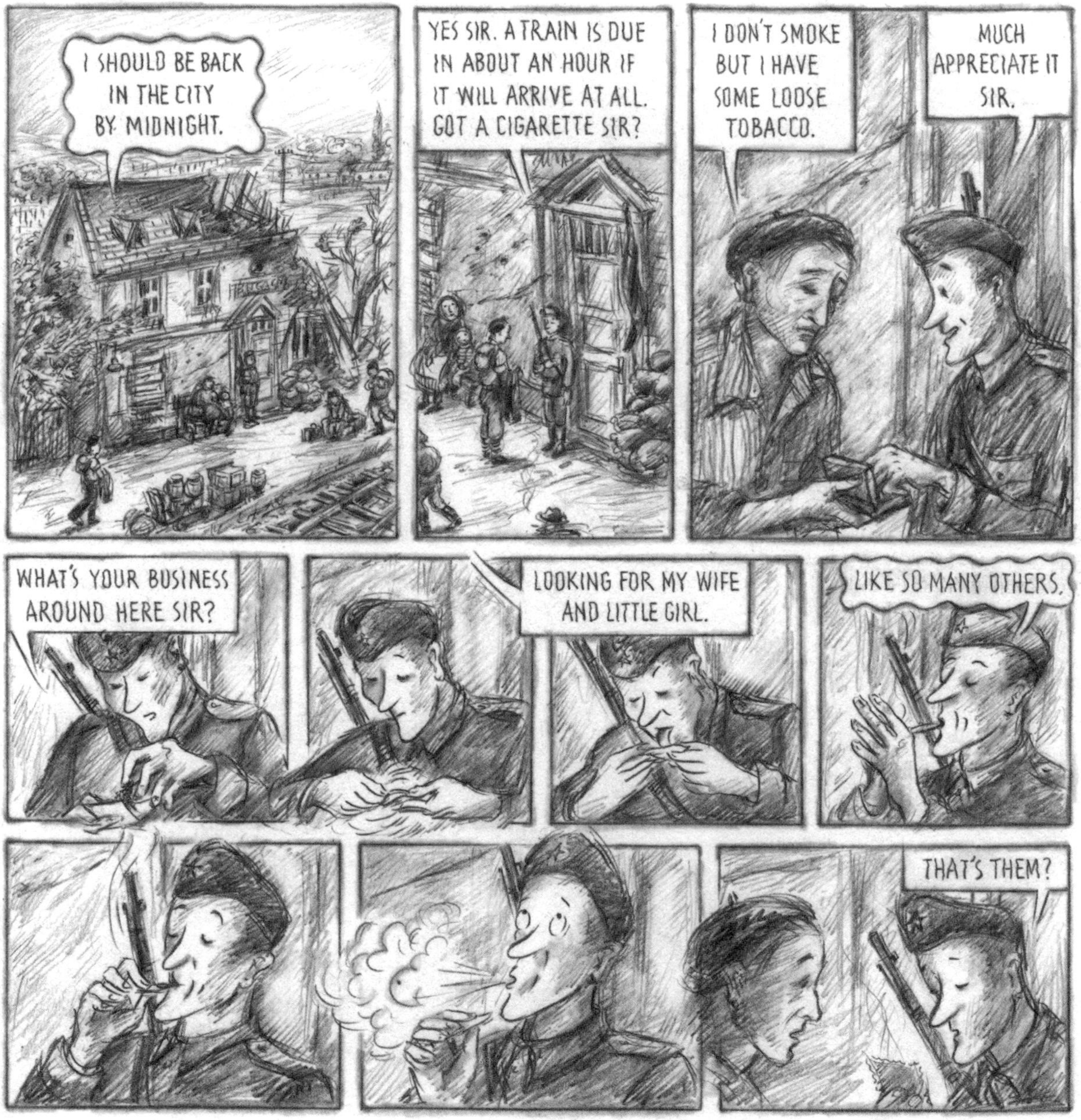
I SHOULD BE BACK IN THE CITY BY MIDNIGHT.
YES SIR. A TRAIN IS DUE IN ABOUT AN HOUR IF IT WILL ARRIVE AT ALL. GOT A CIGARETTE SIR?
I DON'T SMOKE BUT I HAVE SOME LOOSE TOBACCO.
MUCH APPRECIATE IT SIR.
WHAT'S YOUR BUSINESS AROUND HERE SIR?
LOOKING FOR MY WIFE AND LITTLE GIRL.
LIKE SO MANY OTHERS.
THAT'S THEM?

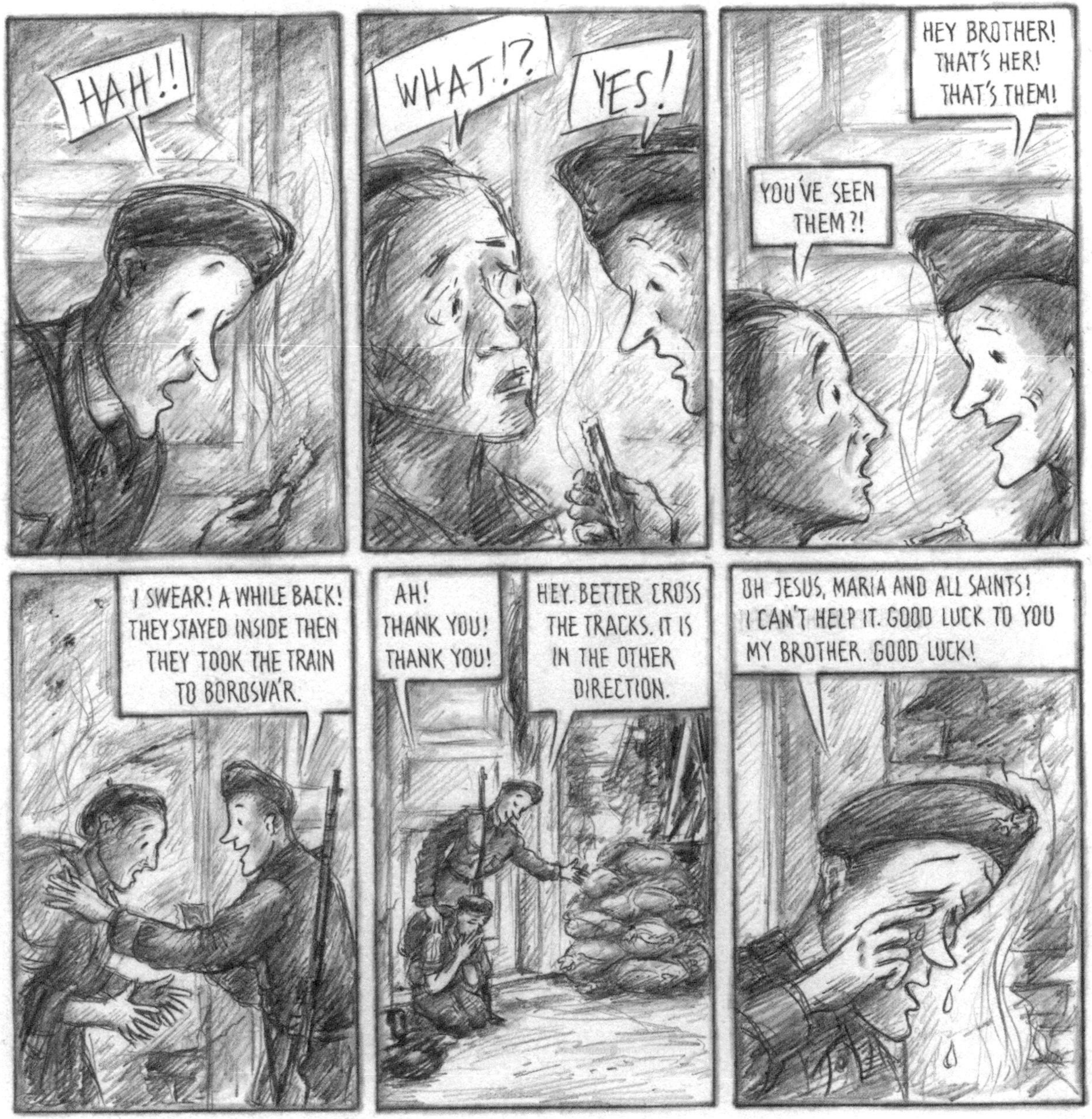
HAH!!
WHAT!?
YES!
HEY BROTHER! THAT'S HER! THAT'S THEM!
YOU'VE SEEN THEM?!
I SWEAR! A WHILE BACK! THEY STAYED INSIDE THEN THEY TOOK THE TRAIN TO BOROSVÁR.
AH! THANK YOU! THANK YOU!
HEY. BETTER CROSS THE TRACKS. IT IS IN THE OTHER DIRECTION.
OH JESUS, MARIA AND ALL SAINTS! I CAN'T HELP IT. GOOD LUCK TO YOU MY BROTHER. GOOD LUCK!

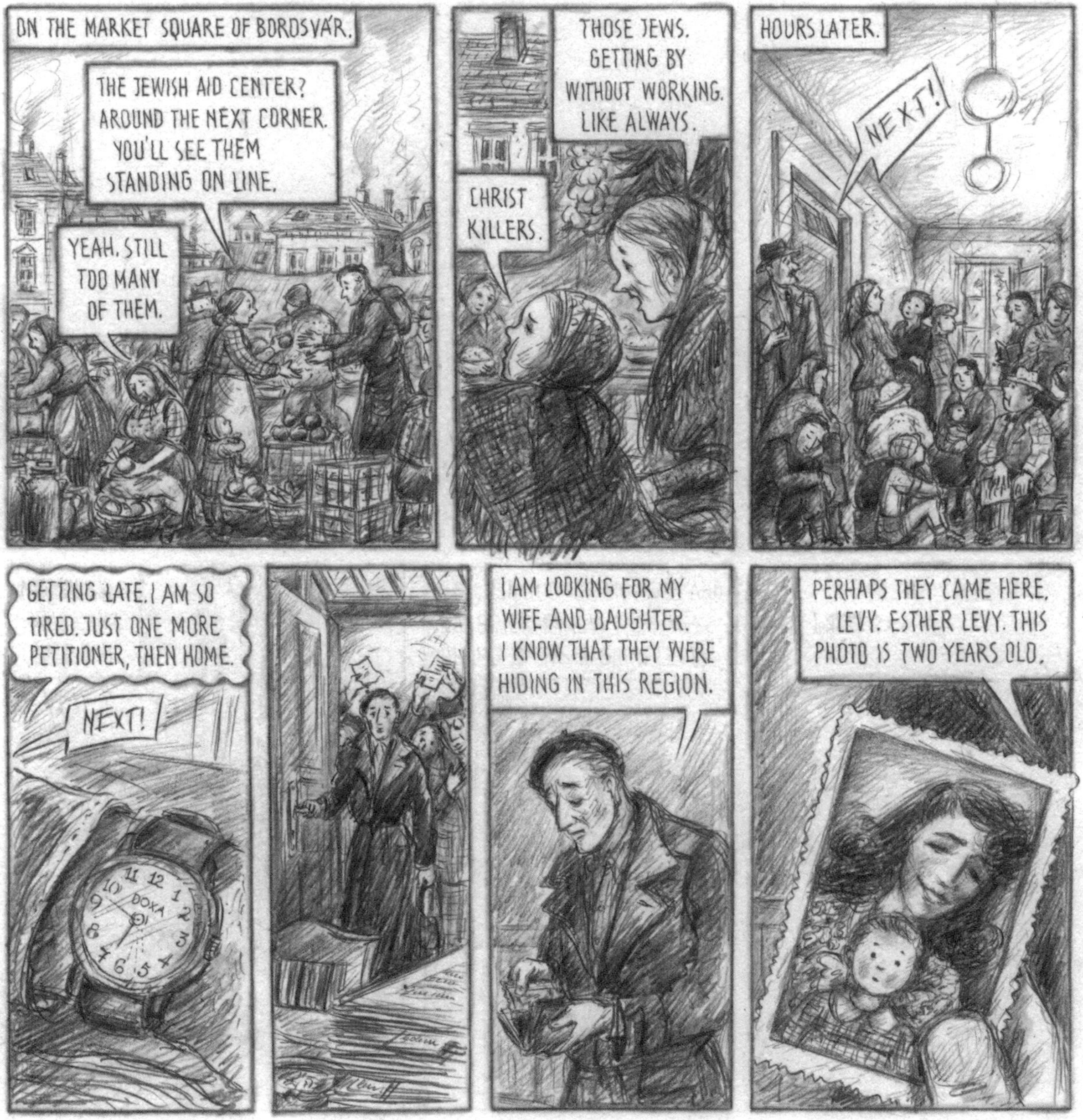
ON THE MARKET SQUARE OF BORDSVÁR.
THE JEWISH AID CENTER? AROUND THE NEXT CORNER. YOU'LL SEE THEM STANDING ON LINE.
YEAH. STILL TOO MANY OF THEM.
THOSE JEWS. GETTING BY WITHOUT WORKING. LIKE ALWAYS.
CHRIST KILLERS.
HOURS LATER.
NEXT!
GETTING LATE. I AM SO TIRED. JUST ONE MORE PETITIONER, THEN HOME.
NEXT!
DOXA
I AM LOOKING FOR MY WIFE AND DAUGHTER. I KNOW THAT THEY WERE HIDING IN THIS REGION.
PERHAPS THEY CAME HERE. LEVY. ESTHER LEVY. THIS PHOTO IS TWO YEARS OLD.

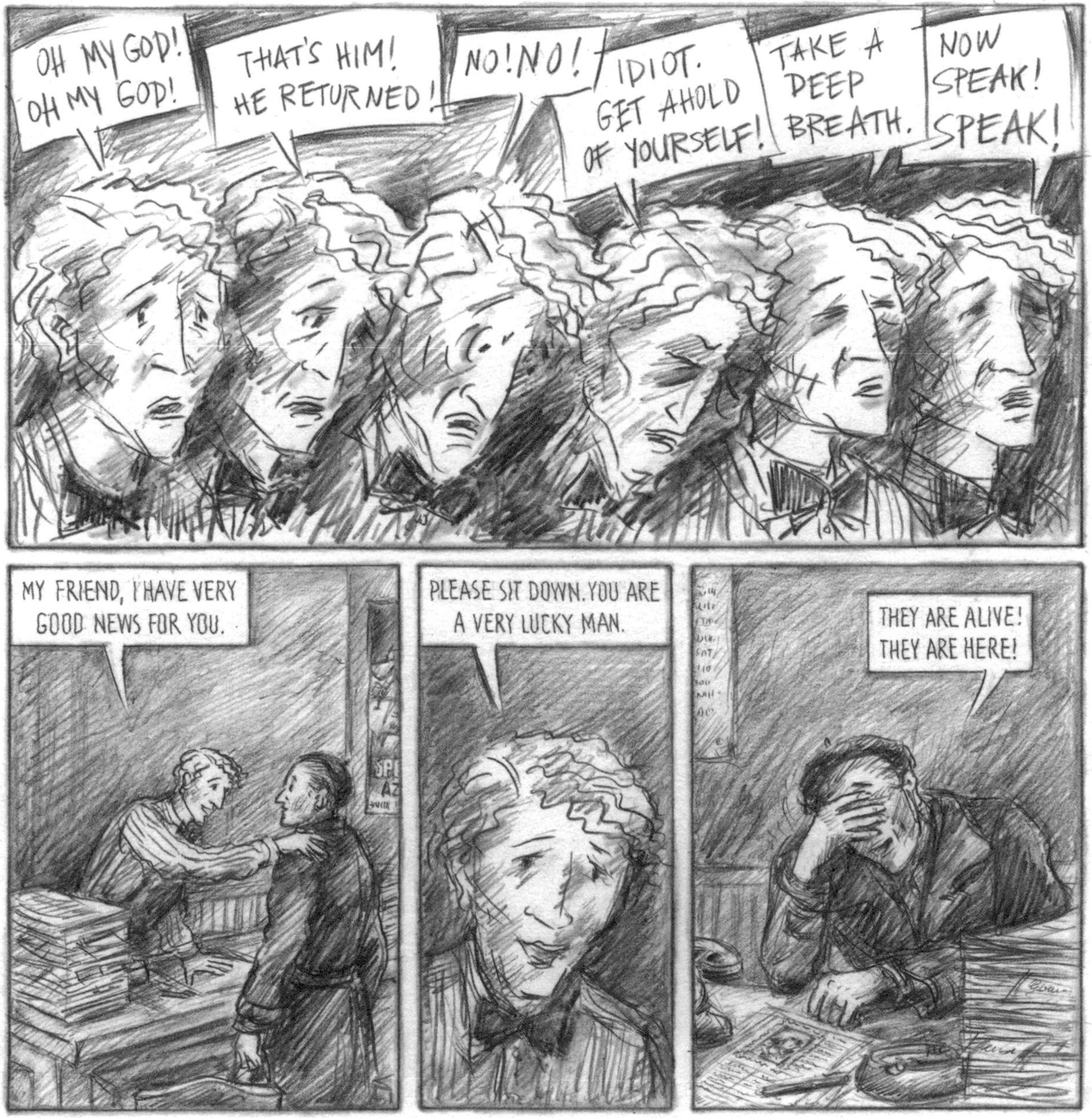
OH MY GOD! OH MY GOD!
THAT'S HIM! HE RETURNED!
NO! NO!
IDIOT. GET AHOLD OF YOURSELF!
TAKE A DEEP BREATH.
NOW SPEAK! SPEAK!
MY FRIEND, I HAVE VERY GOOD NEWS FOR YOU.
PLEASE SIT DOWN. YOU ARE A VERY LUCKY MAN.
THEY ARE ALIVE! THEY ARE HERE!

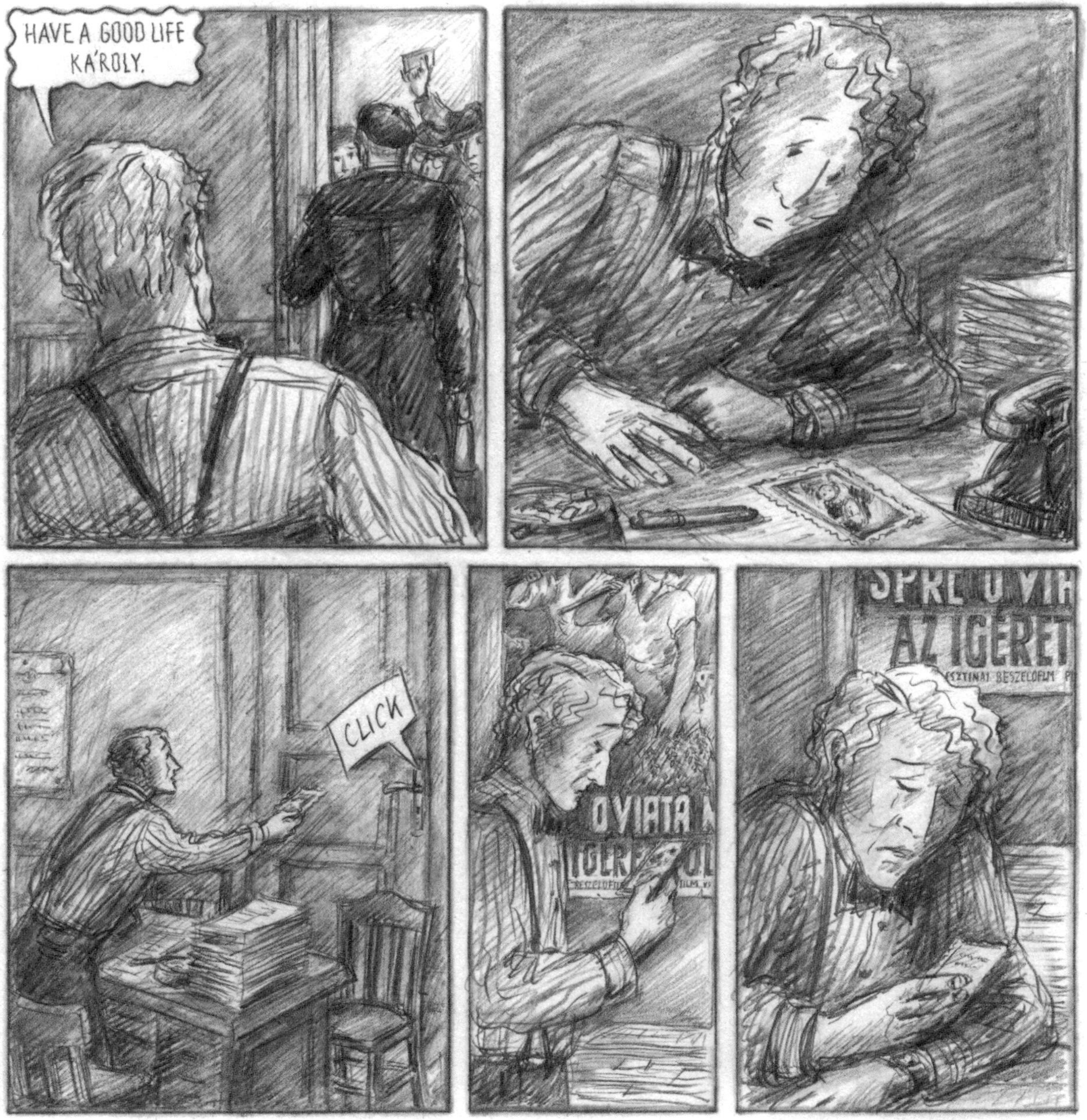
HAVE A GOOD LIFE KÁROLY.
CLICK

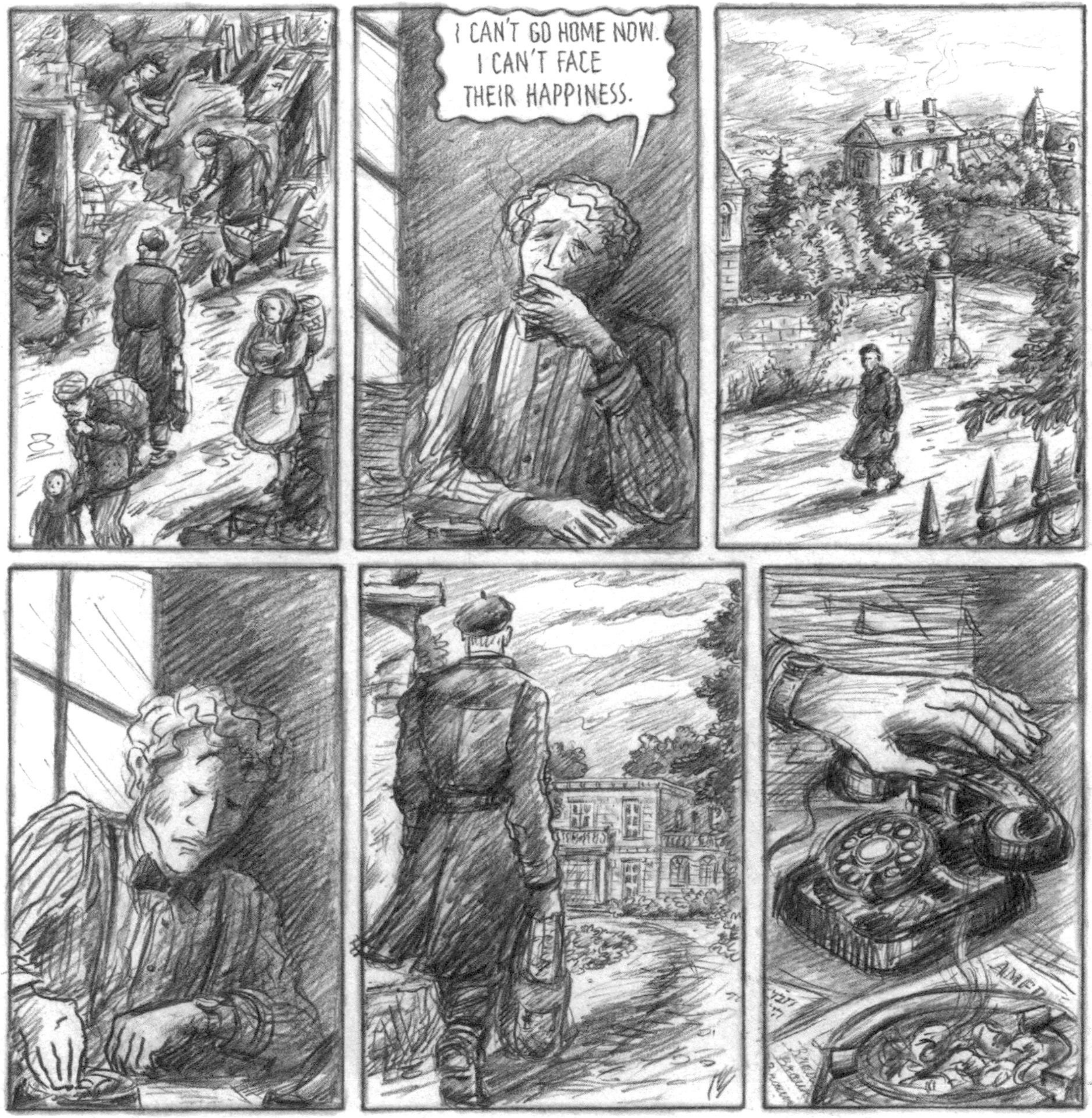
I CAN'T GO HOME NOW. I CAN'T FACE THEIR HAPPINESS.

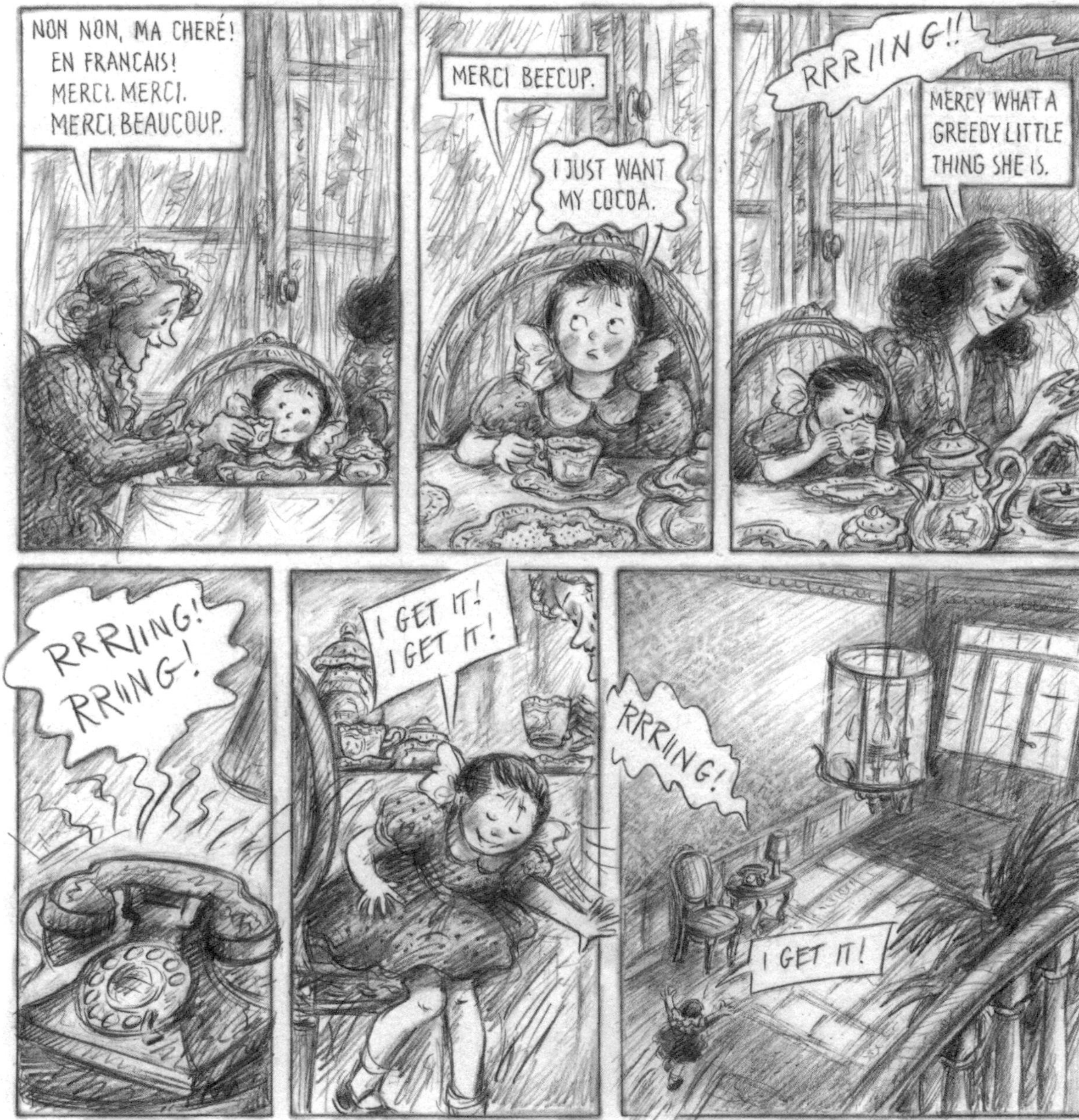
NON NON, MA CHERÉ! EN FRANCAIS! MERCI. MERCI. MERCI. BEAUCOUP.
MERCI BEECUP.
I JUST WANT MY COCOA.
RRRIING!!
MERCY WHAT A GREEDY LITTLE THING SHE IS.
RRRIING! RRIING!
I GET IT! I GET IT!
RRRIING!
I GET IT!

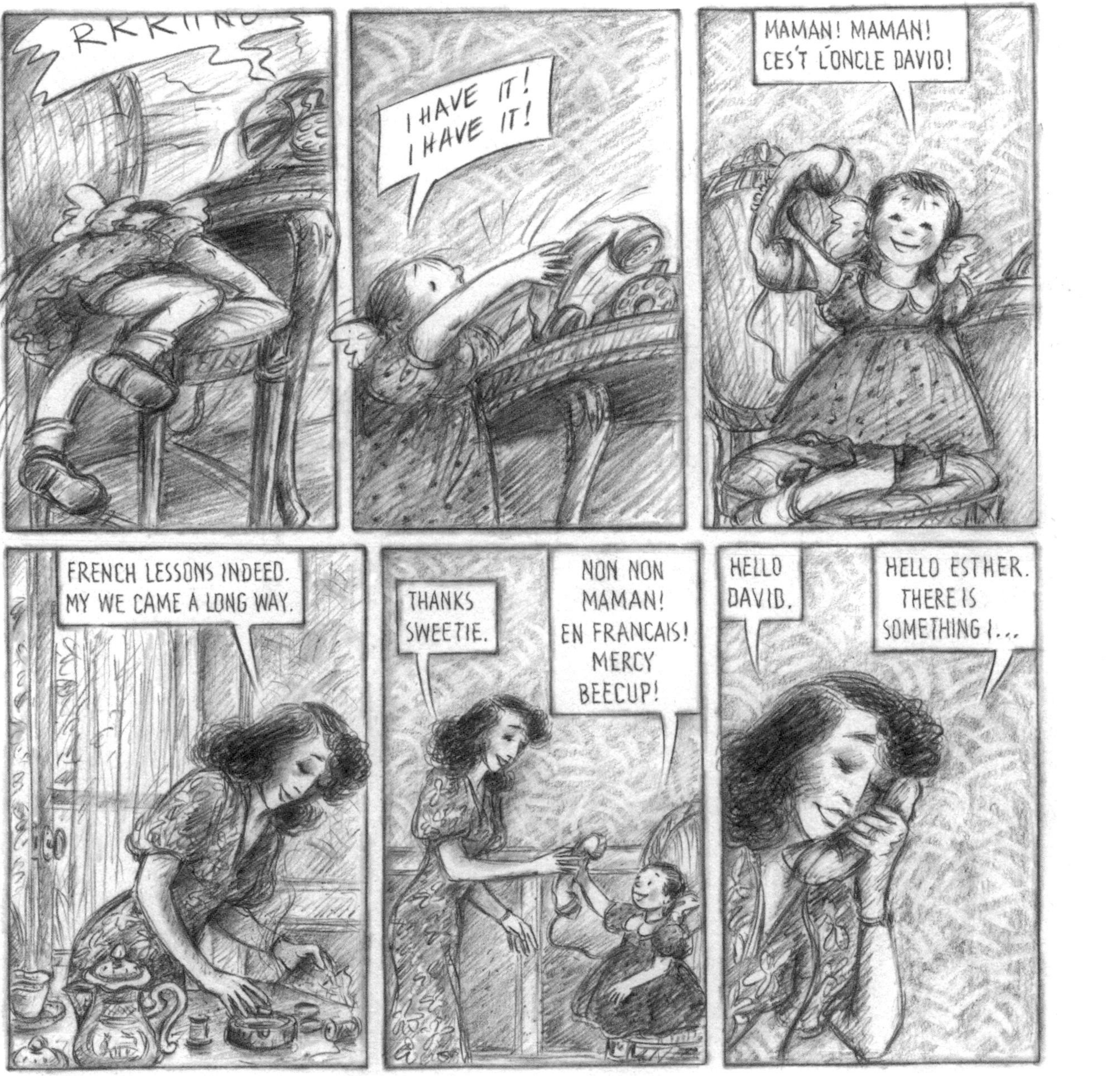
RRRING
I HAVE IT! I HAVE IT!
MAMAN! MAMAN! CES'T L'ONCLE DAVID!
FRENCH LESSONS INDEED. MY WE CAME A LONG WAY.
THANKS SWEETIE.
NON NON MAMAN! EN FRANCAIS! MERCY BEECUP!
HELLO DAVID.
HELLO ESTHER. THERE IS SOMETHING I...

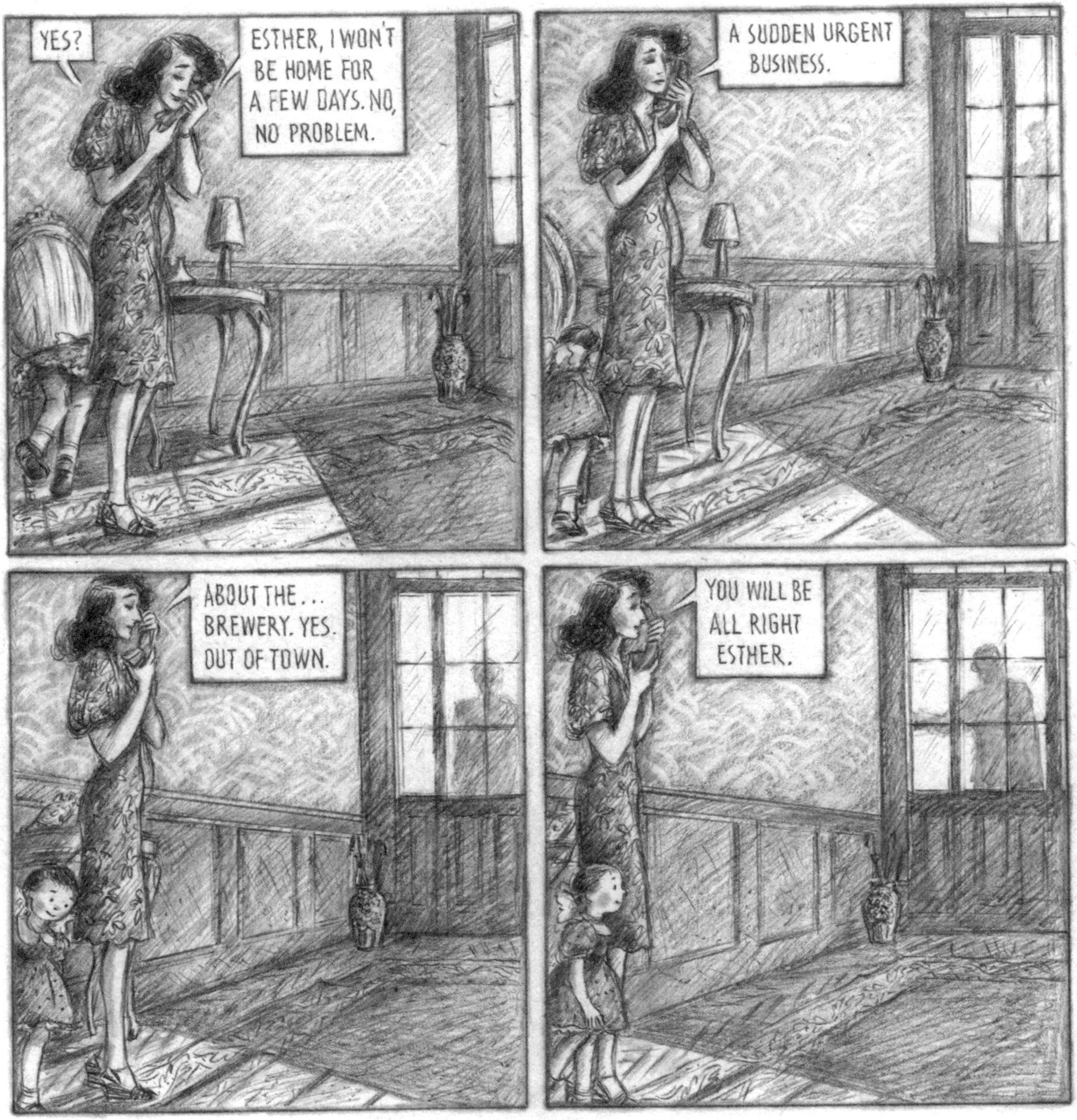
YES?
ESTHER, I WON'T BE HOME FOR A FEW DAYS. NO, NO PROBLEM.
A SUDDEN URGENT BUSINESS.
ABOUT THE... BREWERY. YES. OUT OF TOWN.
YOU WILL BE ALL RIGHT ESTHER.

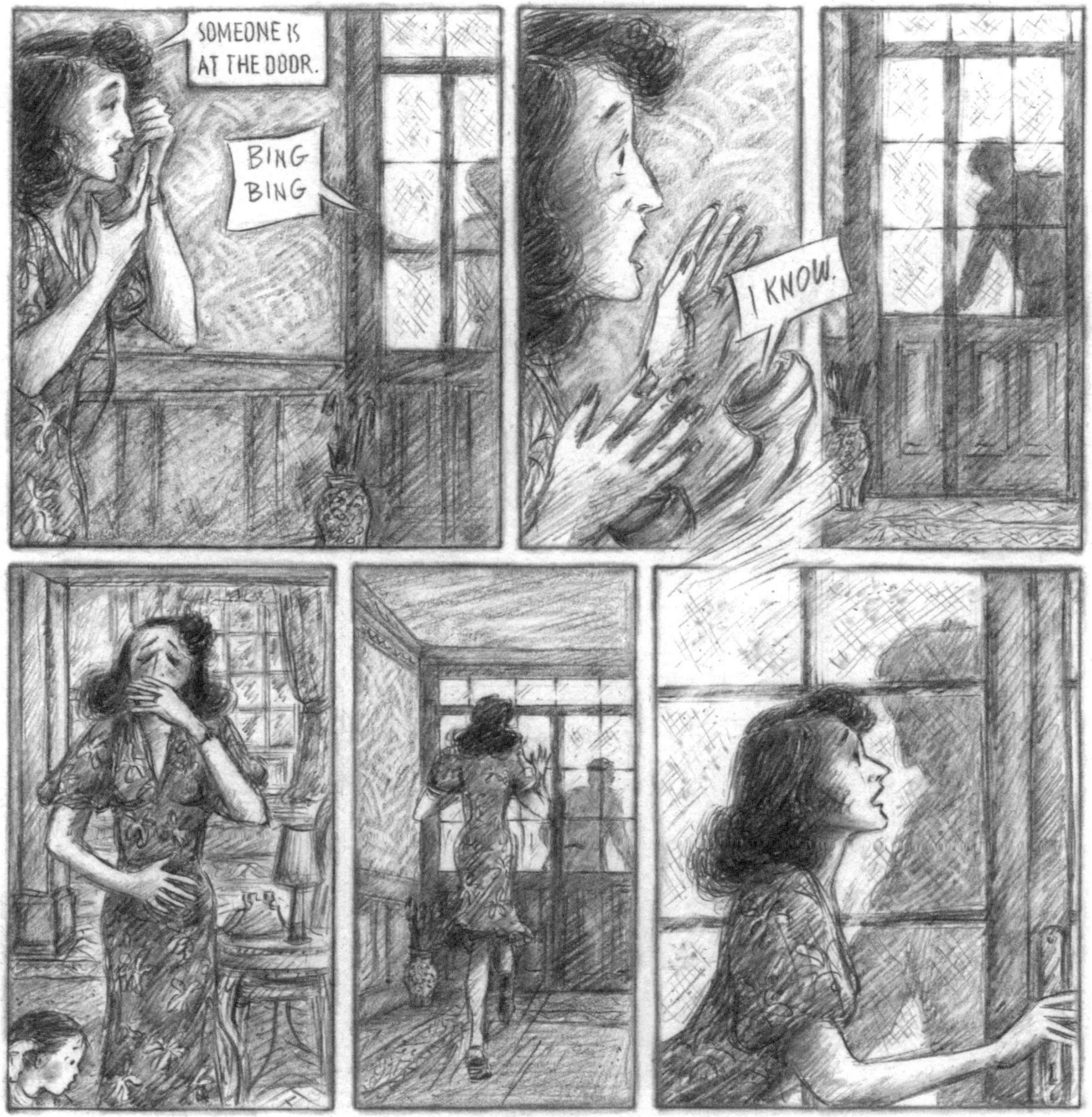
SOMEONE IS AT THE DOOR.
BING BING
I KNOW.

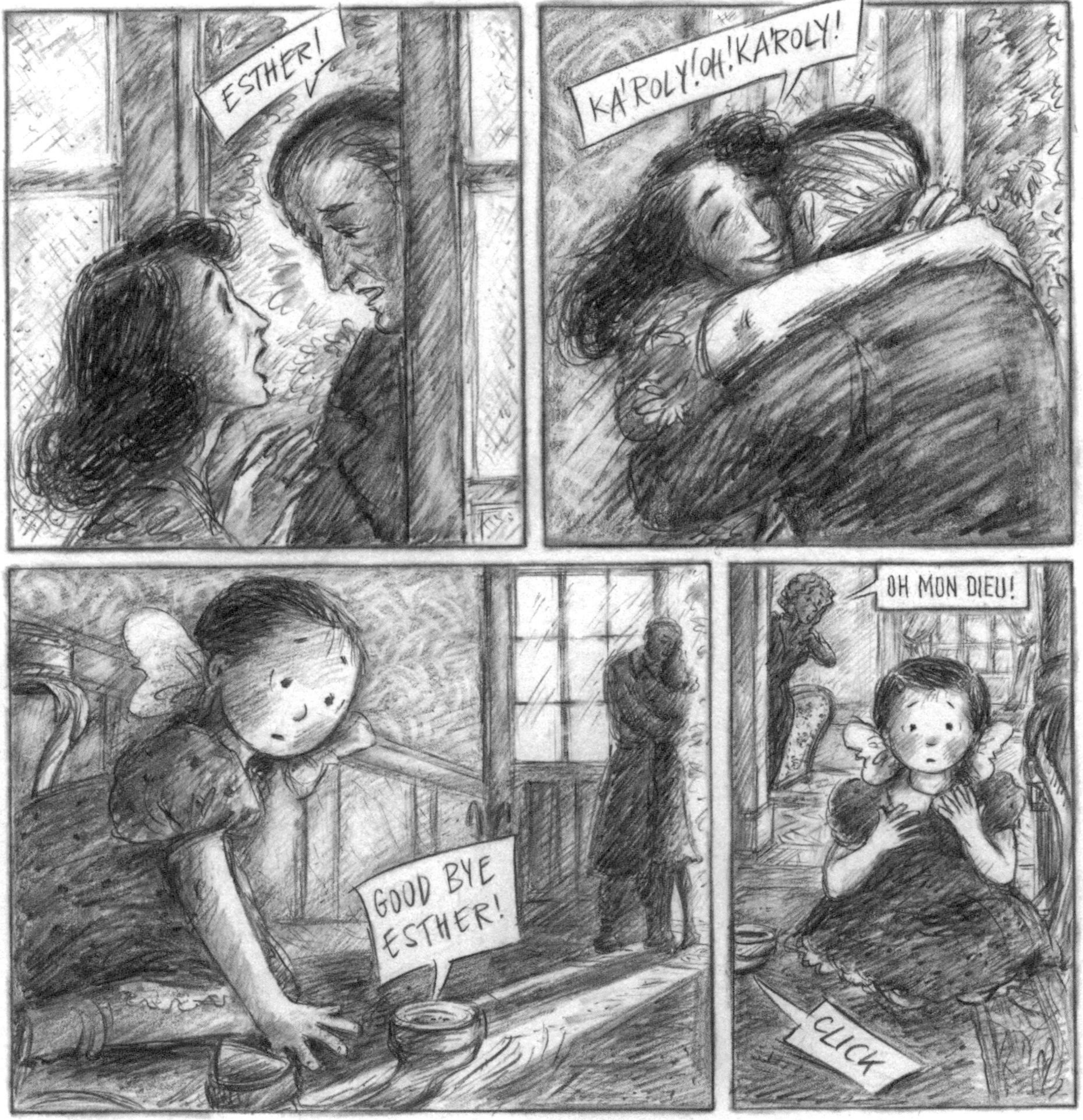
ESTHER!
KA'ROLY! OH! KA'ROLY!
GOOD BYE ESTHER!
OH MON DIEU!
CLICK

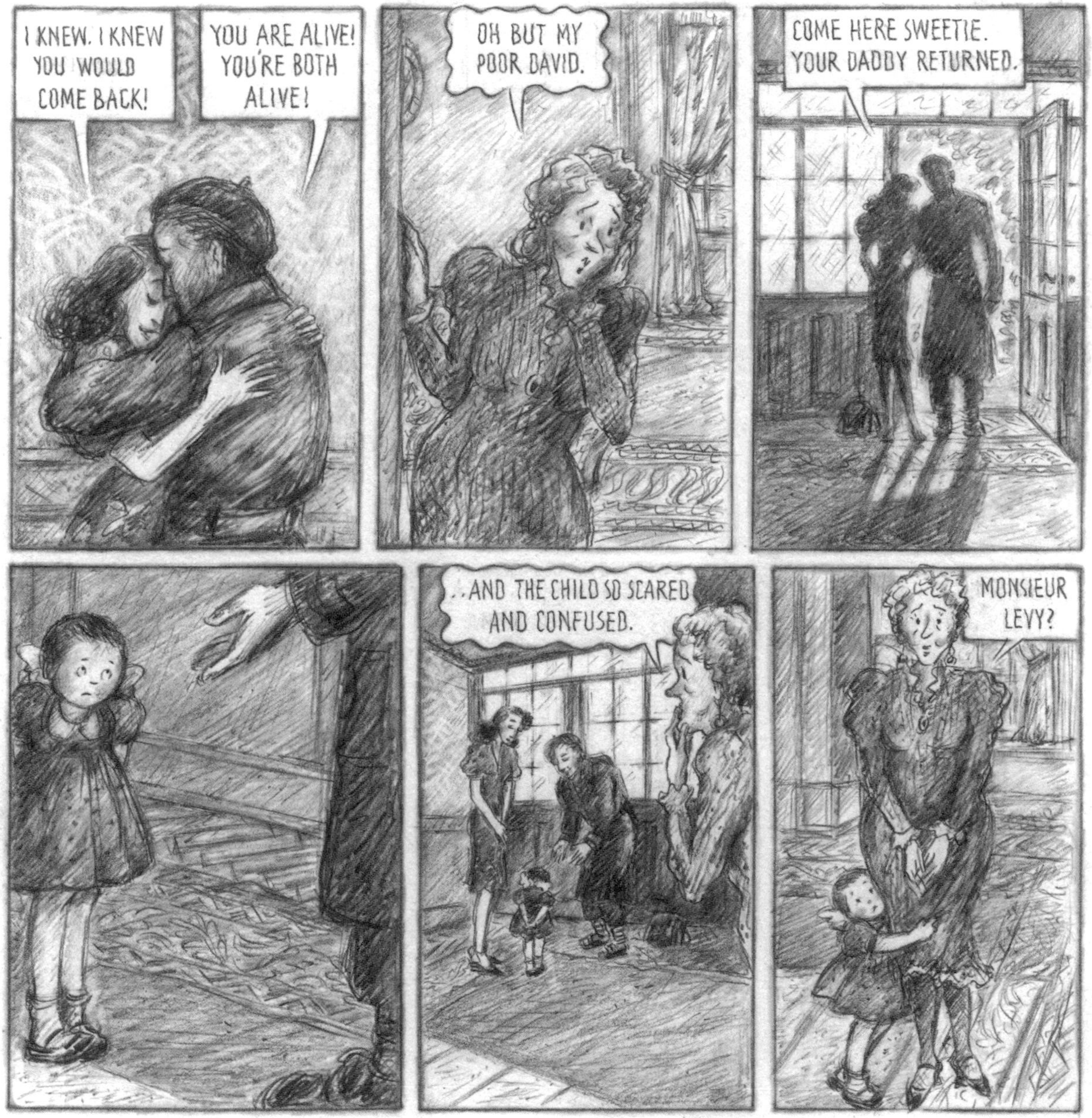
I KNEW. I KNEW YOU WOULD COME BACK!
YOU ARE ALIVE! YOU'RE BOTH ALIVE!
OH BUT MY POOR DAVID.
COME HERE SWEETIE. YOUR DADDY RETURNED.
..AND THE CHILD SO SCARED AND CONFUSED.
MONSIEUR LEVY?

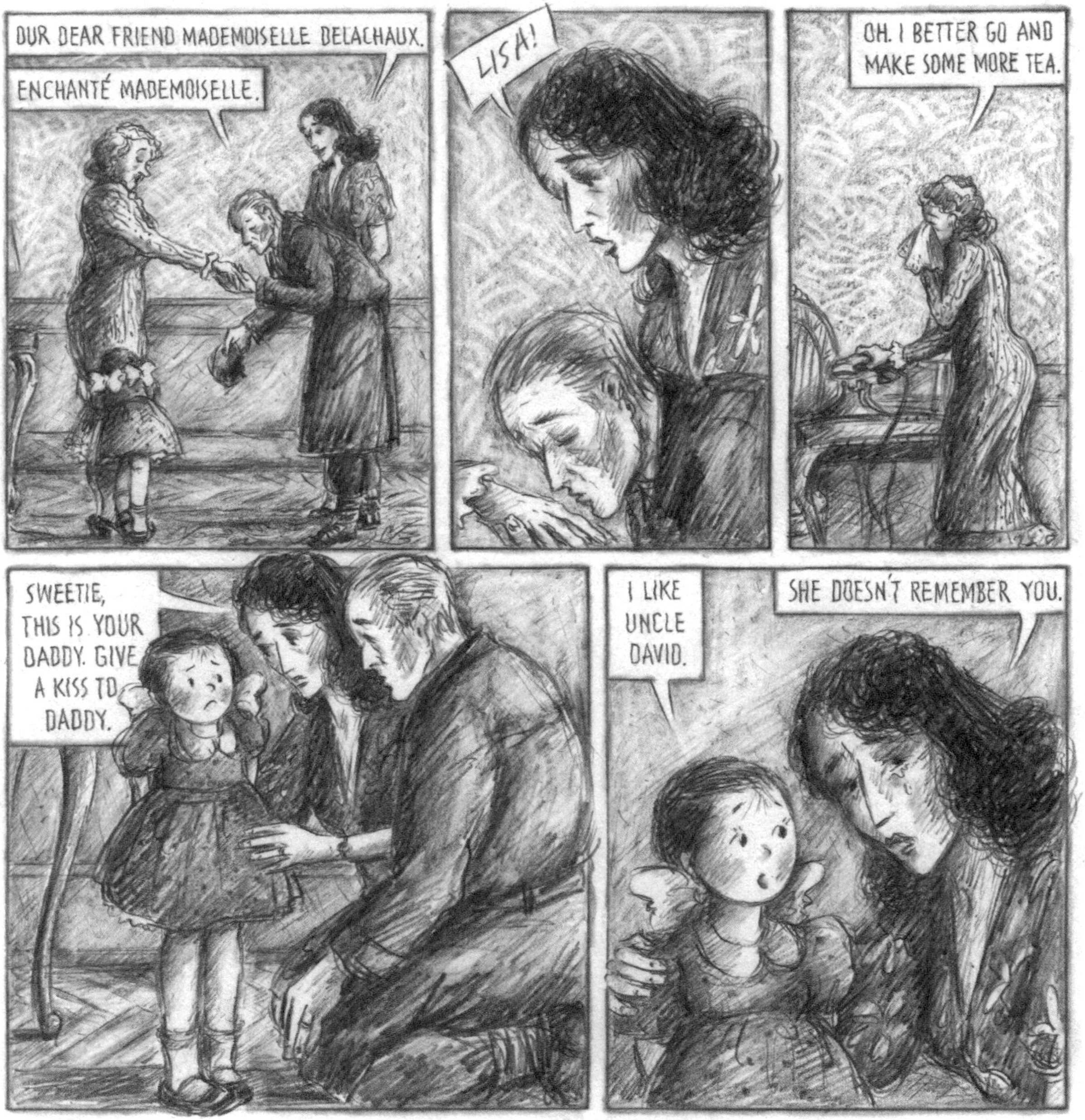
OUR DEAR FRIEND MADEMOISELLE DELACHAUX.
ENCHANTÉ MADEMOISELLE.
LISA!
OH. I BETTER GO AND MAKE SOME MORE TEA.
SWEETIE, THIS IS YOUR DADDY. GIVE A KISS TO DADDY.
I LIKE UNCLE DAVID.
SHE DOESN'T REMEMBER YOU.

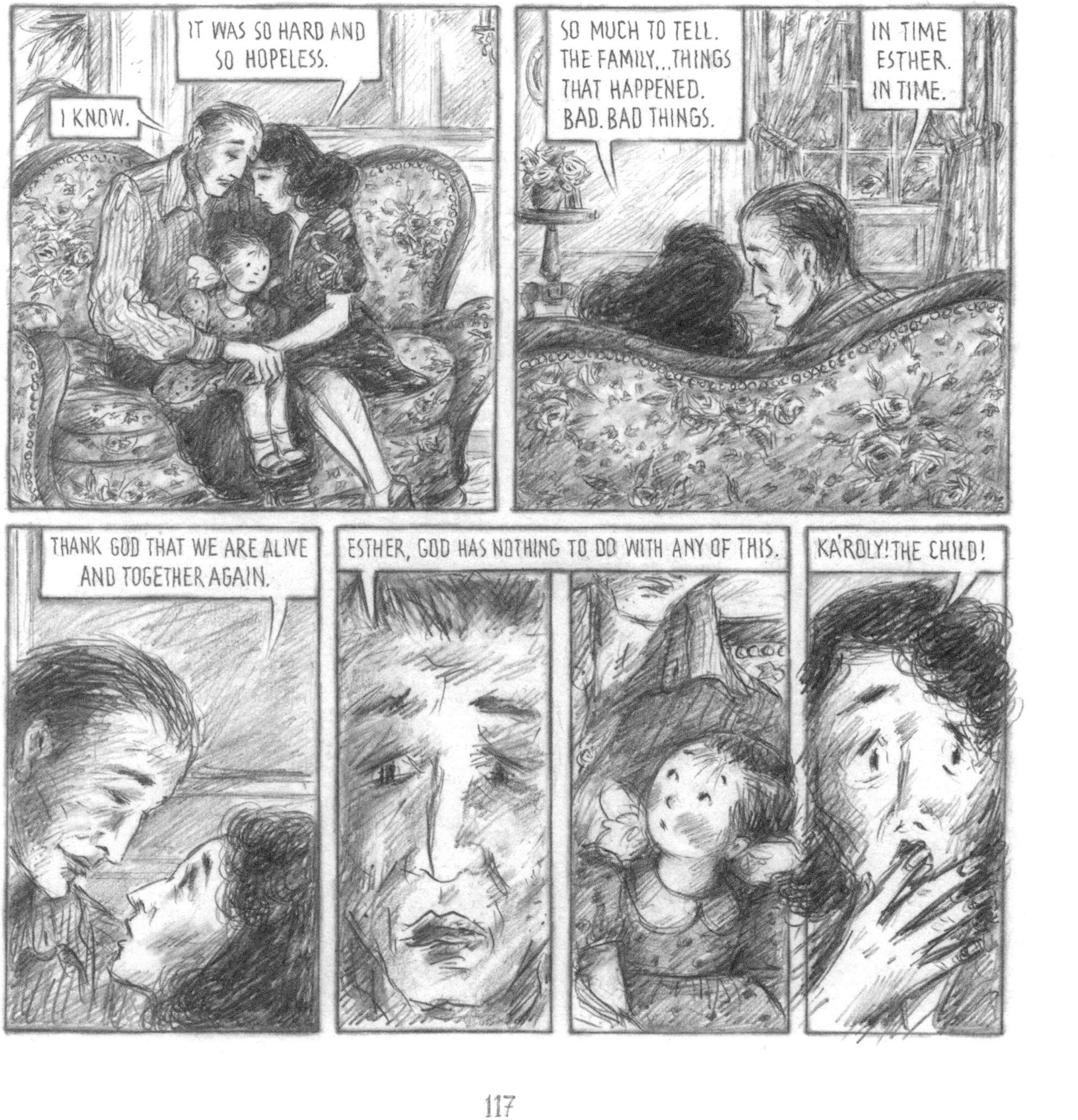
IT WAS SO HARD AND SO HOPELESS.
I KNOW.
SO MUCH TO TELL. THE FAMILY... THINGS THAT HAPPENED. BAD. BAD THINGS.
IN TIME ESTHER. IN TIME.
THANK GOD THAT WE ARE ALIVE AND TOGETHER AGAIN.
ESTHER, GOD HAS NOTHING TO DO WITH ANY OF THIS.
KÁROLY! THE CHILD!

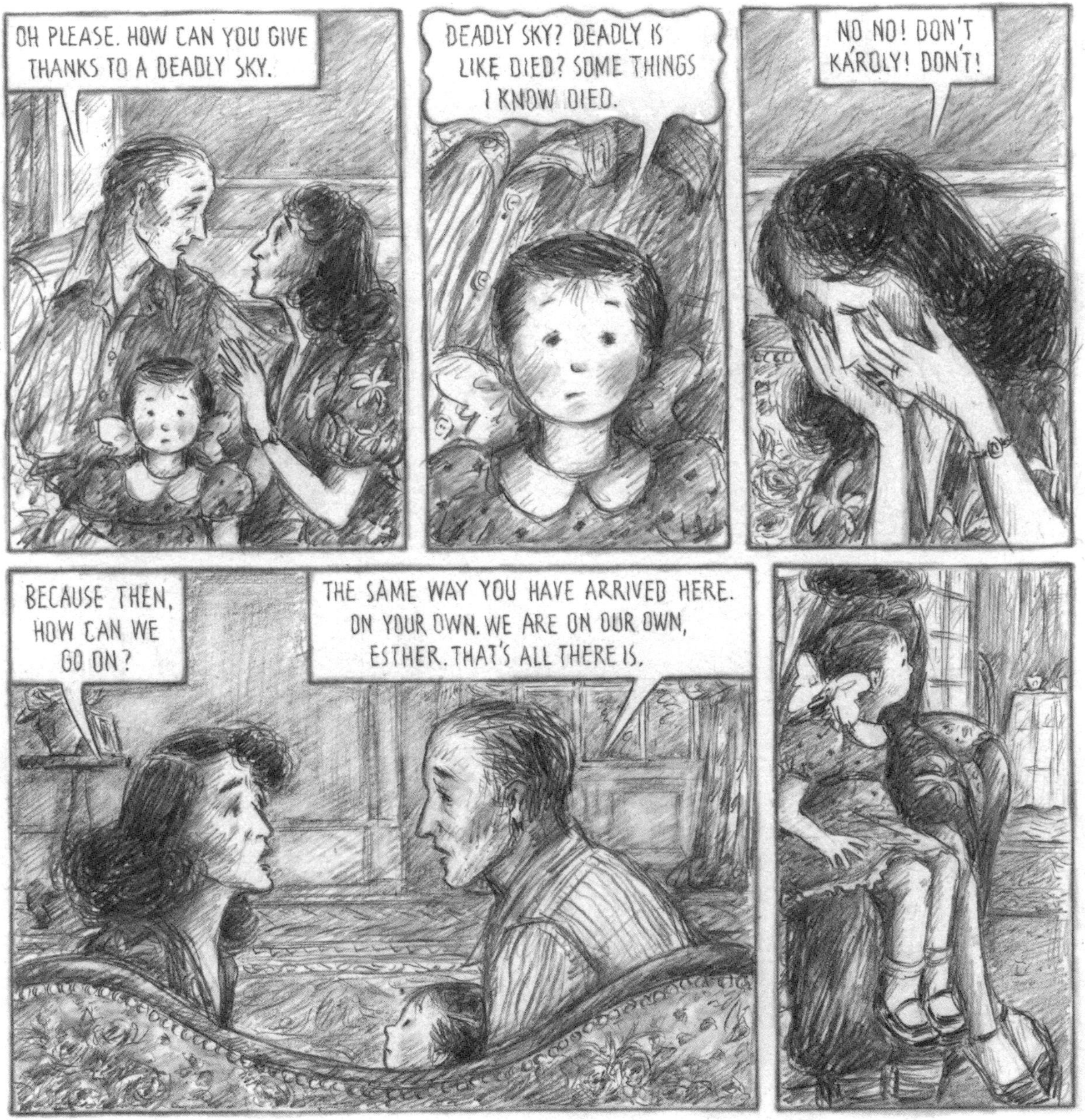
OH PLEASE. HOW CAN YOU GIVE THANKS TO A DEADLY SKY.
DEADLY SKY? DEADLY IS LIKE DIED? SOME THINGS I KNOW DIED.
NO NO! DON'T KÁROLY! DON'T!
BECAUSE THEN, HOW CAN WE GO ON?
THE SAME WAY YOU HAVE ARRIVED HERE. ON YOUR OWN. WE ARE ON OUR OWN, ESTHER. THAT'S ALL THERE IS.

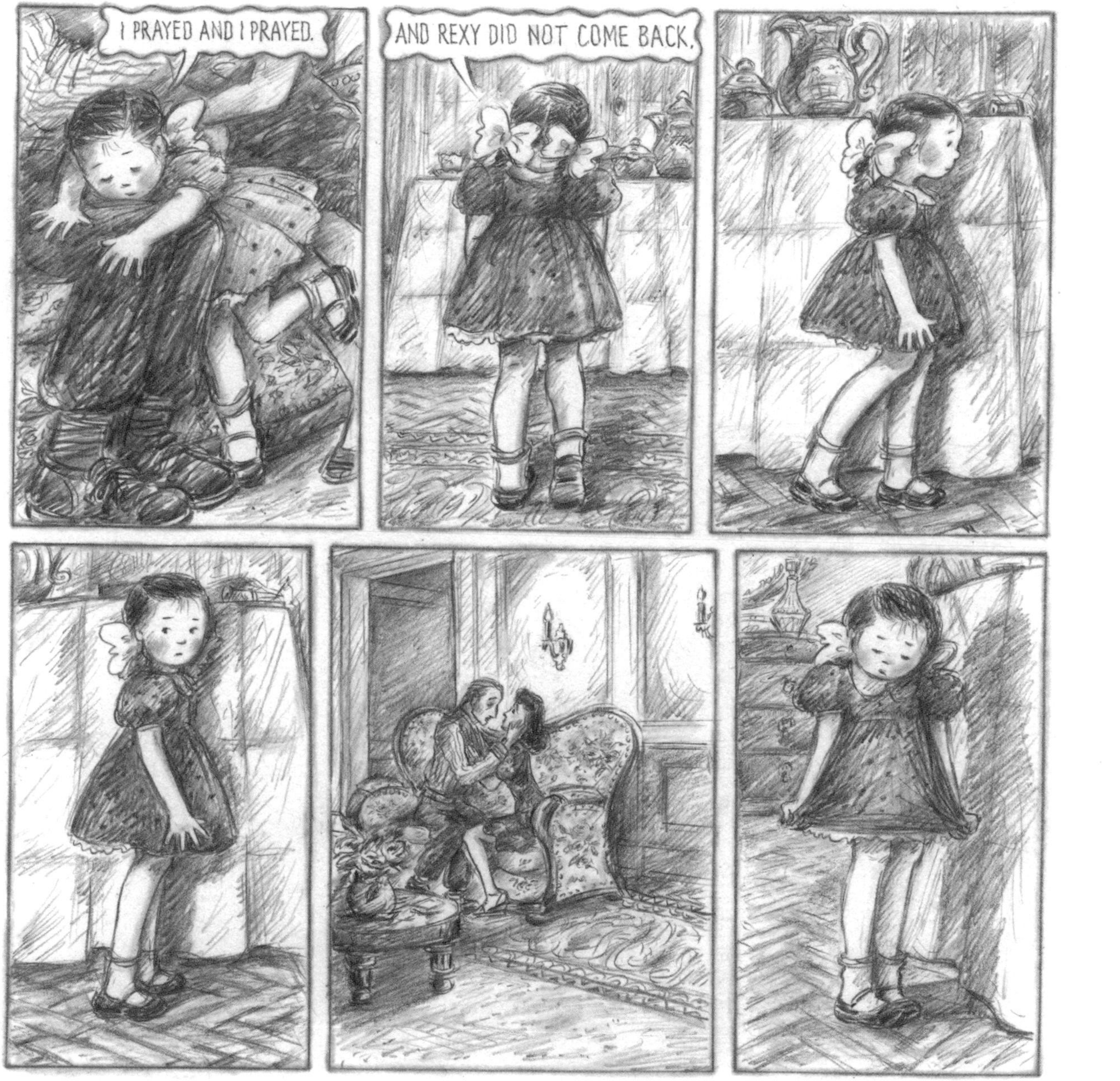
I PRAYED AND I PRAYED.
AND REXY DID NOT COME BACK.

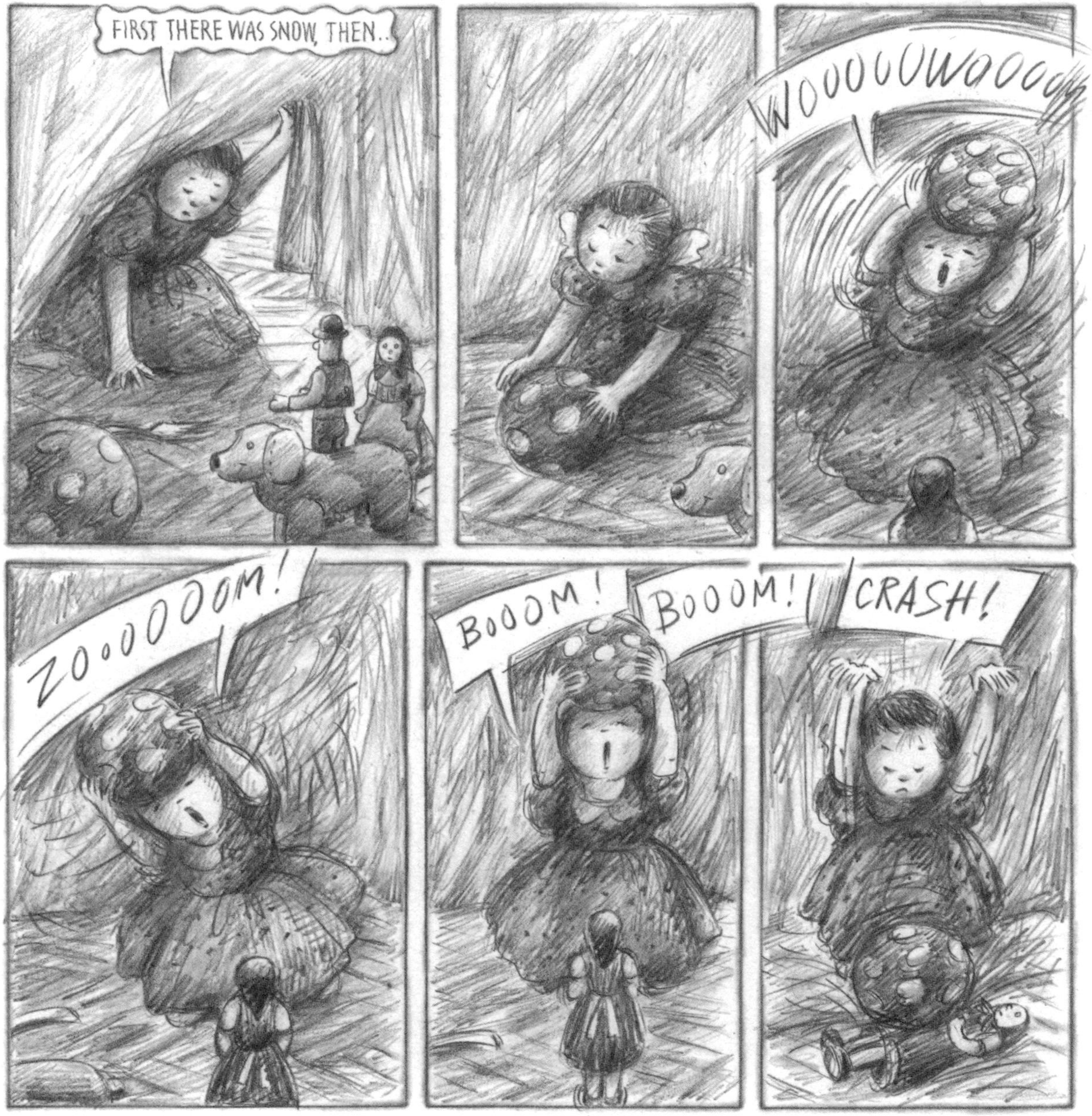
FIRST THERE WAS SNOW, THEN..
WOOOOOWOOOO
ZOOOOOOM!
BOOOM!
BOOOM!
CRASH!

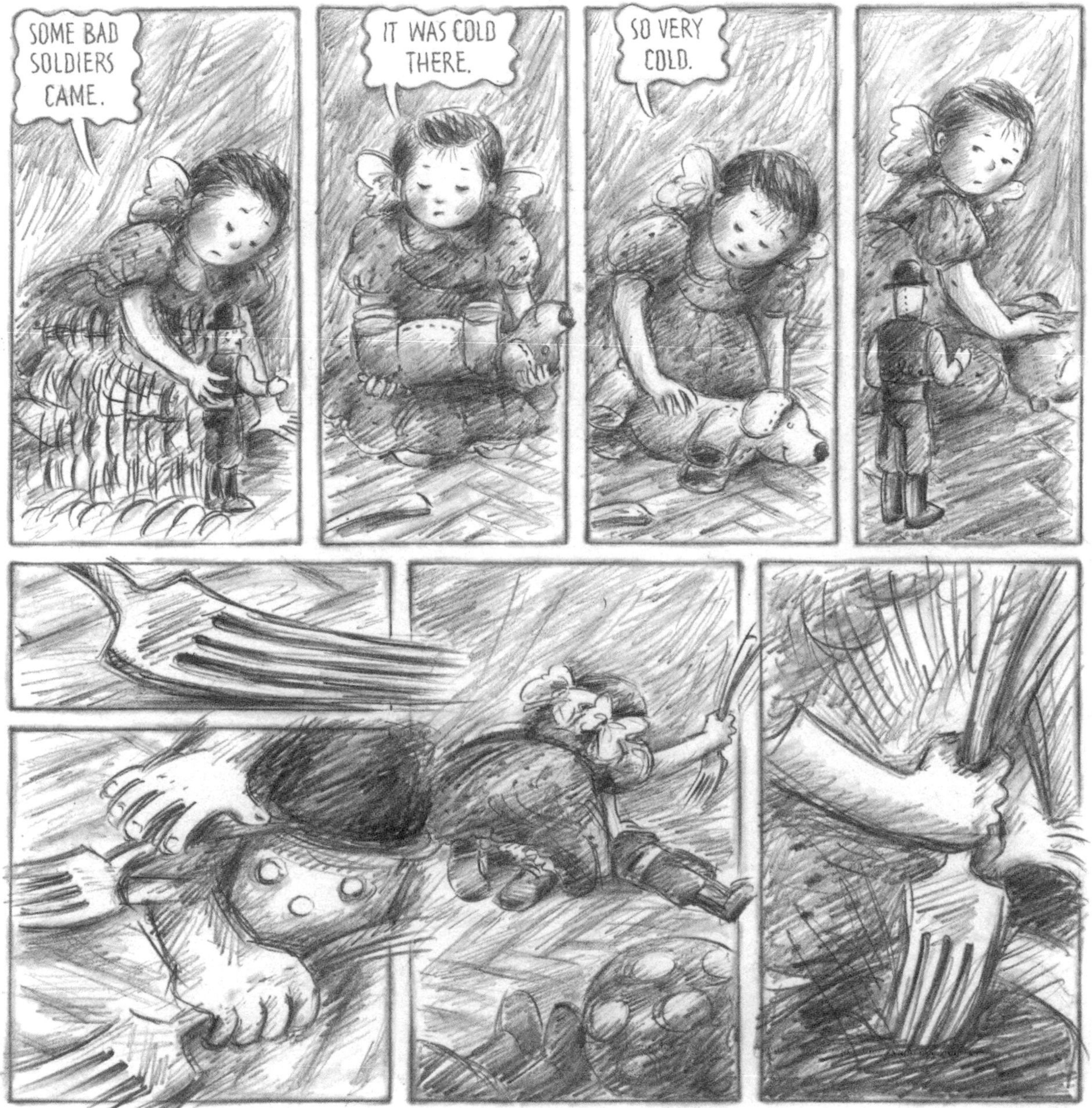
SOME BAD SOLDIERS CAME.
IT WAS COLD THERE.
SO VERY COLD.

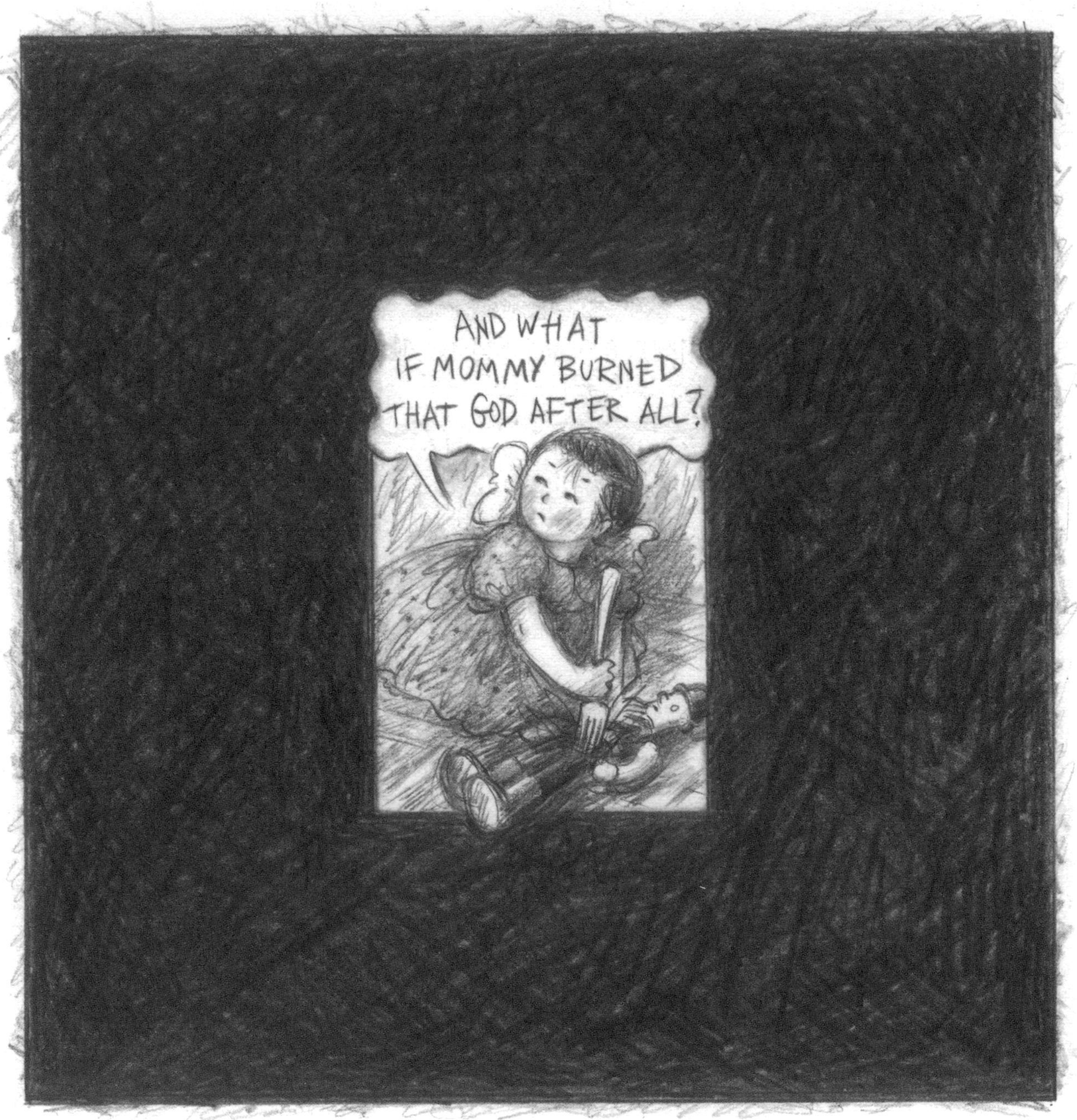
AND WHAT IF MOMMY BURNED THAT GOD AFTER ALL?

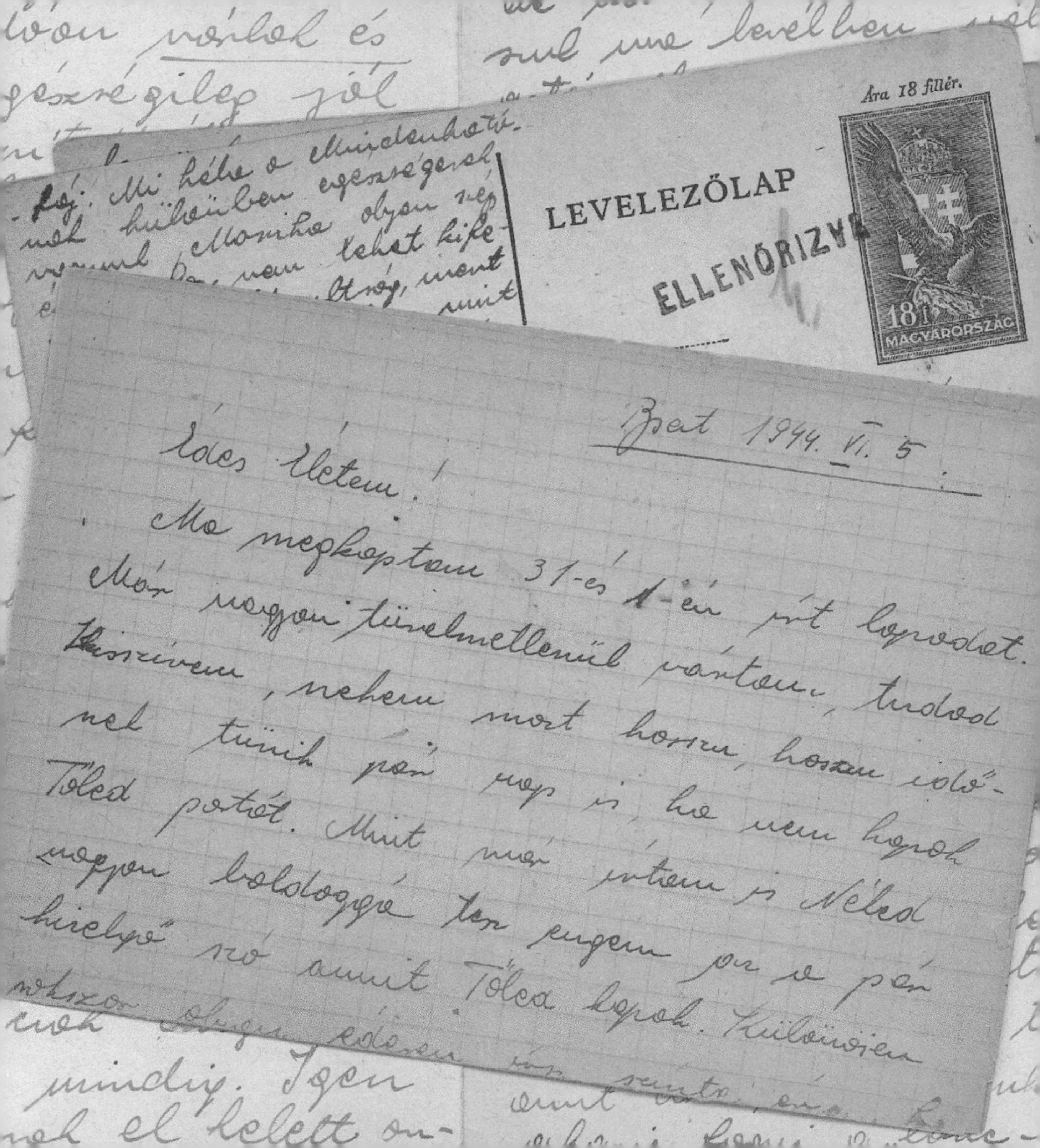

Ára 18 fillér.

LEVELEZŐLAP

ELLENŐRIZVE

18 f MAGYARORSZÁG

Bpest 1944. VI. 5.

Édes Életem!

Ma megkaptam 31-és 1-én írt lapodat.
Már nagyon türelmetlenül vártam. Tudod
kicsivem, nekem most hosszú, hosszú idő-
nek tűnik pár nap is, ha nem kapok
Tőled postát. Mint már írtam is Néked
nagyon boldoggá tesz engem az a pár
kedves szó amit Tőled kapok. Különösen

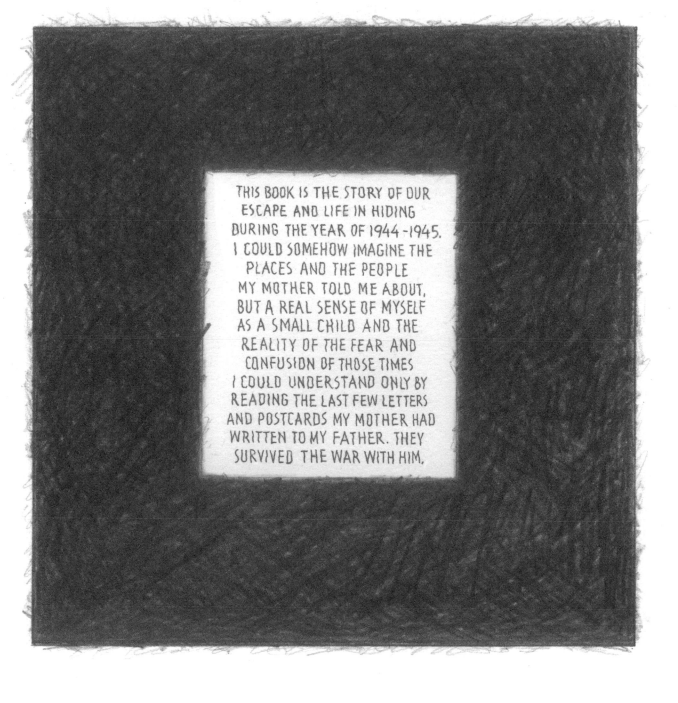

THIS BOOK IS THE STORY OF OUR
ESCAPE AND LIFE IN HIDING
DURING THE YEAR OF 1944-1945.
I COULD SOMEHOW IMAGINE THE
PLACES AND THE PEOPLE
MY MOTHER TOLD ME ABOUT,
BUT A REAL SENSE OF MYSELF
AS A SMALL CHILD AND THE
REALITY OF THE FEAR AND
CONFUSION OF THOSE TIMES
I COULD UNDERSTAND ONLY BY
READING THE LAST FEW LETTERS
AND POSTCARDS MY MOTHER HAD
WRITTEN TO MY FATHER. THEY
SURVIVED THE WAR WITH HIM.

WE RETURNED TO BUDAPEST AFTER THE WAR. LIKE EVERYONE ELSE, MY PARENTS WERE
TRYING TO SET UP A LIFE WHILE COPING WITH THE PAINFUL LOSS OF FAMILY AND
FRIENDS. A GREAT LOVER OF BOOKS, MY FATHER RETURNED TO THE PUBLISHING
COMPANY HE WORKED FOR BEFORE THE WAR. MY MOTHER CONTINUED SEWING.
LIFE WAS HARD IN A WORLD TRYING TO RECOVER, BUT WE LOVED OUR CITY.
MY PARENTS TOOK CARE NOT TO BURDEN ME WITH HISTORY AT A YOUNG AGE.
THE WAR WAS MENTIONED ONLY IN GENTLY SHROUDED WAYS.
I ENJOYED MY CHILDHOOD.

THE 1956 HUNGARIAN UPRISING BROUGHT GREAT CHANGE TO MY YEARS AS A
LITTLE PIONEER. SOON WE WERE ON OUR WAY TO ISRAEL AND I FOUND MYSELF
IN A KIBBUTZ NEAR THE EGYPTIAN BORDER. IT WAS AN EXCITING NEW LIFE.
AFTER GRAY AND MANNERED EUROPE I COULD NEVER HAVE DREAMED OF ALL THAT
SUNSHINE AND FREEDOM. I CONSIDER MY SERVICE IN THE ISRAEL ARMY AS MY
REAL EDUCATION. BY 1963, AT AGE 21, I MOVED TO NEW YORK AND GOT
MARRIED. MY PARENTS JOINED ME THERE LATER THAT YEAR.
MY FATHER LIVED A LONG AND HEALTHY LIFE, STILL BICYCLING AND SKIING
AT AGE 85 WHEN HE PASSED AWAY. HE WAS AN INTELLECTUAL AND A DREAMER.

EARLY IN LIFE I ABSORBED MY FATHER'S ATHEISM AT HOME AND THE SECULAR
EDUCATION IN SCHOOL. MY FATHER, HOWEVER, NEVER DENIED BEING A JEW AND
HELD PRIDE IN THE ETHICAL AND THE LITERARY NATURE OF OUR BACKGROUND.
I WAS ALWAYS COMFORTABLE WITH THIS. LIVING IN HUNGARY AND IN VERY
SECULAR ISRAEL WAS NO PROBLEM. IN NEW YORK, HOWEVER, I HAD TO ALLOW
FOR A MORE CONSERVATIVE APPROACH TO JEWISH LIFESTYLE. YOU HAD TO
BELONG AND SHOW IT. I AGREED RELUCTANTLY BUT HAD GREAT TROUBLE WITH IT.
PERHAPS MY ONLY REGRET IS THAT I COULD NOT GIVE THIS KIND OF COMFORT,
A COMFORT OF FAITH IN THE "EXISTENCE OF GOD," TO MY CHILDREN.
I WAS UNABLE TO LIE.

IN NEW YORK I WORKED IN GRAPHIC ARTS, WE RAISED TWO BOYS AND I KEPT DRAWING THE WORLD AROUND ME.

1981 BROUGHT ANOTHER CHANGE, THE CHANCE TO LIVE IN ISRAEL AGAIN. HERE I WAS IN A BORDER KIBBUTZ BY THE DEAD SEA, THIS TIME WITH MY HUSBAND AND CHILDREN. I JOINED EIN GEDI FILMS, AN ANIMATION COMPANY. WHEN WE RETURNED TO NEW YORK THIS EXPERIENCE LED ME TO WORK WITH JUMBO PICTURES (NICKELODEON), MTV AND THE DISNEY COMPANY.

MY MOTHER IS STILL LIVING IN NEW YORK. NOWADAYS SHE IS SEWING ONLY FOR FUN BUT GRACIOUSLY HOSTING ALL THE JEWISH HOLIDAYS WITH HER FINE COOKING. SHE OFTEN RIDES THE SUBWAYS LADEN WITH SHOPPING BAGS FULL OF HER TREATS FOR HER GRANDCHILDREN WHO SURELY DON'T EAT WELL ENOUGH.

EVERYBODY IS TALKING MORE ABOUT THE WAR THESE DAYS AND SO IS MY MOTHER. THE WORLD SHE FACED SO BRAVELY LEFT HER WITH GREAT MISTRUST OF PLACES, SYSTEMS AND INSTITUTIONS. SHE WATCHED ME CREATING THIS BOOK WITH APPREHENSION. WHEN I WOULD TELL HER, "MOM, EVERYONE FROM THIS STORY IS EITHER DEAD OR TOO OLD TO CARE" SHE WOULD REPLY, "YOU NEVER KNOW. SOMEONE MIGHT SEE IT, TAKE OFFENSE AND COME AFTER US."

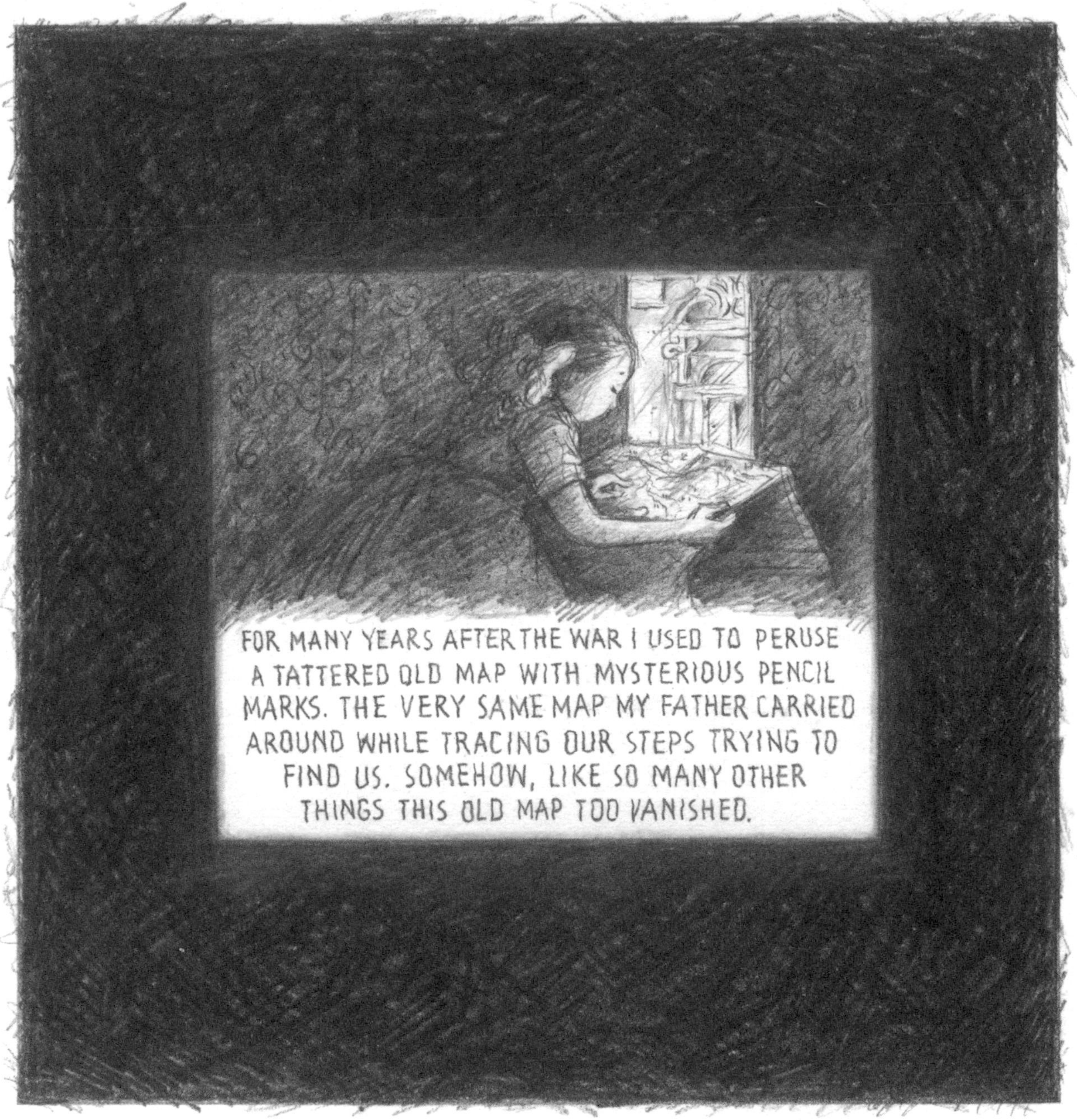
FOR MANY YEARS AFTER THE WAR I USED TO PERUSE A TATTERED OLD MAP WITH MYSTERIOUS PENCIL MARKS. THE VERY SAME MAP MY FATHER CARRIED AROUND WHILE TRACING OUR STEPS TRYING TO FIND US. SOMEHOW, LIKE SO MANY OTHER THINGS THIS OLD MAP TOO VANISHED.

MIRIAM KATIN WITH HER MOTHER.
PHOTO TAKEN IN 1946.